Seeking the God of Ecstasy

A Spiritual Journey of Sexual Awakening

Seeking the God of Ecstasy

A Spiritual Journey of Sexual Awakening

Melina Costello

Foreword by Robert A. Johnson

BOOKS

Winchester, UK
Washington, USA

First published by O-Books, 2010
O Books is an imprint of John Hunt Publishing Ltd., The Bothy, Deershot Lodge, Park Lane, Ropley, Hants, SO24 OBE, UK
office1@o-books.net
www.o-books.com

For distributor details and how to order please visit the 'Ordering' section on our website.

ISBN: 978 1 84694 373 7

A CIP catalogue record for this book is available from the British Library.

Design: Tom Davies

Printed in the UK by CPI Antony Rowe
Printed in the USA by Offset Paperback Mfrs, Inc

We operate a distinctive and ethical publishing philosophy in all areas of its business, from its global network of authors to production and worldwide distribution.

CONTENTS

Foreword by Robert A. Johnson xiii
Acknowledgments xv
Introduction 1
Chapter 1: Awakening Instinct 10
Chapter 2: The Dark Other 41
Chapter 3: Tunnels and Caves 75
Chapter 4: Unexpected Messengers 105
Chapter 5: Relearning Technique 134
Chapter 6: The Soul's Keepers 156
Chapter 7: Falling and Flying 191
Chapter 8: Theater of Dreams 218
Chapter 9: Touching the Wound 244
Chapter 10: Desire and the Forbidden 271
Chapter 11: Consummation 305

Advance Praise for *Seeking the God of Ecstasy*

Melina Costello has entered the winepress and produced from her own alchemy of soul a rare wine to savor. Through bridging the sacred and commonplace, she candidly and intimately fleshes out her dramatic initiation into the paradoxical realm of 'ek-stasis'—the fall into the breathable dance of opposites that is the fragmenting fate of soul—which merges us with the divine madness that is Dionysus.

The archetypes, as Melina makes clear, are the openers of mysterious doors, leading to terror, wonder, wisdom and transformation. Creative dialogue with them requires a shamanic kind of inner strength, shrewdness, imaginal power and moral courage. When approached with the author's brand of creative fire, reverence and vulnerability, this can be a perilous yet exuberant dance at the rim of the Abyss: too much or too little control and we risk being overwhelmed. Melina discerningly avoids either extreme. She both gives herself fully to a raw merging with the rending joy of Dionysus and at the same time wisely distances herself in order to reflect. This is a god we cannot, dare not face till we have ourselves become many faces, many masks, all of them forged through successive deaths and rebirths that render us as fluid as nature's elements and changing forms. Melina makes all this viscerally real and alive in this uniquely exuberant, timely and deeply personal work.

—**Maureen B. Roberts, Ph.D,** Soul-centered Psychiatric and Shamanic Therapist, Co-founder: Mental Health ReEducation and Human Rights Network Australia, Inc.

A captivating journey through the labyrinth of imagination and dreams. Opening to the mysteries of the body, Melina Costello's psychic and somatic relationship with a theater of deities unleashes the alchemical fire of self-initiated awakening—the hieros gamos. Deeply personal and profoundly transpersonal, Seeking the God of Ecstasy provides readers with a radically entertaining learning tool for reaching into the depths of their own souls.

—**Jana Dixon,** *Biology of Kundalini*

Once a Catholic, now a Maenad, Costello vividly recounts her firsthand experiences with the psychic forces of an archetype personified as Dionysus. With courage and aplomb, she willingly walked through a hole in the universe and got an initiation—unique, authentic and life-changing—and crafted a narrative that catches it all.

—**Richard Leviton**, *Looking for Arthur, Santa Fe Light*

C.G. Jung anticipated that 'Man's procreative power is only a special instance of the procreative nature of the Whole.' This deeper procreation and conception process is described in the Hermetic alchemical coniunctio as the sexual unification of the goddess and the god that leads to new creation and incarnation in the universe. However, the human body was not sufficiently included in Jung's theory. Melina Costello has the courage to face this deeply introverted process and shows us that the Holy Wedding is constellated as the unification of the god and the human being. By surrendering to the allegedly destructive demons instead of fighting against them as in Active Imagination, she extends the methodology of Jungian depth psychology and experiences the coniunctio of Hermetic alchemy, which, according to Jung, symbolically represents the unsolved task of Analytical Psychology and the challenge of the 21st century.

—**Remo F. Roth, Ph.D**, *Die Gottsucher (The Quest for God)*

An heroic work. With persistence and courage, Melina Costello has deeply embraced her experience of the archetypal world and offered us a brilliant and poetic account of what she has found there: 'a massive network of opposites twisted inside a powerful column of life reaching heavenward.'

—**James Bertolino**, *Finding Water, Holding Stone*

Living fully as an embodied soul is the great invitation of human existence, but often we find its realization frustrated by a myriad of influences. Indeed, it often seems there is little wisdom in our culture—even in its religious traditions—that addresses how to facilitate the integration of body, psyche and spirit necessary to realize our fullest potential. In Seeking the God of Ecstasy, Melina Costello details her courageous journey of integration and individuation through profound inner work with archetypal characters, who reveal to her the deep-seated fears and disenfranchised parts of herself. By honestly facing these inner forces and what they represent about herself, she is able to reclaim repressed potentialities, as well as discover gifts of creativity and vitality that deeply enrich her life.

—**Philip St. Romain**, *Kundalini Energy & Christian Spirituality*

Powerful and unique. The author's vivid writing style and descriptive ability take the reader into another world. Because the book is written from a feminine point of view, it is extremely timely and will help many people, much needed in this essentially sexually uptight world. The author involves the reader in her experiences beautifully and the dreams are excellent. I know readers find dreams and how they apply to one's life fascinating.

—**John D. Goldhammer, Ph.D**, *Radical Dreaming*

What's rare about this book is the author's willingness, honesty and courage to integrate the tension she experiences between the mundane world of kitchen and laundry, and her soul's journey through the archetypal world with Dionysus as her guide and trickster companion. Her courage inspires us to do likewise. And it's a courage that manifests on nearly every page as she opens to sexual passion and its usefulness in exploring the interior world, the world of relationships and that place where the divine and mundane join in the dance of life and ecstatic union. The author's integrity in opening to the depths of her feeling world lends a profound sense of authenticity to a book that amazes in its ability to probe the hidden nooks and crannies of our psyche as we, her readers, meditate and reflect on our own experiences as we read. This is a book that will endure over time, provide insight and comfort to fellow travelers on the way and serve as a wonderful example of a lay person's ability to enrich the Jungian corpus.

—**Herb Long, Th.D**, counselor and instructor, The Process Work Institute of Portland, Oregon

Seeking the God of Ecstasy

Blew me away! Join Melina Costello on her awe-inspiring journey of individuation and sexual discovery. You'll be amazed by her insights and honesty, and will be tremendously empowered yourself!

—**Gillian Holloway, Ph.D**, *Erotic Dreams*

The author wishes to thank the following publications in which the poems in this book first appeared: *Bluefish* Volume 1 ("Ode To The Unloud"); *Randy Habits* ("St. Bridget's Lamentation"); *Clifton* Magazine Volumes 10, 12 ("In Twilight We Move In Technicolor," "A Freudian Dream In Three Movements").

Grateful acknowledgment is made to reprint an excerpt from *The Picture of Dorian Gray* by Oscar Wilde. New York: Dell Publishing Co., Inc., 1969.

Cover art from an original painting by Emily Balivet, *Eve Swooning in the Garden of Eden*. http://www.emilybalivet.com

Website: www.melinacostello.com

For Ted

It is dawn: the petals close, slightly crumpled; there nests in the soft and secret urn some new happiness, I cannot say what.

— Pascoli

FOREWORD

You are about to read a book that will enthrall and terrify you, a book that will carry you to dizzying heights of ecstasy and cast you into forbidding realms of shadow, woundedness and insatiable longing. The place to which you are going is the place of the soul, and I am honored to have my name associated with this marvelous book.

Melina Costello's inner journeys are driven by a rare nerve that is so often the hallmark of astonishing acts of imagination. It is here that Goethe's words sparkle with renewed meaning: *Whatever you can do, or dream you can, begin it. Boldness has genius, power and magic in it.* The vibrancy of Costello's archetypal encounters with the Greek god Dionysus, made even more compelling by her candid writing, testifies to the quality of daring essential for traveling the inward road—a road that will inevitably lead beyond the tidy features of the rational world. Yet for all its fresh impulse and invention, boldness tends easily toward recklessness and hubris; thus the unwieldiness of the inner sojourn: bringing forth the fruits of the soul is a perilous mixture of uncertainty, daring, self-abandon and wisdom seasoned by numerous wrong turns.

The journeys so meticulously chronicled in these pages take us intimately into the tensions of the human soul, many of which are poignantly familiar. Whether we long to touch the transcendent in ordinary life, realize our chosen vocation, nurture intimacy in relationships, or fill a sense of spiritual vacancy, we are impelled by fundamental forces and drives that significantly shape our behavior. Psychologist Carl Jung called these forces *archetypes*—"first patterns"—and like blueprints, they are the basic human drives and impulses we share with all of humanity.

In Greek myth, the ecstatic impulse that heightens our

instinctual sense of unity with the natural world and connects us to every living thing is represented by the half-mortal, half-god Dionysus. As the personification of divine ecstasy, Dionysus symbolizes the irrational world of the senses as it interacts with the rational world of rules and limitations. To cultivate a harmonious relationship between these two worlds in our everyday lives, we need look no further than to the rich storehouse of myths and their archetypal energies, for it is here we will discover the dynamic, living components of our inner world. When we view myths as pictures showing us how our basic human drives interact, they become inexhaustible sources of insight into our psychological motivations.

Safely building a bridge between mythic reality—the realm of the gods—and ordinary reality is an enormous subject, and I cannot begin to do it justice within the constraints of a foreword. There are many fine books on the subject for interested readers; otherwise, I advise a careful study of the instructions in my book *Inner Work* (HarperOne, 1989) for anyone planning to use this pathway.

Seeking the God of Ecstasy is a welcome adjunct to many psychological writings that fall short of adequately conveying the experience of numinous consciousness and the *mysterium tremendum*—"awful mystery"—as it is apprehended by the human soul in states of divine communion. In the following journeys, the sensuous, intuitive quality of divine ecstasy is returned to the vine, to the flowering garden of earth, to ivy moist with summer rain, to Luna's hypnotic dance on the river Styx. These fertile images leap off the page and burrow deeply into the psyche, not soon to be forgotten.

Blessings on this book and may it have a long and fruitful life.

Robert A. Johnson
San Diego, California

ACKNOWLEDGMENTS

I would like to express my appreciation to the editors of O Books, and in particular to my publisher John Hunt, whose pioneering spirit and vision midwifed this book into print. To Robert A. Johnson, who graciously provided the foreword, I owe a debt of thanks. My thanks to Emily Balivet for her stunning artwork that graces the cover of this book. Wilma Jones' loving insight helped to keep the path lit and my footing steady. I am indebted to the late Dorothy Schlosser, whose boundless optimism and earthy wisdom was my life raft when the journey got rough. My love and thanks to Karen Maier for her companionship, encouragement and generous support throughout the early phases of this work. Marie Barnett's enduring friendship provided emotional nourishment and deep comfort, helping me to bear up under long periods of solitude along the way.

I am deeply grateful for the love and support of my mother, whose birthing into an enlarged awareness of life and Spirit in her own journey hastened my awakening. My love and gratitude to my brothers Tony, Paul, Joe and Dominic for believing in me during times when I did not, and whose outrageous humor kept me whole. My heartfelt thanks to my brother Mike, who helped me break my romance with the pen and initiated me into the world of computers; without his love and devoted assistance throughout the many phases of preparing the manuscript for publication, this book may well have remained sealed in piles of legal pads in which it was first written. For the bright presences of my children Maria and Joey, who were a constant source of joy and sustenance throughout the transcribing of this work, I am truly thankful and deeply blessed. To my partner Ted, who wore every hat in the book as he companioned me along the journey, *tanti baci amore mio.*

INTRODUCTION

No one really knows why the movements of soul compel some individuals to dive into the mystery of its inner storms and others to sculpt, play the piano or stroll under a night sky. Varied as fingerprints, responses to inner life are telling signatures of deeply private conflicts and truces with our humanness. This book is just such an account: an intimate quest for spiritual meaning and transcendence within the gritty paradoxes and emotional assaults of living a mortal existence.

The soul's insistences reveal themselves early in life, erupting like wildflowers through the soil of our childhood imaginations. It is within this primary place of self that we first discover how incipient will and soul interact: who gets to take possession of the golden fleece or wear the queen's crown; who is run through the middle by the sword of vengeance or made to eat swill in a dank dungeon. Both my will and imaginal life were regularly exercised by lively skirmishes with my six brothers as we play-acted popular heroes of the day—Peter Pan, Robin Hood, Superman, and Zorro—but only when I wasn't engaging a more subtle and peculiar realm: the invisible world quietly engulfing nature.

Unlike many children who'd gaze at a tree and see an explosion of foliage, I saw the empty spaces between the leaves. What was hypnotic about the emptiness was the magical invisibility it shared with the mighty realms of Heaven which, for reasons I could never comprehend, no living person was privileged to see. For me this boiled down to a simple formula: emptiness was an imperceptible cloak designed to fool the nondiscriminating eye, for while it kept the glories of Paradise concealed, it had the potential to reveal them unexpectedly. The trick was to watch without blinking at just the right moment and maybe, just maybe, one could glimpse the fleeting face of that mysterious and all-knowing Creator, God. I really couldn't imagine anything more thrilling than to steal a peek at the Heavenly Host, so promising Him I wouldn't breathe a word of His appearance to any of my siblings, I perched myself at the foot of a large maple tree and earnestly begged Him to materialize.

Looking back, it's difficult to believe I was muleheaded enough to think the heavens would part in the way I anticipated, but in the rural Midwest of my childhood, my imagination was left to happily run riot. Nested in a middle class, two-parent home with a couple of Hula-Hoops, a rusty bicycle, some old bocce balls and acres of poison ivy, my world was as simple and guileless as a Christmas snowflake. All those blistering hot summer days of fending off flies and sweat bees while keeping vigil under the maple tree was not only fervent prayer, but hefty sacrifice for a five year-old waiting ardently for the Father of all Creation to knock off the games and get down to business. My faith was deadly serious, joined at the hip with logic: a God almighty enough to create heaven, earth and all the creatures in between could, without the least effort or thought, manifest Himself to me. I waited, but to no avail.

I now can clearly see that from early life, I imposed my will upon the Divine without the slightest inkling I was walking in footprints left by legions of angels as they hurtled toward their fatal fall. Blindness to my predicament followed me like a shadow companion throughout successive stages of my emotional and spiritual growth. By young adulthood, my skulking silhouette had become a full-grown nemesis, stoking the fires of inner tension in which soul and will duked out their stormy differences.

In a quest to ease these conflicts, I began to explore alternative spirituality books that introduced me to the wisdom traditions of the East and the sacred practices of yoga and meditation. The perceptual confines of my Catholic upbringing were greatly enlarged as I drank in the heartfelt simplicity and devotional aspects of the Tao, Zen Buddhism, the Hindu philosophy of Vedanta and the ancient Jewish mysticism of the Kabbalah. The Way, I discovered, was "within." The deeper reasons for one's earthly existence and longing to know God, which had been parceled out in stingy rations by the religion of my youth, could be discovered in prayerful stillness.

Teaching myself how to breathe deeply and rhythmically, I began to observe silence in deep contemplative states that brought to bear the emergence of powerful inner voices. Suspecting the chaos of my imagination was responsible for these seemingly autonomous utterances, I did what the Catholic Church advocated in times of doubt about mysterious indwellings: "Resist the Spirit. If it is really the hand of God moving upon you, your resistance will be vanquished by the power of the Holy Ghost." After months of obstinacy, abject denial and exhausting struggles with anxiety, I surrendered my fear to the awakening of my interior life. Entrusting my soul's care to the tutelage of my inner guides—or guardian angels as they are often called—I was awed by the clarity and coherence of their teachings, the still force upon which revelations were carried to me, and the deep care in which they were imparted. I began to transcribe everything I heard, an endeavor that honed my ability to listen without interfering, and which taught me the wisdom of being still.

Implementing the spiritual teachings that filled my notebooks over the next few years, my inner vision and sense of purpose began to flower, releasing a spiritual vitality that flowed into every area of my life. Intimate experience of the divine Self as an inexhaustible source of love and inspiration crumbled preexisting walls that had defined the parameters of my selfhood. Carried into altered states, I reveled in a boundless wealth of nourishment that replaced time, form and self-knowingness with unnamable life, engulfing soul in a mystery of consecration. My capacity for empathy was acutely heightened by experiences in these states, expanding inner sight and depth of feeling. Rendered highly sensitized to the myriad forces that minister unseen to the human soul, I was able to assist in healing emotional and physical ailments of friends and loved ones through words and touch.

Despite my absorption in an enriching spiritual life, I was continually perplexed as to how I could experience such heightened states of awareness and emerge from these sacred places with my blind spots, weaknesses and vanities still intact. Regular confrontations with this distressing dichotomy made me realize that spiritual growth can and often does pass over the emotional self as though it were a bowlegged kid trying out for ballet—an apparent contradiction I was at a loss to rectify. I viewed my body, personality, passions, appetites, paradoxes, desires—in other words, my humanness with all of its foibles—as impediments to my ability to use the intuitive gifts I'd been given for "the highest good." That my vices would not amend themselves as my spiritual faculties flourished often made me feel like a hypocrite as I indulged in divine favors I'd neither merited nor was capable of using toward conquering my errors. Carrying around an extra measure of spiritual aptitude became a burden, a lopsided equation I could never reconcile against my numerous shortcomings.

To strengthen what virtues I possessed against the onslaught of my faults, I explored meditation and healing groups within my local community where I could utilize my energies toward a worthwhile collective purpose while fulfilling my desire to be of use to others. This period of my life so nurtured my inner voice and commitment to service that for the next several years my private home was a haven for individuals seeking counseling, many of whom were teachers and spiritual care providers in charge of large groups and institutions. Little did I realize how the shadow side of my work was gesturing to me as I witnessed these individuals' public and private selves at agonizing odds:

their inability to allow vulnerability, error and doubt to seep through the highly respected personas they had cultivated in the outer world, and the quiet tragedy of bearing their humanity "under wraps."

I was 28 years old and sorting through the week's laundry when the realization struck that I was not only unhappy in the highly demanding position I'd wedged myself into, I was weary of having no personal life in which to recover from the draining ordeals of listening, caring, sublimating, sacrificing, guiding and tolerating. As I connected with these feelings in myself, laundry began to fly around the room with ever increasing fury. I realized I was as hooked on being needed as others were dependent on my inability to create boundaries around how, when and with whom I shared the gifts of spirit. I recognized that a sense of unworthiness fueled by guilt had flipped me unknowingly into overcompensation and, most painful of all, that being loved by others was as great a motivation for my work as the purpose for which I had intended it—love for God. I surveyed the disheveled room littered with all of my family's dirty laundry and saw it as a statement of my life: my ambition to walk a selfless path found me in collision with the needs of the self.

Weaning myself from the excesses of spiritual service, I withdrew to the welcomed ordinariness of domestic life and enrolled in a writing program at the local university. For the next two years I was a blissful hostage to the creative forces that raged through my pen, yielding dozens of published poems, a position as assistant editor of a national poetry magazine and supportive fellowship in weekly poetry workshops. I'd finally discovered what I was looking for: the exhilarating freedom of the creative process that allowed the soul its off-color truths without a shred of judgment. The self I'd so carefully disciplined during my years of spiritual practice not only had recovered its voice, it had regained its innate earthiness and passion for life—a renaissance for which the accustomed complacency of my nine-year marriage was unprepared.

My husband and I separated just prior to my thirty-first birthday, and until our divorce two years later, I wrestled with feelings that I'd been betrayed by my own life. With the exception of my spouse, no one could have been more blindsided by the irreconcilable collapse of my marriage than I was, a reality I found bitterly ironic: why did my highly sensitive intuition, loving inner guidance and scrupulous efforts to live consciously and truthfully do nothing to forestall the demise of my marriage or intervene to save it? Creating a seismic shift in my foundations, the breakup of my marriage became a painfully warped lens through which I saw myself as having been sabotaged by the very forces that had opened me to treasures of spiritual enrichment. I was beside myself to know why the demands of my process and life were such that I was compelled to break my sacred vows; why did an abiding love fail instead of nourishing the vessel of marriage into which I'd poured trust, faith, prayers and self? These unanswered questions struck to the core of my earliest beliefs in the beneficent guiding forces in my life and universe, and severely crippled my trust. Disillusionment gave way to depression, then to rage. I wrestled my demons—and angels—so furiously that I fell ill for a full year.

Following my divorce, I initiated a blind move to California on nothing more than a gut feeling that whatever fate awaited me there—including earthquakes—was a gamble I had to take. My life had been sufficiently emptied to permit a full embrace of the unknown: an arena in which to test, once and for all, what my soul was made of. Having survived the full-scale ambush of all I revered, my future was a blank page—an invitation to dive face first into the poverty of my freedom and come up singing, whatever the outcome. Even after the dissolution of my marriage and spiritual lifestyle, I was inexorably hooked on the power of faith: the leap into Chuang Tzu's "all encompassing net of love" that every ounce of reason told me wasn't there.

I moved to Palo Alto and for three years lived a relatively undisturbed life with my daughter and new partner in a world filled with perennial sunshine, fruit trees and blossom-scented air. Reacquainting myself with the therapeutic joys of reading, I discovered the quiet soul of Rainer Maria Rilke in *Letters to a Young Poet*, and the refreshing wit, sanity and brilliance of C. G. Jung in *Memories, Dreams, Reflections*. Between contemplating my past and slowly healing from old battle wounds, I wrote and directed plays for children's theater, meditated and had a baby. On a spring day in May, an unexpected energy erupted into my consciousness that felt both strange and exciting. That energy was Dionysus.

My introduction to Dionysus as an archetype occurred one afternoon when I was chatting away with the owner of a bookstore and ended up buying the wrong book. Discovering the mistake when I returned home, I flipped curiously through my error and stumbled upon Dionysus, the god of ecstasy. Although I'd initially planned to acquire information about Psyche and Eros in order to develop a romantic theme in a story I was writing, the god of ecstasy seemed to hit the mark quite nicely.

As I browsed through the book, I discovered visualization exercises demonstrating how one could engage in an inner dialectic with the joy-god Dionysus in order to consciously activate the psychological dynamic by which one's capacity for ecstasy is deepened. I'd never before heard of an exercise like this being attempted, let alone successfully achieved by anyone untrained or ill-equipped to endure the full gaze of a psychically potent giant. I was, of course, viewing the experience from a spiritually oriented background of engaging angels and guides in sacred dialogues, activities of healing and states of profound inner union. The possibility had never before occurred to me that having communed with celestial caretakers of the human soul, I could make a lateral shift on a psychic plane to a psychological dynamic imaged in consciousness as a pagan god.

Excerpts taken from actual experiences were cited in the book and as I read them, their seeming one-dimensionality and lack of numinous substance made me wonder if the exercise could render more power and depth if approached from a deeply meditative, mediumistic state. Not only intrigued by the prospect, I was immensely attracted to the idea that if I pursued the exercise, I could throw spiritual discipline and protocol out the window. After all, what possible rules could a psychological exploration have, especially in the mythological domain of a pagan god? I decided if such an inner dialectic with the god Dionysus could render an authentic numinous encounter, I'd give it a try the following morning. The day I made this decision was to become the last day of my old life.

The next morning after breakfast, I retreated to my office, pulled out a writing tablet and gazed at the clock. Having had years of experience transcribing discourses with angels and inner guides while in altered states of consciousness, I hoped to record the full particulars of an archetypal encounter should one be forthcoming. Using visualization as a means to invoke the sacred held little attraction for me; whatever I held in the mind only consumed energy that could otherwise be utilized by soul toward its own imagining and restricted the movements of inner life to a predetermined agenda. Instead, I focused on what felt like a growing desire in my gut to "break through" to Dionysus' realm.

I was vaguely aware that attempting to enter an inner state from a gut response—raw emotion versus detachment—might catapult me beyond protective psychic boundaries that for years had kept the dark urges of inner life consigned to noninvasive realms. However, setting my intention to make contact with a mythological divinity seemed to require abandoning myself to an emotional force I was unaccustomed to invoking in my meditations. Knowing full well this approach was a radical departure from my well-traveled routes into the sacred, I fully resigned myself to the unlikelihood of realizing anything but a pleasant meditation. Just the same, I earmarked half an hour for the exercise before beginning my day's work. Relaxing in the chair at my desk, I wrote across the top of my legal pad, "Seeking Dionysus: A Journey of the Soul." I then closed my eyes, breathed deeply, and entered an interior place of calm anticipation...

What unfolds in the following pages is a transformative journey into realms of highly charged archetypal life: an intensive two-year journal of raw psychic experience, dreams and reflections—a naked chronicle of a fall into soul.

CHAPTER 1

AWAKENING INSTINCT

The 'other voice,' the 'strange will,' are the 'other,' that is, God or nature with its gods and demons. Inspiration is a revelation because it is a manifestation of the divine powers. A numen speaks and supplants man.

— Octavio Paz

May 26 Session

I close my eyes and see that I'm surrounded by trees in a sunny clearing in the woods. A young man in his early twenties stands several yards to my right, feeding a lion with his bare hands. Advancing closer, I see that he's feeding the lion male genitals. I'm not shocked in the least. The lion, other than being apparently hungry, seems oddly docile. The young man feeds him calmly and in an ordinary way, as though it's just another activity for him. He turns and looks over his shoulder at me. He's not surprised to see me.

"What are you doing?" I ask.

"I am feeding the lion my genitals."

"Why?"

"I am showing you a reflection of yourself."

I step back slightly, wondering how to interpret what I'm seeing.

"This is pretty weird," I confess. "I'm not sure what I'm supposed to understand about myself through this enactment."

"You do not have to understand anything. Just observe."

As I continue watching this fairly bloodless operation, a feeling of resistance begins to gnaw at my insides. Something about this experience feels staged and unreal. Realizing my subconscious might be spinning a distorted image, I grow increasingly uneasy and skeptical.

"Are you Dionysus?"

"That I am."

He continues feeding the lion without looking at me, fully engrossed in the task at hand. My insecurity mounts. I feel a sudden need to challenge him.

"I'm uncomfortable with your ambivalence. I thought you were supposed to be spontaneous, ecstatic."

"You are full of labels, aren't you?"

He resumes feeding the lion. As I watch him, I notice his skin is becoming softly radiant and is beginning to emit a golden glow. Although subtle, the transformation gives him a dreamlike, celestial appearance that somehow disarms my apprehension. At the same time I begin to feel slightly weak and disoriented. Seating myself in the grass, I close my eyes and place my hands, palm-side-up, on my knees. Allowing the sun's soothing warmth to relax me, I breathe deeply, releasing my tension. I glance over at the young man and see that he has finished feeding the lion and now is petting him, rubbing his mouth and nose. The lion seems to like this very much. I notice the man is wearing a white tunic typical of a Greek god. I'm dismayed that my unconscious has portrayed him in such a predictable fashion.

Suddenly I feel the urge to do something unexpected. I walk over to the man, who is seated on a stump, and plunk myself down at his feet. I see that I've positioned myself directly in front of the lion, which stands to my right. The man gazes calmly at me and commences to rub the top of my head. As he does this, I begin to feel like the docile lion while fully maintaining a sense of my own identity. I turn my head this way and that, letting the man rub under my chin and stroke my cheeks. I then take his hand and place it to my right cheek. I hold it there for several moments, feeling a deep sense of comfort.

"I wanted to tell you that I'm not afraid of you," I disclose quietly. "I was being confrontational. I now realize I have fear, but the fear is not of you."

I look up at him and search his eyes. His face is extremely golden and has become somehow larger to me and more defined. I begin to feel in awe of him.

"Go now and rest," he instructs me. "We will talk again."

I'm in accord with this suggestion and feel it's a good stopping point in the experience. Without saying good-bye, I get up and leave, returning to my normal awareness. I retreat to the couch in my office and lie down, feeling suddenly very tired. I hear a voice and begin to sink deeply inside of it.

"You have been trying to reach me, Melina."

"I know."

"I want to show you a better way."

"That's good. I've been confused and have needed this contact for some time. Are you Dionysus?"

"It is not necessary to name me. I am fire, water, earth and air. Look at my cross."

I close my eyes and see a man-angel with outstretched wings. From head to toe and wing to wing, he shows me the four points of himself—the perfect cross. On his left stands the lion, who now has wings. They both radiate and seem beatified. From the angel's solar plexus, a glowing ball of flames dances and spins. As I gaze into its fiery rotations, a sensation of expanding warmth floods my chest and rises into my skull. All my thoughts begin to overlap.

"I do not possess you; you are not of me," I whisper. "You are a messenger. You have come to bring me a message? And the lion. He is your companion. Together, you are the synthesis of something I need."

"You have been seeking me in the moment of your rapture, when you engage in the dance of your sexual energies. You have called to me. I now come to acknowledge you, Melina."

"I'm a little afraid. Are you the one I've been trying to touch in myself? I don't know who I've been calling—only that I must reach whoever it is."

I now look at his body and realize his genitals are exposed. His phallus is erect. Although it has a solid physical appearance, its ethereal luster resembles a shaft of light. I reflect on the beginning of my experience, where the young man is feeding the lion his genitals, and sense there is a correlation.

"Come," he beckons.

I know what is to proceed and what I am to do. I have the utmost feeling of trust, of complete surrender. The flesh on my back begins to tingle along my spine. I feel very clear.

I move closer to the man-angel. His bare feet are positioned slightly apart and his arms are raised out to his sides. As I gaze at him, I recall a powerful dream I had years ago of a faceless man, naked from the waist up and softly luminous, who stood suspended in the sky. Both his arms were raised out at his sides, and from his left breast hung a living heart organ of pure white. He bade me to touch it. As I extended my hand, an electrifying charge struck through my body and sent me reeling in fright back into waking consciousness.

As I face the man-angel, I know this is the same being as the one in my dream. I also realize I'm now ready to touch his power and that remembering the dream is an affirmation, an unexpected gift he has brought to me. In a standing position, I spread my thighs and carefully ease myself onto his phallus.

We now seem to be telepathically communicating to each other; I'm following his instructions to place my feet apart touching his and to raise my arms out at my sides, placing my palms and fingers in contact with his. He then tells me to be very still and to breathe with him. As I inhale, I'm to focus on pulling energy from the ball of fire in his solar plexus. As I exhale, I'm to release this energy through the top of my head, my fingers and the soles of my feet. He instructs me not to look into his face but to close my eyes, telling me that in this way he can impart his fire to me without causing me harm. He also tells me I should never draw his energy to my pineal gland during sexual activity, but to repeat this breathing exercise and visualization in order to bring his heat back down to cooler, safer levels in my body. He explains that balancing energy is critical, and although it may delay the psychic and spiritual development I seek, without it his fire will only bring chaos, anxiety, fatigue, despair and delusion. I somehow understand and I'm not afraid.

I begin to breathe. His fire burns into my solar plexus, filling my body with a sensation so unexpectedly exhilarating I feel as though it could lift me right off the ground. I exhale and feel the energy coursing out of my body through my head, hands and feet. Its electrifying rush through my limbs makes me want to soar, spin and somersault, but my body is held firmly in place by his strong phallus. I begin to sense his phallus as a great tree whose sap is rising and spreading through my veins. My arms, legs and head feel like the branches of this tree: flowering, swaying and shaking from a dizzying height, dazzled by the sun, wind, sky—ecstatic!

I sense the energy has reached a crest and that I must begin to come down. I slow my breathing. As I do this, he instructs me not to break from my experience with him, but to phase out of our contact gradually, breathing myself back to everyday consciousness without pausing to say good-bye. I seem to be able to make this transition easily. While doing so, he assures me that we'll have many more visits together and opportunities to converse and embrace countless experiences. I'm nodding, happy in my body and looking forward to my next journey into the archetypal world.

Personal Notes

After the experience, I feel both strangely charged and fatigued. I notice that a sexual sensation in my womb continues to stir throughout the day and evening.

Shopping at a large supermarket later in the evening, I feel peculiarly irritated as well as extremely empathic; the mechanical, soul-numbing activity of choosing grocery items seems more tedious than usual. The static quality of myself and others performing a life-sustaining, though lifeless, ritual makes me feel somewhat sad—a feeling I experience often. On this occasion, however, it seems someone else is inhabiting my perceptual self, looking out through my eyes at the world. I can feel this "someone else's" power; latent, quiet, merely watching, while I field the emotional effects of this perceptual "other" in myself. Definitely odd.

Far later in the evening, I leaf through a magazine and skim an article about "sexual secrets men don't tell their lovers." This prompts me to ask my partner, Ted, a blunt question regarding his sexual proclivities, which catches him off guard. The energy snowballs into an hour-long heated discussion which seems endlessly convoluted.

At some point during the quarrel, I begin to see Ted's dilemma as a mirror of my own hidden self. His protective shields reflect my own inhibitions and insecurities, while I appear to be rational and blameless, unsullied by anal-retentive behavior. My awareness of this paradox diffuses my emotional intensity and causes me to reflect on my experience in the archetypal world. I realize then how scary it really was sitting on the phallus of some god within myself, riding him into an unknown dimension of my psyche. I also realize that somewhere, in an overlooked corner of my being, I was actually intimidated, just as Ted had been intimidated by my bold invasion into the private domain of his male psyche. I don't know how long I would have been blinded to this feeling in myself had I not been able to see it reflected in Ted's behavior.

I now more fully sense the dangers of entering the archetypal realm, particularly when hauling a load of powerfully repressed emotions into the experience of the ecstatic. Knowing full well there is a downside to every divine experience, I hope to find a way to minimize the repercussive turmoil which follows reentry into ordinary consciousness—that brick wall toward which my elated self is flung when returning from a promising inner journey. God forbid after all these years I should jeopardize what I could learn by regressing to an infant's crib in my innermost self where I'm lashing out at monsters of my own making. Yet I realize that fear and fear's images are networked inside the journey I yearn to walk; something frightening, which is not merely relegated to the infantile self, inhabits those realms. Whatever it is presses and hovers like an infinite entity with a thousand faces. It is this "thing," both horrible and beautiful, of which I am but a cell, a speck gravitating toward the wholeness of the "It" I am and am not.

This feeling-perception kicks around in my gut and promises it is not an abstraction. I feel somewhat nauseated by it, but also compelled to dive in, for I know I've been long preparing for this. God grant me fortitude and a respite from the mental axe I grind. There's no place in there for cold logic or self-inflation. This, I imagine, will be the terrifying beauty of reduction, death in its favorite pose. As I write this, an internal voice is saying, "To hell with glamour. Stop standing in front of the mirror. Strip down and stand in line to be deloused."

May 31 Personal Notes

Since my first experience five days ago with Dionysus in the archetypal realm, I haven't been able to stop what appears to be an ongoing awareness of that internal world and its powerful activities. I'm certain I was not able to pull all the way back from that world into ordinary consciousness, for the visions continue involuntarily. Some part of myself seems to have disengaged from ordinary activities to continue its inner journey despite the complete lack of synthesis to my daily life. This dual involvement has made me feel irritable and touchy, sober and withdrawn. My appetite has decreased and I've been experiencing an unpleasant dizziness that plagues me from the area at the base of my skull. I feel as though my chakras are overloading. I know I'll have to pay more attention to my health, diet and need for rest. None of these unpleasantries concern me at the present time, nor do they dissuade me from engaging in the mysterious inner life that now consumes my heart, mind and soul.

Over the last few days I've realized it isn't so much stumbling into the horrible in myself that frightens me. I'm far more afraid of confronting the Divine in myself. "Fear of the Lord" comes to mind with a new meaning, bringing to bear the frailties of my creaturehood. This awareness churns up feelings of dread as though an ordeal is at hand. How I've trembled all my life in the face of radiance, shrinking back whenever the power of Love blasted through the stasis in which I ordinarily embrace its life. When the light I ask for comes, I bolt for the door, the closet, the unmade bed. I feel this inner paradox down to the core of my being as if it were the mustard seed from which has grown the huge tree of all I call myself—gnarled, glorious; strong, vulnerable—a massive network of opposites twisted inside a powerful column of life reaching heavenward.

May 31 Session

I close my eyes and see that I'm once again in a sunny area of the woods. A cool morning breeze rustles the trees and everything sparkles with a clean, clear radiance. I walk forward a bit and see that off to my left is a long table covered by a white tablecloth. The table is set for some sort of meal. A number of small silver dishes are set at each place, and upon each dish is a bunch of beautiful green grapes. That is all. I'm tempted to count the place settings, feeling the number is significant, but I somehow lose interest in pursuing this.

No one is around and I'm somewhat relieved to be here alone. As I gaze at the place settings gleaming in the sunlight, I start feeling a sense of anxiety. The table looks too meticulously arranged and once again I have the sense of being inside something unreal. I grow uncomfortable and don't know what to do with myself. I meander around a bit, feeling ambivalent to my surroundings, then grow tired and sick to my stomach. I sit down on a stump and stare into the grass, wondering if this is all just a game I'm playing.

At this point in the meditation, I get up from my desk and lie on the couch in my office. I feel extremely tired and close my eyes. A very old woman appears to me, curiously dressed, babbling something I don't understand. She is a nuisance. I begin to wonder why I'm surrounded by trees in these internal scenarios. I decide I don't like that. The woman goes up to one of the trees and proceeds to kick it. I observe her antics and gradually fall asleep.

Personal Notes

As I write this, I'm eating my lunch. Thankfully my appetite has returned. I napped well for perhaps an hour. When I awoke, I was immediately struck with the word "obsession." The dictionary describes it quite aptly: *the domination of one's thoughts or feelings by a persistent idea, image, desire.*

It's clear I must do my utmost to shake off the archetypal world's hold on me if I'm to continue to return to it with an open mind and senses intact. For five days I've been mesmerized by a highly absorbing, dynamic inner state which I still can't say I understand. It's like reentering the same dream night after night without having fully awakened. I need the juxtaposition of distinctly separate states of awareness if I'm to evenly distribute the load of these energies throughout my waking consciousness. If I can't pull this off, I have no business seeking entrance into the world of the gods. But how will I accomplish this? Archetypal intrusion into everyday consciousness can't be controlled merely by the "I." I'll have to find Dionysus and ask him to help me.

Perhaps he can hold the energy once I leave his world and keep it safe while I'm away. What am I doing trying to lug its weight through my kitchen and bedroom? Yes, it's fascinating and powerful, but also deadly. This somehow reminds me of Persephone. Too late for her. She was had by the chain gang god and now only gets to come up for air once a year. Not me, Pluto. Not me.

Undated Session

I close my eyes and see that I'm seated upon a hardback chair in a dimly lit room. Dionysus is sitting to my left. His hands are folded relaxedly on his lap and his head is bowed, almost as if in readiness to hear me. He looks mature here, not youth-like.

"Why didn't you warn me that all of this could become an obsession?" I ask.

"Another's words are lost on you. Your own experience is not."

"But don't you think it's a bit dangerous letting me plunge headlong into experience that's potentially hazardous?"

"You have enough common sense to sidestep the pitfalls, even when you are right on top of them. An impulsive nature such as yours craves the danger as well as freedom from the craving. This is a terrestrial dilemma."

He pauses and studies me to see how I've taken what he's said. He looks genuinely concerned.

"Let me add that your impulsiveness suits your path and your nature," he continues, "yet it is often reckless and impatient, naive and demanding."

"Is there anything good about it?" I ask, exasperated.

"It has brought you here."

"So now what?"

"You have heard of the senex."

I mentally trip over the word "senex" and wonder if I heard him correctly. Vaguely recognizing it as a psychological term for the archetype of age or "oldness," I nod, even though I really don't know what he's talking about.

"Do you mean that babbling old lady?" I ask, feeling my dislike for the old woman.

"Talk to the senex," he advises firmly. "She can help you. Without her you will perish here."

Growing uncomfortable with the somber mood of our discourse, I start to fidget.

"Lighten up, Dionysus."

Dionysus leans forward in his seat and gazes at me thoughtfully, then undergoes a sudden transformation. His hair begins to move and gather into thick locks. Horns erupt from either side of his head. His chin and cheekbones narrow and become bearded, while his eyes appear smaller, wilder. This all happens so fast I can do nothing but watch. He stands up with a jolt and I see that he has a tail and the legs of a goat. From his pelvis to his cloven feet, he is covered with coarse hair. He prances in a strange manner away from me, then turns about swiftly, cocking his head at me in the queerest way. He holds up some sort of flute and waves it back and forth in the air. I'm breathless, but not shocked.

"All right, so you're Pan," I remark dryly. "I don't get it."

He continues to caper about in a weird, crazy way. As I watch him, deep green images loom in my peripheral vision, crystallizing into the familiar wooded setting in my previous journeys. He skips away from me to a stream just ahead of us. I do not follow. He stands at the water's edge with his back to me and sways in a provocative manner, his arms wrapped about himself. He keeps peeking over his shoulder to see if I'm watching him. Of course, I am. I start to feel strangely unsettled. I walk to a nearby tree and place my back against it for support. I'm not sure why I'm doing this, why I don't flee. He watches me lean against the tree and smiles, seemingly quite pleased. He then advances toward me, swaying and leaping and cocking his head from side to side. At once, on closer inspection, I realize he is hideous, yet it is not a hideousness that's easy to define. I feel simultaneously repulsed and riveted. He is not devilish to me, not malignant or foul. I don't feel he can harm me or has any intention of doing so; yet I do feel he is mischievous and somewhat mad, possessed by something magical I can't understand.

"Do you want to know me?" he asks, slowly swaying from side to side.

He throws his voice like a ventriloquist. High and whiny, it seems to come at me from everywhere. He's stooping awkwardly now, looking up at me from one extreme angle then another, grimacing and smiling. I notice his teeth are very straight and white. Amazed, I don't know what to say. I'm thinking this is some kind of proposition and that he would like to rape me, but I sense he will not do this without my consent. Nonetheless, I'm beginning to think it would be "rape" even with my consent. I'm starting to feel flustered.

He giggles and leaps up, then trots off to the stream, yelling and whooping and flinging his arms toward the sky. It's obvious to me as I watch him that he's experiencing a delicious pleasure I know nothing about. I'm envious of his abandon and the way he grabs the air, delighting in whatever it is only he can see. I want to join in, but I don't know how. He then turns swiftly around and runs toward me, leaping and gesturing with his arms as he approaches. His theatrical overtures look so comical that I burst out laughing. He peers at me quizzically, then breaks into laughter as he spins and pirouettes and skips. He works this into running in a large circle while blowing his flute. He is so crazy-looking that by now I'm really laughing hard, enjoying everything about him. Suddenly he breaks from the circle and runs toward me, placing his face very close to mine. He is breathing hard. He holds the tree behind me with both his hands so that his arms surround me but do not touch me. He then sways back and forth in front of me, watching me intensely with a wild grin.

I immediately close my eyes and hold my breath. I don't want his scent to pervade me, which seems to be precisely his intention. I can't keep my eyes closed. I notice his torso and arms are damp with perspiration. Catching my breath, I smell his body musk. It is strong but not unpleasant. I can feel something happening in my brain as I inhale his scent. It is scrambling my thoughts, replacing them with an awareness of my own body. My skin tingles as though electrified. My nipples harden and I become aware of the weight of my own breasts, how they rise and fall as I breathe. My legs feel suddenly heavy as though they're filled with warm fluid. The sensation of something sinking in my brain brings my body to a wild alertness. My respiration quickens.

"You do want to know me, don't you?"

He says this in an almost hiss and I'm reminded of the forbidden fruit, that this, he, is the forbidden fruit. I'm ashamed of my need to want to know him, to touch the forbidden in myself. I feel I'm betraying some sacred code, that I'm weakening, falling prey to an abyss in myself. I think of a way to justify what I'm doing but I can't. He takes both my arms, lifts them above my head and holds them against the tree behind me. Some part of me is glad he is doing this, that he is taking control where I dare not. Suddenly I feel cool tendrils encircling my wrists and arms. I look up and see that vines of lush green ivy are moving and curling around the tree, securing my arms to it above my elbows. A heavy, coarsely-textured garb hugs my body. I look down at myself and see that I'm wearing an animal skin garment. The sight of it sends blood rushing to my head with such force that I can hardly breathe. Gasping, I look into Pan's face and see nothing less than the personification of raw desire staring back at me. Both fear and excitement strike hard in my stomach as he tugs the garment from my body. My sudden nakedness engulfs me like cool rippling water. Some part of me thrills to be naked, stripped free at last, exposed. I yield to this feeling and discover that I really do want this experience more that I realized.

Here I pause. I'm seeking counsel and find myself seated with Dionysus as before. I'm glad for the respite. I look into his face and detect a trace of annoyance, although his manner is calm.

"I'm having problems with this," I confide nervously.

"With what?"

"This Pan thing, this scenario I'm in."

"What troubles you?"

Embarrassed, I stare into my lap as I struggle to articulate my feelings.

"I'm starting to get off on all this. It worries me."

I wait for a response but Dionysus says nothing. Assuming he didn't understand what I just said, I take a deep breath and force myself to look into his eyes.

"I'm becoming aroused."

Dionysus looks at me blandly.

"That is the whole point, Melina."

"To get off?"

"To open to the life of your body and the power of your instincts. It has been a hidden world for you."

I gaze down at my hands. I realize this is true, but I don't trust the manner in which it is playing out with Pan. The whole thing feels uninhibitedly wicked, even depraved.

"I notice I'm experiencing this detail for detail," I remark. "Is that really necessary?"

"Necessary for what? What is 'necessary,' Melina?"

Dionysus studies me as I grope for an answer. Disappointed in myself, I shrug.

"I don't know," I admit weakly.

"This is an area you least trust about yourself."

"I know. I guess I just needed to check this out with you."

"Do not seek my permission. Seek it from yourself or not at all."

I'm becoming aware of a part of myself that dislikes the body, physical functions, appetites, sex. This awareness is annoying and increases my feelings of discomfort.

"Why is all this taking place within a sexual construct?" I ask pointedly.

"I cannot answer that right now."

I find his evasion frustrating. I bite my lip, trying to control my rising tension.

"Look, it seems that I'm being deliberately set up by this experience and I don't like it. I don't like the fantasy-seduction theme thrown in with the lure of spiritual union and ecstasy. The mixed metaphors are confusing and they're throwing me off balance. Let's be clear about this from the start: I didn't come here to be seduced by some animal for enlightenment's sake, at least, not in the way... I mean... oh! You know what I'm trying to say. This entire experience is making me mad."

Dionysus gazes at me quietly. His face is utterly expressionless.

"You are wasting your energy here. Either rest or re-engage with Pan."

"Just like that?" I explode. "What do you think I am, a robot?"

"You can shift, Melina. All you have to do is desire it. It is really that simple."

I leave, grumbling to myself. Navigating my way back to Pan, I find myself walking through a tunnel of semi-darkness that echoes whenever I make a sound. Trudging along slowly, I wonder if I'm just inventing this anger as a cover to disguise my own horniness, my darker sexual nature. Disgusted with this thought, I throw it out, feeling it is much too transparent. I dig deeper. I wonder if I've stumbled upon stored unconscious anger somehow related to the sexual experience. I soon realize that isn't it either. This is all a smoke screen for something else; what, I have yet to find out.

The tunnel is thinning out and I can now see that I'm approaching the woods. I slacken my pace, then remember something Dionysus said to me that I forgot to write down: if I wish to touch knowledge in his world, I'm going to have to part with my judgments and embrace nature instead. I think about this as I peer through the trees to the spot where Pan still stands. I see myself, arms strapped by ivy to a tree, gazing at Pan. He is fondling my breasts vigorously, pulling at my nipples. I look at my face and see quite plainly that I'm excited by what he's doing and breathing heavily. I suddenly enter into myself. I'm moving my backside in a rhythmic motion against the tree. I sense Pan wants me to do this as a signal for him to enter me. My body responds immediately to this awareness and I'm swept completely into my cells, my own heat, the wide circling rhythms of my pelvis rocking back and forth as I anticipate his entry.

At this point I break from the experience, realizing it's late and that what I need is contact with a real flesh and blood human being. I also feel this scenario has gotten just about as intense as I can stand. I shower, slip into bed with Ted and make love for what seems like hours. I'm more receptive than usual to my body's rhythms and needs, as well as his. The experience is very deep and gratifying for both of us. I tell him afterward that I need to lose more control during our lovemaking. I ask him if he'll help me. Ted seems to understand completely and consents. We fall asleep in each other's arms.

June 1 Session

I close my eyes and see that I'm once again in the woods. Morning sunlight spills through the treetops, drenching the grass in a sparkling wash of gold. I spot Dionysus at the edge of the stream several yards in the distance. He's strolling with his arms folded, his right hand propped under his chin as though he's immersed in thought. Catching sight of me, he walks toward me. He is not smiling.

"What's going on?" I ask.

Dionysus studies me for several moments.

"Why are you here?" he asks in a serious tone of voice.

The way he's eyeing me suggests I'd better have a good reason. Caught off guard, I can't think of a legitimate excuse for my being here. I'm struck with the thought that I've inadvertently done something wrong. Dionysus' brow is deepening.

"Do you want me to leave?" I offer, hoping this might rectify some error.

"You have unfinished business with Pan."

"Unfinished business?"

"You must complete what you have started. If you choose not to do this, you must leave."

Staring open-mouthed at Dionysus, I can feel the blood rushing to my face. My mind begins to race in a hundred directions. It's all I can do not to give in to a feeling of rebellion.

"Why must I complete this thing with Pan?" I cry. "Hasn't it gone far enough? I don't understand what you want!"

"It is you who does not understand what *you* want," he replies with equal force.

"Okay, I'll admit that. But why do I have to get involved with Pan again?"

"It will not be possible for you to go any further if you do not complete the experience."

"But it is complete!" I insist. "I went as far as I thought necessary!"

I stop and listen to that last word. Dionysus is staring intently at me. I think back to yesterday's discourse on the word "necessary" and feel caught between a rock and a hard place. My irritation escalates.

"What's the point to all of this anyway?" I snap.

Dionysus quietly turns away from me. I can see that his patience is wearing thin. He slowly paces, then turns around and faces me. His eyes look very sober. I'm beginning to feel frightened and don't want him to leave me. I'm also aware that my face is very hot. I feel like I'm going to cry.

"Look, I don't want to go back there with Pan," I explain. "It's really weird for me. It's embarrassing! Don't you understand? I don't know this guy! I'm not used to this!"

"What did you think you would encounter here, Melina? Certainly you realized you were entering a world of the unfamiliar. Now you want only those experiences with which you have grown accustomed? If so, go back into the other world that comforts you."

The moment he says this, I realize it's true. Somehow I'd forgotten the potential value of embracing the unfamiliar, one of the main reasons I came here in the first place. I can hardly comprehend how I'd gotten so sidetracked. I begin to reconcile the fact that if I want to continue my journeys here, I must finish this thing with Pan. I then wonder if I've invented all of this conflict and anguish for myself merely to appease my code of ethics, which won't allow me to enjoy the forbidden fruit without due punishment. The thought is nauseating. I glance over at Dionysus and see the hint of a smile playing on his lips. His eyes are sparkling. I break into a smile and suddenly feel very stupid.

"Well, I have to say I don't like the fact that I have no privacy in here," I confess in a calmer voice. "Invisible eyes seem to be everywhere in this place. I feel as though everyone is looking over my shoulder."

"Who?"

"You, for one!"

Dionysus bursts out laughing, shaking his head from side to side.

"My, my, what a serious girl you are."

"I do like my privacy," I emphasize.

"There is no privacy here. You know that."

"What?"

"You are autonomous only in the other world."

He pauses to study my reaction.

"Do not think about the meaning of this now, Melina. It must come to you from a place other than your mind."

He winks at me. Feeling shy, I stare down at the grass. I start thinking of Pan and feel uneasy.

"May I talk to you more about Pan?" I ask.

Dionysus sighs. I know this is a cue that I must keep it short. We both sit down on a low smooth rock.

"I don't really like him, you know? Something about him is disgusting. I want to throw a rock at him."

I look up at Dionysus, hoping I haven't said anything that might offend his sensibilities.

"Why do you want to hurt him?" he asks.

I pull up some grass and start tearing it up and twisting it around my fingers. I'm troubled by what I've just said.

"I don't know," I mumble. "It seems he's trying to pull me down to his level. He doesn't seem to have any conscience about this."

"What level?"

"The level of an *animal*," I stress, irritated by the question.

"Why does this bother you?"

I fling the grass aside and turn to face him.

"Are you a ghost, or what? Can't you get what I'm talking about? Don't you understand what it is to be human and live inside a body?"

A long interval of silence ensues. I'm convinced he can hardly be an authority on the subject, as he's a god.

"You are not going to like my saying this," he warns, waiting for my full attention. "It is you who does not understand what it is to be human. And certainly, you do not have the faintest idea what it is to really live inside your body. How can you? You have been punishing it all your life. It is the rejected 'other' you merely put up with."

"That's not true," I argue. "I do like my body."

"Your whole notion of your body is an illusion. You are not

dealing with a body. You are dealing with fear. Your fear creates a picture, effectively blocking out whatever it does not want to see. To do that it must cut off a few fingers and toes, an eye, a breast, a rib. It inserts a mutilated picture of you into your mind's eye. You see the picture and accept at face value the half of what you see. But what of your wholeness? What of your dismemberment, and where have those pieces of you gone?"

As he asks this, an image of Pan comes to mind. Somehow the words "dismemberment" and "pieces" seem to describe him, although I'm not sure how. I'm fascinated with the link. Dionysus continues.

"Those pieces gradually sink to the sublevels of self where they resume their respective lives and functions with or without you. Your fear keeps them relegated to those realms where they cannot be seen. In order to prevent your curiosity from dredging them up, fear posts warning signs at the threshold of their realms. Thus, these realms become the forbidden zones of your own internal landscape, threatening untold agony and death to whomsoever would tread therein."

I gape at his exaggerated choice of words but can't refute anything he's said.

"It seems fear is a formidable enemy to life," I remark, overwhelmed by his portrait of my psyche.

"That is another discussion."

He folds his hands on his knees and quietly studies me.

"What happens when one of your dismembered arms or legs floats to the surface from the realms of the forbidden?" he asks.

"I imagine it would look ghastly," I venture.

"And?"

"I suppose I'd want to get rid of it somehow."

"Would you say such a dismembered leg or hand would disgust you, repel you?"

"Yes, I'm sure it would. I'd probably think it was evil, harmful."

"How would you get rid of it?"

I imagine a hand floating in water.

"I guess I'd try to sink it with a rock, or whatever was handy."

I stop. Something pulls inside my stomach as an image of Pan appears in my mind's eye. I see myself throwing a rock at him. He cowers and throws his hands up to his face to protect himself. I suddenly feel sorry for him, sorry I threw the rock. I want to apologize to him. I look over at Dionysus. His eyes are very clear as he watches me; they radiate an intelligence beyond my ability to describe. I want to put my head inside of his and experience his thoughts. Unable to take my eyes off him, I begin to feel self-conscious and avert my gaze to the grass.

"You said before that Pan pulls you down to his level and seems to have no conscience about doing this," Dionysus continues. "He seeks to reunite with you from the only life he knows. In his world he is pure for he is truly and utterly being the life of himself, the life of the instinctual realm. This is his only purpose: to manifest the qualities of his realm. He is not capable of making the transition to your world without your help. However, you are vastly capable of making the shift to his world by becoming aware of his existence and receiving him into your conscious life. Then and only then can the body and all its parts be restored to wholeness."

As I turn his words over in my mind, I realize it will take me a long time to fully digest their meaning. I think of Pan and notice the tension in my stomach has subsided. I can't say that I view him with much liking, but I'm somehow more sympathetic to him.

Reflecting on the instinctual realm, I wonder why our Western culture has left so little room for its expression in our daily living. I wrestle with pangs of regret as I contemplate the strictures orthodox religion has imposed on consciousness and behavior, particularly my own, where angels bless and devils damn from their appointed sides of the fence. Aquarian Age or no, these forces are just as lively, colorful and argumentative as they were back in the Middle Ages. I look up and see Dionysus, his arms folded across his chest, enjoying whatever he's picking up from my reflections. I smile at him.

"Come," he says, his voice suddenly buoyant.

He takes my hand and helps me up from the rock. My behind is sore and I massage it. He smiles down at me.

"Do you want to go on?" he asks.

I pause and consider what he could mean.

"I think so."

He places his arm around my waist, takes my hand and dips me to one side as though we're dancing. I'm startled by his quick change of mood.

"Are you sure?" he asks, smiling down at me.

"Yes, I'm sure!" I laugh.

He places his right hand in front of his face and removes it quickly. I'm suddenly gazing into the wild eyes of Pan. I catch my breath and step back. The transformation is complete. A fluttering sensation steals through my stomach and chest as I adjust to his overriding presence. He is amazingly dark and physical, like a tree or a rock. My first impulse is to move away from him, to quickly put space around myself. I do this instantly, as though my brains were in my feet. He reaches out and grabs me by the back of my neck, then pulls me toward him even closer than before. I'm looking straight into his grinning face and notice his teeth again, how beautifully white and straight they are. I'm completely speechless.

"Where are you going, little lamb?"

The strange quality of his voice hits a delicate chord in my brain. I don't like it, yet I'm somehow lost inside of it as though it were an invisible web he has spun around me. Suddenly he sweeps me off the ground and carries me in his arms across a clearing in the woods. I notice he's heading for the stream. Grabbing onto him, I realize I'm stark naked and that my right breast is pressed to his chest. I feel very vulnerable.

"What are you doing?" I shriek, strapping my arm around my breasts.

His breathing gets very hoarse. He looks at me, apparently pleased with himself. He smiles and snorts but says nothing.

"Would you please put me down?" I plead, trying desperately to be civil.

He ignores me, enjoying my efforts to maintain my composure. Rapidly approaching the stream, I can now see that it's the size of a small lake, far wider and deeper than I thought. I'm wondering if I should start punching him so he'll drop me to the ground. I'm afraid to do this, not knowing in what perverted manner he might interpret my blows.

"Put me down!" I shout, pushing at his chest with my fists.

I really don't like this; in fact, I hate it. I hate being helpless. I hate not having control over my own physicality. I hate dumb brutes who think they can literally sweep women off their feet. He starts singing raucously, paying no attention to staying on key or putting the lyrics in any kind of order. This is maddening to me. I grit my teeth, getting ready to punch him no matter what the cost to myself.

He stops abruptly and I see that we're standing at the edge of the stream. The sun on the water is blinding. I turn my eyes from it and, in so doing, face Pan who is gazing at me with an expression of dead earnestness. Bewildered by his change of temperament, I relax my grip. He looks as though he's preparing to say something serious. Afraid he might behave rashly if he thinks I'm resisting him, I try to affect a composed demeanor. It's difficult. I don't like looking into his eyes and I'm trying to hide it as best I can.

"Can you swim?" he whispers hoarsely.

"What?"

He suddenly lets out a loud whoop, swings me high into the air and lets go. I hear myself scream as my back and rear-end smack the water. It is shockingly cold. Water rushes up my nose as I plunge deep. I swiftly paddle to the surface, gasp for air and push the wet hair out of my face. I can hear Pan laughing and spot him standing mid-calf in the water near the bank's edge. He's slapping his thighs and pointing his finger at me, howling loudly. I realize my feet aren't touching solid ground. I start to dog-paddle and feel like a fool.

"You idiot!" I scream shrilly.

I feel completely ridiculous and resolve that I'm never coming out of the water. I paddle out even farther.

"What are you going to do about the eels?" Pan yells at the top of his lungs, gesturing at the water.

Suddenly he raises his hands and starts wringing them in distress.

"Eels! Eels! Yii! Yii!"

"What eels?" I shout.

Uncertain if he's kidding, I carefully search the water. I imagine eels biting small chunks of flesh out of my breasts and thighs. I cover my breasts with one arm and try to dog-paddle with the other. I lose my balance and go under. When I come up I see that he's running out of the water, shrieking. Frightened, I swim fast toward the bank.

"Hurry! Hurry!" he cries, wringing his hands more desperately.

I feel something rub against my ankle. I jerk my leg in and flounder in the water. I think I'm not going to make it out, that I'm going too slowly.

"Help me!" I scream, fighting a wave of panic.

"I can't!" he yells back. "I don't know how to swim!"

My arms hit the water like propellers as the adrenaline rushes through my brain and limbs. My body feels amazingly alive and charged as my arms and legs slice the water like razors. I'm frightened out of my mind. Reaching the bank, I scramble up fast, then drop to my knees in the grass as I struggle to catch my breath. In my peripheral vision I can see Pan standing off to my left, watching me. I turn my gaze in his direction. His hand is cupped over his mouth and he looks as though he's stifling an urge to laugh. Dazed, I watch him for several moments, then turn around slowly and face the stream. Energy is draining out of my arms and legs as I study the water's smooth glassy surface. I see nothing remotely menacing out there, nothing at all. Scanning the water's edge near the bank, I can see clear through to the bottom. No insects. Not even a fish. I then realize I've been had.

An involuntary force deep within my chest begins to churn like a slow-rolling ball. It is a heavy feeling and grows stronger. I can feel it push through my back and spread across my shoulders. Everything in me sinks into it. Everything in my head fades out. Its gravity intensifies, penetrates like a harsh angle of light exposing an unhealed wound. Pressure gathers in my throat. I drop my face into my hands and feel a river pushing behind my eyes. All at once something breaks loose and I'm sobbing. Every muscle, every bone in my body is convulsing, shaking the grief loose. I don't know what is happening to me. I don't know why I'm so sad.

Pan is leaning over me and pokes my hand with his finger. I look up at him and see that he has his mouth turned down at the corners and is wagging his head from side to side in a comical way. I can't stop sobbing. I cover my face with my hands and slowly rock myself back and forth. Pan is still leaning over me and makes a strange sound. I glance up at him and see that he is handing me a flower—a black-eyed susan. Dazed, I take it from him and gaze at its childlike, simple loveliness. A deep quiet falls over me, numbing my feelings of sadness with exhaustion.

I lie down on my side and hold the flower to my chest. Pan walks several feet away and begins to pull up handfuls of grass. I watch him gather up a small pile and carry it over to where I lay. Taking one handful at a time, he sprinkles it slowly over my naked body. The grass falls like tiny feathers and begins to form a soft blanket. I feel warm and close my eyes. Sleep comes swiftly.

Personal Notes

A jarring transition: it's late in the evening when I pull back into ordinary awareness. I'm very tired. I walk into the downstairs kitchen and find dirty dishes and leftover food from dinner lying helter-skelter all over the counters. The garbage is overflowing and bits of cat food decorate the floor. My daughter has long since put herself to bed, forgoing my good night kiss and hug. I feel guilty about having abandoned my family.

I peer into the den and spot Ted sprawled out on the couch reading a book he hasn't been able to put down for days. I'm certain he's had his nose stuck in that book for hours. Feeling resentful, I march into the kitchen and grudgingly clean it up, banging cabinet doors and pans. I'm sure Ted hears this but doesn't come to help. I feel overwhelmed and wonder how I'm going to be able to continue to write and maintain a family and household as well. I begin to feel like a maid.

I've finished cleaning the kitchen when Ted makes his entrance. Of course there's nothing more to do and the irony of this fact doesn't escape me. He puts his arms around me and begins to tell me how much he's missed me. I interpret this as being his way of appeasing me, as he knows he's neglected doing his part of the chores. I push him aside and recite a litany of complaints about the kitchen being a wreck.

The next thing I know, we're in the den playing tug-of-war with a basket of clean laundry that needs to be folded, contending for the title of domiciliary competence. We're both yelling at each other as clothes fly in all directions. I'm surprised to see how angry he is and how vehemently he detests my "making a mountain out of a molehill." I, on the other hand, see him as really making the mountain out of a molehill over my making a mountain out of a molehill. I can't stand to be in this dilemma. To complicate matters, I don't know how to clarify what I'm feeling without adding more fuel to the flame.

I explain to Ted that my frustration is due to the fact that he's neglected to do his part to clean up. He replies with much disdain that I have one set of rules for myself and another set for everybody else. For a split second I can see this clearly; I allow myself the privilege of being holed-up in my office all evening, exempt from normal duties in order to transcribe the events of my inner journeys, yet I do not allow him to spend his evening with the same exemptions, enjoying the adventures of a good book. I attempt to justify this by reminding him that I write for a living and the time I spend in my office comes under the heading of "work." As I hear myself saying this, I realize it's not adding up no matter how I examine and weigh the facts. Growing increasingly flustered, I try to get a grip on where the flaw in my perception lies, without success.

Meanwhile, Ted's anger has increased enormously. A torrent of choice names spews from his lips and hurts me deeply. I become enraged and warn him to stop. For a millisecond we stare at each other, knowing full well that we're both doomed to drink this cup to the bitter dregs. Ted suddenly erupts with a host of verbal assaults, boldly aiming below the belt to prevent me from getting the upper hand. Incensed at how belligerent this tactic is, I start punching his arm, yelling that he stop being so "disrespectful." As the word ricochets off the walls, I feel conspicuously like one of my parents. Towering over me, Ted holds me easily at arm's length and I know I can't faze him no matter how hard I punch him with my skinny fists. I also know he has to use extraordinary self-control not to simply pick me up and sail me into the next room. Thank God he doesn't disappoint me.

We exchange more unpleasantries as he heads for the stairs to take his shower. He tells me there's nothing more horrible to him than my anger and that he's simply not going to put up with it. On that note he leaves.

I stare down at my hands mechanically sorting through clothes strewn about the floor. Dazed, I recall how I punched Ted and feel very badly. I also recall how I wanted to punch Pan as he carried me to the stream. Something gives way in me and I begin to sob. The tears are profuse, unearthing feelings of sadness that seem strangely linked to my experience with Pan. I collapse on the couch and close my eyes. Completely exhausted, I fall asleep instantly.

An hour later, I wake to the sound of Ted's voice gently nudging me out of sleep. Kneeling on the floor beside me, he takes off his shirt and drapes it around my shoulders, then hands me a glass of juice. I sip it in a stupor and feel oddly small. He then helps me up from the couch and holds me, asking me if I'll talk to him. I want to talk to him but my brain is not functioning that way. My feelings are in my hands. I gently stroke his back.

Together we walk slowly up the stairs to our bedroom. I enter the dark closet where my nightgown is hanging and stand there in half-sleep. Ted feels his way to me in the darkness and begins to undress me. Suddenly he kneels, wraps his arms around my waist and buries his face in my stomach. I stroke his hair and feel a deep tenderness for him. We go to bed and lie in each other's arms. I want to sleep but my hands are filled with a desire to talk to him, to caress him. We communicate this way for a long time.

An hour later we're lying in bed talking over our quarrel. We've made love and I'm particularly aglow with good feelings. This is the first time since my initial meeting with Pan that I've allowed him to join Ted and me in our lovemaking. Although I'm still not certain what this means, I'm aware that I'm less threatened by whatever Pan represents in myself, permitting him to become a more conscious, expressive dynamic in my lovemaking experience. Also unusual is the frequency with which Ted and I have made love since my first journey into the archetypal world. While I don't expect this to continue unabated, it is the quality of our experience I find most sustaining. My ability to channel needs, desires and drives through my body, and the freedom and strength of my focus, is a powerful emotional release and healing for my soul.

Soul force. That's what I've been trying to channel to the physical level all these years, especially to the most fragile area of my being: my sexuality.

June 2 Session

I close my eyes and see that I'm standing in a darkly shaded forest. I immediately notice it is a very different place from the woods in my previous journeys. The trees are immense and aged, reaching mightily toward the sky. The sun filters through the treetops and dapples the leaves with a soft golden light. I'm standing alongside a wide dirt road that bends to the right through a thicket of trees. It's very peaceful here. I feel as if I'm inside a cathedral.

I become aware of a sound in the distance—the soft clippety-clop of a horse slowly advancing from the right. I turn and face the bend in the path. I wait. Out of the thicket, a man approaches on a black horse arrayed in medieval attire reminiscent of the period of the Crusades. The horse is quite awesome-looking in its formal regalia. I like the animal at once. The man is young, perhaps in his early thirties. He has a handsome face but seems to be sporting a self-aggrandizing smirk that makes me suspicious of him. He's clothed in tights and a dark tunic set off by a fancy collar which is gathered at the neck like the petals of a flower. I notice he's wearing gloves straight out of the Civil War. I'm bewildered.

The man dismounts unhurriedly and gathers the reins of his horse. He's wearing a full-length velvet cloak of deep crimson which is unbelievably beautiful. As he walks over to a nearby bush, I take note of his shiny brown, knee-high boots. His curious mixture of clothing gives me an uneasy feeling. I suddenly want to get this encounter over with. Not knowing how to address him, I name him X.

"Who are you?" I ask loudly.

He is several yards away and looks over at me casually. He then plucks a blossom from the bush and slowly raises it to his nose, gazing at me in a strangely deliberate manner. I'm now sure I don't like him.

"Dionysus," he answers languidly.

I'm certain he's an impostor. Instantly the muscles in my body grow taut.

"You are not," I challenge him.

He walks over to me and hands me the blossom, smiling at me. I take it. It is small and pink with a yellow center. I'm not impressed.

"All right," he shrugs. "So I'm not. Who do you want me to be?"

I dislike his indifference, particularly his disregard for naming himself. I stare at him, feeling more and more critical.

"Don't you think you've confused your centuries?" I remark, gesturing at his clothing.

He looks himself over and smiles.

"What, this?" he asks, raising his cloak.

"Who are you?" I demand.

"I told you. I'm whoever you want me to be. Lancelot. Gawain. Dionysus... "

He lowers his chin and raises his eyebrows.

"Even Pan."

He lifts one edge of his cape like a wing, holds it in the air momentarily, then lets it fall in all its velvet glory back to his side.

"How about a horse's ass," I offer, my voice laced with sarcasm.

Instantly I grow afraid. My face begins to flush and I stand there hoping I haven't said something I'll regret. He walks over to me, still smiling.

"You really are a feisty bitch, aren't you?" he hisses.

The word hits me dead between the eyes. I hate the word "bitch" more than anything, particularly when a man calls me that.

"What do you want?" I ask again, trying to hold his gaze.

"It is you who wants me. After all, you are here, aren't you?"

My mouth opens involuntarily. His arrogance is beyond belief.

"I don't have to put up with this."

I turn on my heel and head for the trees. I haven't the faintest idea where I'm going and I'm beginning to feel sick to my stomach. I keep walking, driven by a mounting sense of dread. I stop, sit down on a rock and try to pull into my feelings, but everything is whirring inside. A crazy feeling seems to be taking over my brain. I feel very strange. I try to conceive of who this man is, what he represents. All I feel is fear. I'm sickened to think he is some part of me.

Personal Notes

After coming out of this experience, I feel deeply troubled. I'm confused as to why I've had an encounter as disturbing as this one, especially when I've been feeling so good about how I've been able to process my experiences thus far.

My abhorrence for X deepens as I go about my usual activities of the day. I have no desire to meet him again, yet I realize if I don't allow myself to explore this experience further, it will only plague me with anxiety and interfere with my future journeys. Meeting him has definitely put me in touch with my own feelings of darkness and insecurity. When I try to analyze this, I find that a mental approach only increases my feelings of anxiety and confusion. I can't seem to find another way in.

CHAPTER 2

THE DARK OTHER

June 3 Session

I close my eyes and see that I'm standing in the forest where I first met X. Everything looks precisely as it did before. Even the slant of the sun pouring through the treetops hasn't changed. The forest is very shady and peaceful—too peaceful. I don't like this. Feeling nervous, I wish I were somewhere full of sunlight and noise.

I hear the slow trot of a horse approaching on my right. As I turn and face the bend in the road, I get an ominous feeling of a bad dream repeating itself. My feet feel strangely frozen to the ground. I spot X approaching on his black horse and my heart begins to race. The horse is decorated in the same medieval style. X is wearing the same red cloak, the same black tunic. I realize I don't like this combination of black and red. It vaguely reminds me of something, but I can't put my finger on what it is.

X dismounts a short distance away. His manner is seemingly casual. He tosses his cloak over his shoulder as he gathers the reins of his horse. I notice he's wearing a wide black belt fastened by a large silver buckle. I'm certain he wasn't wearing it during our last encounter. On the right of the belt hangs an ornate silver dagger which stands out prominently against his dark tunic. He looks over at me with some purpose in mind. I'm gathering my nerve, trying to prepare myself for whatever he might say to me. I wonder why he's wearing a dagger and assume it must be but another ornamentation to enhance his sense of masculinity.

He advances toward me. Studying his features, I'm struck by his pale gray eyes and colorless complexion. A sudden chill races down my back. I clench my fists and realize my hands are like ice. He halts a few feet before me, then places his hands on either side of his belt. A short riding crop hangs from his belt on his left side. It is black and braided tightly. From the end of it hang several thin straps of leather. Seized with fear, I quickly turn my eyes from it. He smiles at me knowingly. I look back at the riding crop and see that he's fondling it.

"Look familiar?" he asks, smiling at me.

My mind races wildly. I've never seen a real riding crop before. I don't know what he means. He starts to laugh.

"Don't worry. I won't hurt you," he says reassuringly.

He reaches up and pulls a leaf off a nearby tree. I'm desperately confused and feel very emotional. I keep telling myself this is not real, that I have nothing to worry about. I'm breathing heavily. He slowly paces in front of me, then throws me a sidelong glance.

"And now you'll have to tell me all about yourself, won't you? Why you're here. What you're thinking... "

He stops pacing and studies me. I watch his eyes fall to my breasts. He stares at them brazenly.

"What it is you really want."

I wince, then feel a surge of anger. I realize I'm here of my own free will. I'm not a puppet and I don't have to take this kind of treatment from anyone. I can feel the anger sucking all my fear into it the way fire devours oxygen. Something pops in my brain as wild currents of energy shoot to the top of my skull. The muscles in my body tingle as though they're expanding. I begin to feel huge and enormously aggressive. I turn my gaze on him. I hate him intensely.

"You dumb fuck asshole!" I cry fiercely.

A strange look flashes across his face. His mouth parts, revealing teeth that are set closely together and have a glistening gray cast. His mouth suddenly widens to a grin. His eyes are alert.

"That's good. Very good!" he applauds, visibly delighted.

He walks a distance away from me, his step quick and determined as he removes his gloves. Taking them in his hand, he smacks them hard against his open palm, then spins around and walks back over to me. His eyes are gleaming and he's very excited.

"There are rules to this game," he warns, waiting for my full attention.

I try to relax my facial muscles. I'm very tense.

"Rule one. I can't touch you. You can't touch me."

He brings his face close to mine, opens his mouth and slides his tongue slowly across his lower lip. Repulsed, I draw back.

"I don't understand," I stammer.

"Of course you don't, whore."

He starts laughing. It is very low and raspy. I struggle to hold my breath so his vileness won't invade me.

"I can't touch you here because your body is in your other world. For the same reason, you can't touch me. But... "

He stares at me long and probingly. A self-contented sneer begins to play at the corners of his mouth.

"I can touch your mind."

A feeling of anxiety knots in my stomach. My mind races to an image of Pan holding my arms against the tree. I remember clutching his shoulders as he carried me to the stream. I'm very confused.

"But what about... "

X draws back suddenly.

"Pan?"

His face flushes with anger.

"That's different!"

He resumes pacing. His whole presence seems somehow darker, more sinister than before. He sees that I'm staring at him and turns away from me.

"Yes, Pan," he murmurs, regaining his composure. "A mindless bastard."

He pauses, then starts to giggle. It grows very high-pitched and dissolves into laughter. Suddenly he whirls around to face me, throwing his cape over his shoulder.

"You want to fuck him, don't you?" he shouts.

My eyes bulge with a sudden pressure as blood rushes to my face. I see he has his hand on the riding crop. He slowly takes it from his belt and holds it close to my face. My heart begins to race as I struggle to push it away. I can't seem to move my hands toward it no matter how hard I try.

"Tell me you haven't seen this before," he says in a low voice.

He twirls the riding crop in front of my eyes, savoring my discomfort. A sense of shame burns my face. I close my eyes. He places his mouth close to my ear.

"All women want this," he whispers. "All women are whores and cunts. You do know what I'm talking about, don't you?"

Suddenly I feel as if my hands were tied behind my back. My feet are bound and I can't move. As I struggle, the rising panic in my chest breaks loose and spills into my brain. I start to scream. X laughs wildly.

"Look!" he cries, pointing to a tree several yards across a clearing.

Tied to it is a woman dressed in medieval clothing. Her delicate face is framed by a white veil which wraps under her chin. She is pale and frightened. Striding towards her, X swiftly raises his arm and strikes her face with the back of his hand. Her piercing shrieks fill the woods as she strains against the rope that binds her tightly at the waist. X laughs hysterically at the sight of her helplessness. Filled with dread, I can barely breathe.

A dark shape invades my peripheral vision. Glancing to my left at a figure stirring in the trees, I recognize Pan moving stealthily through the woods toward the woman. I'm trying desperately to think what Pan means to do. Unaware of Pan's presence, X is turning away from the tree and putting on his gloves. All at once he spins around and spots Pan. Pan quickly moves to the rear of the tree and begins to untie the woman. A thick braid of rope falls to the ground and her arms drop to her sides. She leans over, exhausted, then gazes at X, her face twisting with terror. Swiftly gathering her skirts, she flees into the woods.

X walks away from the tree and finishes putting on his gloves. His manner is smug and casual. Pan stands to the side of the tree. He looks at me and then at X.

"What are you doing here?" X asks Pan as he smoothes his gloves into place.

His tone of voice is serious, almost businesslike. Pan stands there and looks at him. He says nothing. X turns away from him and walks over to me.

"What are you waiting for?" he shouts, gesturing at Pan. "There he is!"

Flustered, I look over at Pan. Less animated than I remember him, he simply stands there and says nothing. X begins pacing the area between me and Pan, clenching his hands behind his back as if he were immersed in thought. Twigs snap loudly beneath his boots in the silence. Suddenly he stops, raises a fist and smacks it hard against his hand.

"Do you know who that is?" he screeches at me, pointing to Pan.

I don't know what to say and feel extremely anxious. X laughs nervously, his finger rigidly pointed at Pan.

"That's my brother!"

My eyes widen in disbelief. I look over at Pan and then at X.

"Yes, my brother! Can you believe it?" he cries, nodding emphatically.

His whole body seems jerky and intense. He grabs the edge of his cape and quickly walks over to Pan. He studies him impatiently, swinging his cape to and fro.

"So, brother, fuck any pigs lately?" he asks loudly.

Pan gazes at him in silence. His arms hang motionless at his sides and his face is expressionless. X laughs disdainfully.

"What's this? Did some bitch bite off your tongue?"

Pan says something to X but I can't hear it. X gets right up into his face.

"What's that you said?" he shouts.

Pan says nothing. X turns away from him in disgust. He paces back and forth restlessly, then turns angrily to me.

"Well, why don't you fuck him?"

His eyes look wild and crazy. I'm frightened and don't know what to do. I want desperately for Pan to stop him.

Personal Notes

I pull back into my ordinary awareness feeling somewhat numb. I don't realize how exhausting this experience has been until later in the evening.

I walk downstairs to the den and play with my infant son. He is fat and happy. I hold his creamy smooth body close to mine, diving gladly into his simple uncluttered world. While I play with him, I mentally review my experience with X and still feel slightly numb. I don't know why I'm not experiencing emotional reverberations from the ordeal and wonder what is responsible for my detachment. All I know is I'm grateful for the respite with my son. Even with the television blaring and toys scattered from one end of the floor to the other, the world inside this room seems blissfully calm.

Later in the evening after dinner, I share with Ted my experience with X. As I read the material aloud, I grow increasingly uncomfortable. I plow through it anyway, pausing uneasily at all the expletives. After reading it, I take a deep breath and look at Ted, anxious to know his response. He seems unusually calm, which somehow disturbs me. I immediately assault him with a flurry of questions. Soon we're caught in a language web filled with psychological jargon, disagreeing with each other's definitions. This is not where I want my experience with X to wind up. Wrestling with an onslaught of conflicting emotions, I'm feeling much too vulnerable to get hung-up on semantics. I know if I don't succeed at removing the language barrier with Ted, these emotions will spill out in anger. He begins to sense this and makes a gallant shift.

Ted advises me to stop looking at X merely as an archetype belonging to the collective unconscious and to begin viewing him as a psychic component of my personal interior world. I initially resist the word "personal," insisting that if ten women were sitting in the room with us, all ten women would be able to recognize some aspect of X's dark energy—rapist, sadist, demon lover, etcetera—as an underworld dynamic alive and well in their own psychic make-ups.

Ted then asks me, "How many women do you think have fantasies inhabited by a Nazi wielding a riding crop?"

I'm surprised by his word "Nazi" and don't know what to say. I sit quietly and stare up at the ceiling.

Ted offers that the way I've internalized the psychic dynamic represented by X is unique to me. The way I perceive him is filtered through my own conditioning and private judgments about myself. As I listen, I know there's some truth in what he's saying. He then reminds me of the dialogue I had with Dionysus in which he talked of "dismemberment." Ted speculates that X is one of my truncated legs floating up to the surface of my awareness. I remark that if X is one of my dismembered legs, then Pan is my other.

Recalling how X addressed me as a "whore," I ask Ted if he thinks somewhere deep in the sludge of my unconscious, I perceive myself this way.

"If you're using the word 'whore' in a patriarchal, pejorative way to mean a woman who enjoys sex," he answers, "I'd have to say yes; your desire for sexual pleasure flies in the face of your early moral conditioning and probably stirs up old voices of judgment from the past. Maybe X is one of those voices buried so long that it has become a mutated version of itself, a 'phantom of the opera' whose genius has become twisted to the point of madness."

He then reminds me that in our lovemaking, my capacity to surrender to the forbidden in myself increases excitement, and that the escalation of sexual pleasure might be unconsciously experienced in direct proportion to the furor of old moral voices that brand such behavior as "whorish."

Squirming with self-consciousness, I know it's futile to resist this notion of myself. I realize when I'm fully enjoying sex, I'm also engaging my lust, an aspect I relegate to the world of X with all its seamy undertones: white into gray, gray into black, and black into blackest. As I peer into this face of my sexuality, I imagine it to exist within a convoluted underworld where things frighteningly twisted and perverse lurk in shadowy camouflage behind a psychic iron grate, howling to be let out. How does anyone truly know what can be let out safely and what needs to be held in check for the sake of one's daily psychic maintenance and overall sanity?

An array of sexual taboos begins to dance before my mind's eye, emphasizing the psyche's seemingly innate gravitation toward a fantasy life of sadomasochistic eroticism. This awareness is distasteful to me and instantly puts me on the defensive. Ted listens quietly as I vent my views on the subject, arguing that no one is spared the intrusion of the psyche's dark side into his sexual fantasies. I speculate that the majority of Western society has been rigorously conditioned to cosmeticize their chthonic urges; bleach them clean of perceived blemishes and adorn them with a sweet-smelling garland of benignity—and why not? How many of us possess the conscientiousness of genuine self-honesty, let alone the guts, to jump into the excruciating ordeal of confronting the dark underworld's implied amorality and violence in ourselves?

On the other hand, I suggest there are those who feel perfectly comfortable with the forbidden aspects of their sexuality, allowing dark impulses to penetrate their intimate experiences without the slightest sense of shame or conscience. Finding this latter posture baffling, I confess that it's all frightening to me; that despite—or in spite of—the fact that I enjoy sex, I've never been able to reconcile the dark side of myself, nor have I ever really understood how it is threaded into the pleasure principle.

Ted tells me that my own experience and perception of its darkness is something I should look at more closely. As I search my conscience, my mind becomes overlaid with images: the Virgin Mother-sacred goddess partnered by the whore-bitch. They are joined by an invisible commonness like two sides of a coin. As I reflect on these images, a memory dislodges: I see myself as a young girl struggling to read my sins off a piece of paper in the dim light of a church confessional, enduring the humiliation of disclosing my "impure thoughts" under the heading of "venial" sins. Then came the priest's inevitable question.

"Did you touch yourself while you were having impure thoughts?"

Holy Mother of God I had indeed, and more times than I could possibly remember.

"And were you with someone when you performed these acts?"

No, but the question provided new food for thought and fuel for later fantasies.

As I recall this episode from my past, I realize how moral self-scrutiny became a vicious circle that tormented me for years and filled me with guilt. Sighing heavily, I want to leave this saga of my girlhood behind but another memory invades: I'm 19 years old and spending a rainy afternoon with a distant relative who shows me how to inhale a cigarette. I like it and later buy a pack so I can experiment. I leave the cigarettes lying around and my father finds them. He is enraged. Grabbing the pack, he waves them furiously at me, shouting that smoking makes me no better than "a streetwalker who wears red lipstick and shows off her breasts and fanny." He informs me that if I continue to smoke, I'll have to move to another state so I won't shame him in front of his family. He throws the cigarettes into the garbage and turns on his heel, leaving me in a humiliated, tearful heap.

Grief-stricken that my father would sooner have me out of his life than wrestle with his embarrassment over the fact that I smoke, I jump in my car, find a drugstore and buy a pack of cigarettes. I light one up and smoke it between sobs. As I inhale, I try to detect whether an insidious inner transformation is taking place; if my sensibilities are dissolving into a muck of moral decay. I feel exactly the same, "as myself."

Ted is gazing at me from across the room and I realize I've been quiet for a long time. We begin to talk of Pan, how his impotence in the face of X seems somehow appropriate. Ted remarks that it is impossible for Pan, with his instinctual innocence, to meet X on the level of "calculated mind." I agree. The fact that they are brothers is fascinating to me. I wonder aloud why X hates Pan. Ted suggests I ask him, that he will have to answer me. I tell him I'm not ready for that. I will find out in my own good time.

This morning when I awaken, I realize I've spent my night in the archetypal world. Images pour back to me in a powerful but unrelated way. I feel energized and happy. I go out to the garden and cut some roses. While I'm arranging them in a vase, a large ugly spider flops to the countertop from one of the petals. Terrified of spiders, I quickly raise an object to smash it, then stop in midair. Finding a paper towel, I gently scoop it up, open the screen door and shake the spider loose into the sun. This is the first time I've allowed an arachnid to exist peacefully within my swatting range. Surprised at how easy it was, I feel the pull of the archetypal world and know there's a definite link.

June 4 Session

I close my eyes and hear someone shouting. I recognize the voice as X's. As the image of a forest sharpens around me, I spot X and Pan at a distance. X has grabbed Pan by the hair and is forcing his head back as he shouts at him. I can't make out what he's shouting. Pan's face is contorted. I see that he is in pain but won't raise his hands to loosen X's grip. It's pathetic to watch and I'm feeling powerless to do anything.

All at once X reaches for his dagger. He holds it out to his side and waves it menacingly as he shouts at Pan. It is bright silver and has wavy edges. I want to help Pan but my feet are locked to the ground. I can't seem to move and don't know what to do. I realize I can't touch X to pull away the dagger. I try to shout, but I have no voice. My eyes strain at their sockets as I struggle to free myself. X turns his face in my direction. He's still gripping Pan by the hair. His face looks very fierce.

"Don't worry!" he shouts. "I can't kill him!"

He smiles in a most evil way, tilting his head back and opening his mouth with frantic abandon. Suddenly he plunges the dagger into Pan's chest. Terror explodes in my body as Pan's deafening, anguished roar fills my ears. He is down on his knees, twisting and jerking as X turns the dagger in his flesh, delighting in Pan's torment. Screaming, I pull wildly at my clothes to free myself. My feet break loose and I race toward Pan. X sees me approaching and releases him. He quickly steps back as Pan falls to the ground.

"Get out of here! Get out! Get out!" I shriek, glaring at X.

My face is engorged with blood and I'm trembling uncontrollably. X looks at me blandly. He takes out a scarf and wipes the blood off his dagger, then casually drops the scarf to the ground, sporting the same self-aggrandizing smirk as on the day I first met him. I feel both shock and loathing. He mounts his horse unhurriedly, then looks down at Pan as though from Mount Olympus. His eyes are filled with pleasure at the sight of Pan rolling in his own blood. Suddenly X jerks hard on the horse's reins. The beast rears, then charges down the road at a full gallop. They quickly disappear in a cloud of dust.

I gaze down at Pan clutching his chest. His hands and arms are soaked with blood. I kneel and pull his arms aside to see his wound. Gasping, I quickly cover my eyes, trying to shut out the sight of a gaping hole oozing thick dark blood. I'm starting to feel faint and place my head between my knees. My hands stick to my face and I realize they're covered with blood. Pan begins to groan more loudly. I reach for his hand and look back at the wound. I'm breathing fast and feel sick to my stomach. The wound is deep and close to his heart. Panicked, I look around frantically and see no one, nothing. I clutch Pan's arm.

"What should I do?" I ask desperately.

Pan is still groaning. I grab his face in both hands and shake him.

"Tell me what I should do!"

He looks up at me. I can tell he's having difficulty focusing and I'm terrified he's going to pass out. I bite my lip to hold back the tears.

"Dionysus," he rasps weakly.

The name leaps into my brain and brings a sudden clarity.

"Where is he, Pan? Where can I find him?"

Pan groans loudly. He clutches his chest and rolls onto his side. Afraid of losing time, I jump up running, having no idea where I'm going. A pressure builds in my head. My brain feels as though it's splitting in two as I force my mind to reveal a direction.

Personal Notes

I pull back into ordinary awareness feeling drained. I know I've exhausted much psychic energy during the ordeal with Pan. Some part of me wants to continue, while another cannot. I simply don't have enough energy.

I feel quiet and withdrawn for the rest of the day. By evening I sense an anxiety building. I try to ignore it but it continues to build. Finally something snaps and I find myself questioning my entire experience in the archetypal world. I'm afraid I'm just making everything up, that all the archetypal images and activities are mere inventions, fascinating toys with which my imagination is masturbating. I question how I'm capable of such vivid imagery and riveting plots, why my own involvement is so intense. I begin to suspect this is all a maniacal creation of my ego; that if I continue, I'll inadvertently shake loose some latent psychosis which will suck me into it and devour me. Feeling cynical, I conclude that stumbling naively into my own psychosis could be the landmark of my first real experience in the archetypal world—that all the mesmerizing drama is but a ploy to that end, well-drafted by some hideous unconscious mechanism. This thought freezes in my mind and fills me with dread. For the first time, I examine to what extent my own gullibility has contributed to the ongoing inner productions. This examination sets off an inner alarm; I mentally slap myself awake and command myself to *get real*, resolving that I will not be duped into mindless compliance with the seductive illusions of my inner world.

I imagine this thing I call "Dionysus" and place him in my mind's eye. I then batter him with questions, determined to obliterate his persona in my psyche so that the true substance behind the projection can reveal itself. He is silent. I keep battering him. He looks at me with a haunting expression that fills me with the memory of a picture which used to hang on my bedroom wall for years: a melancholy rendering of Christ sitting on a large rock under a moonlit sky; spread out below him, the lighted city of Jerusalem lies hushed beneath dark enfolding clouds. His presence is filled with ineffable calm and surrender as he gazes upon his beloved city, his face betraying a quiet sorrow.

I go to bed feeling troubled and tell myself I need some confirmation about what I'm doing. I need to know if I'm heading in the right direction, if what I'm doing is right. A voice moves quietly in my mind and asks, "What is 'right,' Melina? What is 'right'?"

June 5 A Dream

I dream that I'm with a small group of people, both men and women. One of the women is my real-life sister, while the others are unfamiliar. It seems we all work together, but this isn't clear. One of the men in the group is black, another is a short, jumpy nervous type. I feel a sense of camaraderie with these people except for one: a tall dark-haired man dressed in black, who has a penchant for drama and acts extremely weird. Ghastly pale, he looks exactly like Bela Lugosi. He gives everyone the creeps, but we humor him and try to put up with him.

We go to someone's house in which there is a small room off the main parlor that resembles a laboratory. From the parlor, I can see an intelligent-looking man holding a hypodermic needle in the small room. Someone tells me we're all going to be injected with a drug that will alter our consciousness. Everyone seems excited about this prospect except for me. I hate hypodermic needles and ask if it will hurt. Someone shows me how it is done and says it will only feel like a mild prick, then it will be over. I'm worried the drug won't be "clean" and that I'll experience negative side-effects. He assures me it's very clean. I'm still worried.

"What if I never 'come down' or come back into normal awareness?" I ask. "What if I lose control?"

He assures me it won't be like that, saying that once I'm in the altered state, I'll be feeling calm and ecstatic and all my fears will vanish completely.

"But what if I die?" I ask.

He tells me if I die it will be absolutely painless, and that the transition from my altered state to afterlife consciousness will be as calm and gentle as going to sleep. I tell everyone I'll go last, that I first want to study how the drug affects each of them before I make a final decision.

The dream shifts and all but the Bela Lugosi character have been injected and are sitting together in a circle in one of the rooms. I sit next to them and observe them closely. They definitely seem "altered" and are smiling and talking quietly. Their eyes appear large and filled with light. They're very kind to me and understand my apprehension as I question them about their experiences. They entreat me to join them, telling me it's beautiful where they are and that I'll love it. Suddenly my sister remarks that my nose looks very large. Feeling self-conscious, I start crinkling up my face because my nose feels fleshy and awkward and I don't know what else to do.

The dream shifts and I find myself in the small room with the Bela Lugosi character who is preparing to be injected. A wild look flashes across his face and I know that it's done. As the man with the needle turns his back to him, the dark-haired character raises his hands menacingly behind him as though to attack him. Then he opens his mouth near the back of the man's neck and bites the air. I know he's "miming" that he's Dracula, only his manner is even more strange and obsessive than before. He proclaims loudly, "I feel as free as a bat!" and rushes out of the room.

The dream shifts and I find myself viewing the backside of the Bela Lugosi character. I notice he's wearing a black cape. I'm now very frightened of him and feel he's lost all control. All at once I see a hand floating in midair above the man's head. Unattached to a body, it is holding a short, very pointed dagger. The hand brings the dagger down hard and plunges it into the top of the man's head. The hand continues to strike the man's head and face forcefully, although his face is turned away from me. Blood is squirting everywhere. He staggers around and stumbles to the ground, his face covered with blood. I see that he won't die and keeps getting up. Suddenly he runs out of the room.

I look around at the frightened people in the room and notice a young fragile boy lying on a bed. His face is pale and his eyes are filled with terror. We begin to discuss the presence of the hand, where it came from and whether it means to hurt us. We realize it belongs to a force we can neither see nor understand.

"I knew this house was haunted all along!" I exclaim.

The young boy gasps with fright and I realize I should not have said this to him. We all agree we're now more frightened of the hand than of the Bela Lugosi character.

The dream shifts and I'm somewhere in the city. A woman's dead body has been found in the trunk of a car and the police are looking for the murderer. Joining the hunt, I'm told the murderer tries to lure elderly women while they are shopping in department stores. I enter a department store and see an old woman holding a large shopping bag. I know she'll be his next victim.

Personal Notes

I awaken from this dream feeling very crabby. My thoughts are imprisoned by the dream's images and I can't shake them loose. I'm miffed that I've dreamt of Dracula, a thinly-disguised projection of a woman's negative animus, as it is so-called. It's clear to me the dream is about X, but does my psyche really have to borrow from Hollywood to drive the point home?

I attempt to disassemble and analyze the dream, but I soon feel too tired and overwhelmed by its overlay of meanings. Trying to discuss the dream with Ted, I'm met with reluctance. It's Sunday—his ritual day of leisure—and understandably, he wants the luxury of not having to tax his brain. Nevertheless, I feel abandoned. I don't want to wade through my private hell alone.

I retreat to my upstairs bedroom and dive into bed, nestling deep under the warm comforter. The morning sun spills over me through the overhead skylight and feels wonderful. I try to empty my mind, but it's impossible. X parades boldly through my thoughts. Accompanying him is the "hand" hanging in midair, holding the dagger. As I watch X, I begin to feel small and worthless. I try to keep these feelings in check. I don't want my Sunday with Ted to go down the toilet.

I close my eyes, hoping I'll fall asleep so my heavy mood will shift. Instead, I find myself wondering how I'm going to get a handle on my interior world which is bulging with images. I keep seeing the hand and realize it's my own. The word "dismemberment" bangs in my brain. I suddenly recall a poem I wrote years ago that rose out of a darkness I now realize belongs to X. The title crystallizes in my mind: "A Freudian Dream In Three Movements."

I leap out of bed and search for the poem in my office. As I leaf through several poetry magazines, I see other verse I'd written during that time period which also seem "X possessed." Viewing my Freudian poem from this revealing new slant, I read it carefully.

A FREUDIAN DREAM IN THREE MOVEMENTS

1
A filthy man is eating
my rice. He points
to the rain-splattered
eyeglasses of a monsoon
escape

always midnight when the man
face down stalks her shadow
with a pillow open belly
open window the man only

happy with the sight of her
third rib in water gentle
boil and alluvial blade
precisely curved as her left
and only ear

"See the rain on his glasses?
It means the blood of Mr Smith
will save you."

2
I'm having Mr Smith
with tea. He knows
a lot of songs. I press
a cut lemon to my tongue

always midnight when the man
grins splinters from his gums a torn
scarf pulled from her dresser
drawer to stop bleeding
hands on the bedstand red
stain on her bedclothes he
whispers to her left
and only eye

"See the chain link fence on his belt?
It means the crime of Mr Smith
will save you."

3
Mr Smith is grinding
coriander for mother.
She reads the morning
obituaries out loud

always midnight when the man
ties up the cemetery willows,
smears their bark
with bright thin blood
of pomegranates
in moonlight the smooth
edge of his blade taps her left
and only leg

"See your heart in his boot?
It means the love of Mr Smith
has saved you."

As I finish reading the last line, the knot in my chest tightens. I close the magazine, realizing it has been seven years since I wrote the poem. Thinking back to that period in my life when my creative self-expression was at its most prolific, I now feel acute pangs of self-consciousness: how utterly transparent I was. How visible were all my wounds.

I go back to bed, burrowing like a crab beneath the covers. At once my mind gravitates to a disturbing meditation I had nearly a year ago during my last trimester of pregnancy. I see it very clearly: I'm lying on my bed in the late afternoon, exhausted with the weight and size of my body. I close my eyes. Instantly I find myself in the woods, staring at a grotesque tree stump which is alive and grimacing at me. Gnarled fleshy roots are growing all over it and I can scarcely believe how ugly it is. Suddenly it opens its very large mouth and says, "I'm going to crush your flesh and bones between my teeth, swallow you and shit you out my other end."

I look to my inner guide who is standing on my left and ask, "Will it be painful?"

My guide answers, "No, the process itself is painless."

I sigh with relief.

He then says, "Be warned. It is your fear which will cause the pain."

Gazing at the grimacing stump, I try to imagine what it would be like to be eaten. I conclude that having my flesh and bones crushed and digested in the realm of the abstract couldn't possibly hurt. I feel confident I can handle it. I then remember what my guide said about my fear. I imagine what it would be like to be an excretion, to be a "pile of shit." I begin to feel troubled and move out of the meditation.

The darkness of what I now call "X" and the idea of being "shit" begin to resonate familiarly alongside of each other. As this awareness deepens, I grow terribly afraid. I feel an urgent need to flush X out; to come to terms with whatever he represents in myself, which for years has lurked in a shadowy world behind a wall of fear.

Later in the week, Ted and I browse through a large old bookstore. Searching for the philosophy section, I wind up on a remote, musty-smelling floor of the building and notice a nearby area marked "Sex and Psychology." On one of the upper shelves is a fat hardback book entitled, *The Marquis de Sade: The 120 Days of Sodom*. Unfamiliar with Sade's dark legacy of prose, I take the heavy book down and leaf through it. Instantly my senses are bludgeoned by language and images so foul that I panic, slam the book shut and nearly throw it back on the shelf. I pace about, toying with other books while my eyes continue to stray to the fat book. Looking around to see if I'm alone, I pull the book off the shelf and open it. I'm appalled and fascinated. This combination of feelings in me smacks of X, his dark invasions into my sexual fantasies. I'm compelled more than ever to know why.

June 8 Session

I close my eyes and see that I'm standing in the forest in the same spot where I first met X. I look up and see that X is already advancing toward me on his horse. He rides with a deliberate casualness. As I watch him approach, everything seems strangely blurry. Suddenly I remember Pan and look to the spot where I last saw him. A long narrow mound covered with dead leaves suggests that someone has just been buried. I try to sense whether it could be Pan, then realize he cannot die. I wonder if Dionysus covered him with leaves to keep him warm.

X dismounts and walks toward me. I'm feeling somewhat numb and unafraid, for I can't imagine X capable of greater treachery than what I've already witnessed. X pulls his velvet cloak aside and I see that he's wearing the black belt. A scroll is tucked into it on his right side. I do not see the dagger or the riding crop. X takes the scroll from his belt and hands it to me. I take it cautiously while studying his face. The barest hint of a smirk plays around his mouth, but somehow he seems more serious. He turns away from me and mounts his horse. They leave as slowly and casually as they came.

I'm now alone and examine the scroll, which is made of thin, gray-white parchment. As I unroll it, the paper crinkles loudly. At once I see large, black ink calligraphy. I stare at the writing and can't make it out, as the letters keep going out of focus. I close my eyes and try to quiet my mind. I look again at the letters and see "I AM." I can't make out the rest.

My heart is beginning to beat rapidly. I close my eyes and tell myself that I will be able to read the words, that I must be calm. I open my eyes and see "I AM SENT." I shift my focus slightly to the left of the next word and it suddenly comes into view: HEAVEN. "I AM SENT FROM HEAVEN." There are more words but my mind is starting to reel, blurring the letters.

I look away from the parchment and take a deep breath. I'm worried it may bear a message that will frighten me. Maybe it will say something I don't want to know. I look back at the parchment and see the word "HEAVEN." Suddenly more words appear: "TO LIVE IN THE BOWELS OF HELL." I stop. I'm stuck on "BOWELS OF HELL" and think I'm mistranslating what I'm seeing. I look back and still see "BOWELS OF HELL." Then, "THIS IS MY MISSION." There are no more words. I read the message again: "I AM SENT FROM HEAVEN TO LIVE IN THE BOWELS OF HELL. THIS IS MY MISSION."

Instantly my mind races to find a meaning. The language in the message strikes me as metaphorical, hinting at a deeper underlying alchemy. I wonder what "bowels of hell" could refer to. And why "mission?" Why not "purpose?" The choice of words seems significant.

I roll up the scroll and try to put it in my pocket, but it isn't deep enough. I tuck it into my waistband and head into the forest to look for Dionysus. I think of Pan momentarily and feel a strange ambivalence. The mound piled with leaves flashes in my mind. I don't want to go back and look at what might be there. I tell myself that Pan is resting, that I can't help him without Dionysus anyway. I touch the scroll at my waist and peer ahead through the trees. I don't know where I'm going and have a terrible sense of direction. I decide not to think about it and allow my feet to go wherever they're so inclined. I know I'll eventually find Dionysus.

As I walk, I reflect on the word "mission" and improvise a definition: *that which one is appointed to do.* How is it different from "purpose"? I imagine a snake; one of the purposes for its existence is to keep nature's rodent population in check. But is this the snake's "mission"? Is a snake conscious of its role in keeping rodents from running amok? I decide that "mission" implies a conscious consent or willingness to carry out a plan of predetermined importance, whose means and effects fulfill a perceived purpose, individually, socially or otherwise.

I think again of X and the message on the scroll. If X is conscious of having been sent from heaven to fulfill a mission by living in the bowels of hell, then it stands to reason that he possesses divinity and is a collaborator with whatever or whomever sent him in the first place—God? If this is so, then X can't truly be evil. This leads me to thinking about Lucifer. As I reflect on his name, Lightbearer, I imagine his light falling like a lantern from heaven into hell's abyss. If I were to gaze deep and long into whatever chasm he roams, would I be able to see a glimmer of light? And if his light is there, and has been there all along, what is it doing to this thing we call "hell"? I can't imagine it would have no effect. If light exists even in hell, what the hell is hell, anyway?

I suddenly remember a passage that was dictated to me years ago by an inner Voice while I was in a deep state of meditation. I pull back into ordinary awareness and storm through several boxes in my closet. I finally locate the passage in an old notebook.

"The Creator then bade the Spirit, 'Go into the lands where my people dwell and bring to them my staff upon which the serpent shall lay, who shall gather to himself all desire for consummation. Thus shall my people's burdens be carried by the serpent, who shall take into himself all manner of density until his entrails burst. In that moment shall they know their God who sent them, for when the serpent's entrails burst, they shall hear a loud voice cry out across the land, yearning for life's renewal. And in the serpent's death shall be their regeneration unto Life, which shall blossom in the Tree central in the Garden.'"

I close my eyes and reenter the forest. I see that I'm walking in a specific direction, although I still have no idea where I'm going. I reflect on the passage and think of X, remembering the line, "Thus shall my people's burdens be carried by the serpent, who shall take into himself all manner of density until his entrails burst." Is this X's mission: to take my density into himself and become my very darkness? Visualizing his red cloak and black tunic, I wonder if he's wearing my anger and my fear.

I'm growing very tired and don't want to walk anymore. As I look around for a place to rest, I notice the forest has thinned considerably and now has the familiar appearance of the wooded setting in my previous journeys. I find a soft patch of grass beneath a large tree and sit down in it, placing my back against the trunk for support. Overhead, the afternoon sunlight pours like honey through the thick leafy treetops. I watch the leaves dance and sparkle as my eyelids grow heavier. Slowly closing my eyes, I feel as though I could sleep for a thousand years.

It seems some time has passed before I hear a voice. I think it's Dionysus, but I can't open my eyes. I feel very subdued, as though some part of me is sleeping while another part remains awake. I sense Dionysus is seating himself before me. Trying once more to open my eyes, I have the peculiar sensation of dreaming—that I'm dreaming of trying to open my eyes. I find myself surrendering to this strangely surreal state the way one would breathe effortlessly under water in a dream. A blurred image comes into view like a reflection in rippling water. All at once it stills. The features sharpen and I now can clearly see Dionysus as if my eyes were open.

I study what he's wearing: a long string of wooden prayer beads hangs from a belt of rope tied loosely around his waist. The beads are perfectly round and smooth and appear to be made of sandalwood. The texture of his ankle-length tunic is distinctly rough-looking like crudely spun wool. His entire appearance rings of an age in the long-ago past. Feeling disoriented, I stare more fixedly at him. Suddenly I'm struck with the fact that he looks like a monk. As I try to imagine why he's dressed this way, I grow uncomfortable; I don't like the religious overtones of his garb. Dionysus gently takes my hand and in it places the beads. They clack together softly and remind me of the sound of a prayer wheel.

"Remain relaxed and hold these in your hand," he instructs me.

I want to ask him why, but I feel too relaxed to move my lips. I also want to ask him why he's wearing monk clothes. It then occurs to me that his choice of attire is intended to address some part of my consciousness of which I'm unaware. I suddenly realize I would do well to yield to whatever part that is.

"Have you received the confirmation you were looking for?" Dionysus asks.

My mind is a blur. I don't know what he's talking about. I think maybe he's talking about the scroll.

"Your dream," he prompts.

My dream. The hand. Bela Lugosi. The images flood back quickly, yet it seems I had the dream a million years ago. I now remember the fit I threw that night before falling asleep, how I requested confirmation of what I was doing.

"Dreams will always mirror your own truth," he says quietly.

I try to respond but my mouth feels as though it's somewhere miles away.

"Release these thoughts now, Melina. Release everything. We are going on a journey. It is time to move back into your past."

The moment he says this, I remember an experience I had years ago: absorbed in a deep state of meditation, I find myself walking along a road flanked by tall narrow trees that stretch off into the horizon. I'm anxious to see where the road leads, for the landscape is strongly reminiscent of the Appian Way. My inner guide appears out of nowhere, takes me by the shoulders and turns me in the direction from which I just came. Pointing his finger at the road, he says, "Your path lies back there." He then disappears. I stand there wondering what he could mean, then abandon the meditation.

"It will be easy for you to do this, Melina. Touch the child in yourself. She will help you to reenter your early life."

A heavy feeling balloons in my stomach. I don't want to go back into my early life. I've ransacked my childhood a thousand times searching for bits and pieces of myself and I feel I've acquired enough information. My lips begin to move.

"I don't want to go back there."

"X lives in your past," Dionysus informs me. "We must find him."

This news comes as a revelation and makes me extremely curious. A dizzying sensation begins to flood my body, impelling me backwards through a long tunnel of dark swirling clouds. Instantly I experience a peculiar sensation of my mind narrowing or becoming smaller. The experience feels strangely claustrophobic. All at once the darkness clears and I see that I'm standing in the old kitchen where I grew up on Hopper Hill Road. I examine myself: my arms and legs are skinny and dark and I'm naked from the waist up. I'm wearing hand-me-down shorts and a pair of my brother's old gym shoes. I can't stand being here, being in the body of this girl. My hair feels ratty and sticks to my neck.

"How old are you?" Dionysus asks.

"Five."

"What do you feel?"

I feel frustration. I don't want to be here and I'm growing impatient. Breathing rapidly, I gaze around the kitchen. Suddenly my mother walks into the kitchen from the hallway. She's wearing a baggy red shift and blue sneakers. Her hair is tied back with a bandanna. It looks as if she's pregnant.

"Get me out of here," I plead to Dionysus.

"No, you must stay."

"No, I'm getting out of here."

I run out the kitchen door. Outside, the sun is baking the asphalt in front of the house. I can hear cicadas whirring in the trees and hate that sound. I run around the back of the house. I'm looking for a way out of here.

"Melina, you cannot go anywhere since your past is yourself. There is no place for you to escape."

The agitation in my body seems to be pressing against my lungs. I feel hemmed in, trapped.

"What do you want me to do here, hang around until my

mother finds a reason to punish me?"

I wait for an answer. Moments pass.

"Yes."

"Well, I'm not!"

I run back into the house. I suddenly remember I've hidden my brother's socks behind the laundry hamper in the washroom. I see that my brother is looking for them and is very upset. It's nearly 10:00 a.m. and *I Love Lucy* will soon be starting on TV. If he doesn't find his socks, my mother won't allow him to watch the program. It's our favorite TV show. We watch it together every morning like a ritual.

"Why have you hidden your brother's socks?" Dionysus asks.

"I hide them every day."

"Why do you do this?"

As I search for an answer, the program's opening music begins to blare from the television set. I dart into the washroom and quickly retrieve Mike's socks from behind the hamper, then rush out excitedly and show him that I've found them, exclaiming that he can now watch the show. Nearly in tears, he is so grateful that he hugs me. He tells me I'm the best sister in the world. We're both suddenly very happy. I want this feeling to happen to us every day.

"You love your brother very much, don't you?" Dionysus asks softly.

"Yes. He is my best friend. He's the only one who understands me. I protect him from my other brothers."

"How many brothers do you have?

"Six."

"You are the only girl?"

"Yes."

"What happened after you found your brother's socks?"

"My mother is suddenly standing there. She is suspicious. Every day I find my brother's socks for him. I think she is on to me. She questions me. I try to make up a lie, but I'm too nervous.

I finally tell her I've been hiding the socks on purpose."

"What does she do?"

My legs are tightening. I'm aware that I'm gripping the prayer beads very hard. I feel extremely uncomfortable and don't want to go on.

"Forget it!" I snap.

"You have not forgotten it."

"I don't have to tell you!"

"You must tell yourself, now, here."

As I resist, I can already see what's happening next. My mother reaches up to a high shelf and pulls down a thick black belt. She tells me to follow her. We go into her bedroom. My brother has followed us and stands outside the open doorway. He's very curious. My mother brings me to the side of her bed. She tells me in a very cool, calm voice to pull my pants down. I start to cry. I do not want to pull my pants down and feel very humiliated. I start to sob and beg her not to make me do this. I see by her face that it is her intention to make me feel humiliated, as well as to spank me. It is all part of my punishment. This has never happened to me before. I think she must truly hate me to be so cruel. I feel like I'm going to throw up.

"It is all right, Melina," Dionysus comforts me, touching my hand.

I quickly pull my hand away. I can't bear to be touched feeling this way. I feel very dark. I see my mother's face. I do not see anger. It has been replaced by something I've never seen before, something I don't understand. It's as though she's wearing a mask, for her face doesn't exhibit the usual anger and frustration that accompanies a spanking. The mask is physically beautiful, as my mother is. Her beauty and coolness has become a power. This is what is behind the mask. She seems to be aware of it. It is feeding her, shaping her posture towards me. I am filled with fear.

"Look again," Dionysus urges. "Are you certain this is what

you are seeing?"

I look at my mother's face. I'm trying to see something other than what I've just said. I imagine her today. I don't want to hurt her or cause damage.

"Melina, stay in your past. Stay inside your experience. It is all right. Your mother today knows it is all right."

"She was lonely and frustrated," I explain tearfully. "Too many kids and not enough hands; no one to turn to and constantly tired, pregnant, overwhelmed. She didn't like her life and felt trapped."

"Melina, you must continue. You are very strong now. Move back. You are in your mother's bedroom. You are looking at her face."

I look at my mother's face. It's clear I'm seeing something very dark about her. I'm more afraid of this than of being spanked. Something around my navel loosens. All the sacred feelings I have for myself and my mother are unraveling. It feels as though they're being yanked, ripped. This is what is making me feel nauseous. I pull down my pants just slightly. She tells me to pull them all the way down to my ankles. As I do this I see my brother watching me from the doorway. I'm so ashamed. I'm certain my mother knows he's there. Suddenly she walks over to the door and lightly pushes it with her hand. It closes but doesn't shut. It swings open just far enough for me to see that my brother is still watching from the hallway. My mother then tells me to lean over the bed. Placing my body and exposed behind in this humiliating position causes me to scream with emotional pain and embarrassment. I'm screaming loudly before she even hits me. When she does, it is horrible. I've never felt the sting of leather on my naked flesh before.

"What did you do afterwards?" Dionysus asks calmly.

"I hid in the woods."

"Do you recall your thoughts?

"Yes. I hate myself."

"Do you hate your mother?"

I think this over. I'm confused.

"I don't know. All I'm thinking about is how much she must hate me, how bad I am. I can't understand what made me hide my brother's socks. I wish I could disappear and feel ashamed."

"I want you to look closely again at your feelings, Melina. Do you really feel your mother hates you?"

"I think some part of her hates me and some part of her loves me, but I think she loves me because she has to, because she's my mother."

"Do you hate your mother?"

"Some part of me hates her and some part of me loves her."

"What do you do with the 'hate' part?"

I draw a blank. Dionysus gently places his hand on my foot.

"What do you think your mother does with her 'hate' part?" he asks.

"She spanks me!"

"What do you do with your 'hate' part?"

I'm looking for my "hate" part. I can't find it in my brain where I think my mind would put it. It seems I have to burrow down deep in my body to find it. I sense it is somewhere below my navel. The place down there is dark and swirls around.

"Can you go into that dark place and tell me what you see?" Dionysus asks.

"I will have to get very small to go in there."

"You can get very small."

Already I'm shrinking and dropping down inside my body as though I were gliding on a parachute. Suddenly my feet hit something firm. I look around. It feels as if I'm in a cave. Dark clouds swirl around and around.

"Where are you?" Dionysus asks.

"I'm in a cave."

"What part of the body do you think this is?"

I look around. Suddenly I know where I am.

"It's my womb!" I respond excitedly.

"What do you see?"

"Clouds. It's dark in here."

"Look in your hand, Melina. You have a flashlight."

I peer into my hand and see a flashlight. Examining it closely, I can just barely make out that it has a red handle.

"Turn it on and shine it around," he instructs.

I hesitate. Suddenly I feel fear.

"I don't think I can do this."

"You are very strong, Melina. You would not be in there if you were not."

I look around in the dark. I'm trying to see if I can identify anything without having to turn the flashlight on. I can't make anything out.

"But what if there's something horrible in here?" I worry aloud. "How will I get out?"

"The same way you got in. Use your mind to locomote."

I feel for the switch on the flashlight and turn it on. Shining the beam directly in front of me, I watch the light pierce the thick swirling clouds. I can make out that the cave narrows slightly and reopens into another chamber off to my left. As I inch my way forward, I notice my surroundings are damp and clammy. Listening to the wet sound of my footsteps, I wish I'd taken my shoes off before I entered this place.

"How are you doing?" Dionysus calls.

His voice seems to penetrate the darkness from a faraway place.

"I don't see anything yet."

I'm now walking into the chamber to my left and notice the swirling clouds have dissipated. In the center of the chamber is a large rock with a smooth flat surface that looks vaguely like a primitive altar. Resting upon it is something wrapped up in a white blanket. I move closer, place my flashlight on the rock and pull back a corner of the blanket. There in the half-light is a round-cheeked baby with large brown eyes looking up at me. I'm surprised she doesn't cry at my sudden presence. Placing my hands beneath her small bundled body, I gently pick her up and cuddle her. She feels wonderful in my arms.

"Dionysus! I found a baby!"

I hear no answer. I walk the baby around and talk to her. Her soft eyes focus on me easily. I study the surroundings, wondering how she got here, who takes care of her, how she eats. Suddenly I notice the far end of the chamber. It narrows considerably into what appears to be a passage or tunnel. I place the baby down and fold the blanket around her. Taking hold of the flashlight, I walk to the far end of the chamber, crouch down and aim the beam into the tunnel. The light pierces deep into the darkness, but I can see nothing at all. I notice the passage is just large enough for a human body to crawl through it. A feeling of claustrophobia suddenly grips me and I gasp for air. I slow my breathing and try to calm myself. I shine my flashlight once more into the tunnel. Again I see nothing. My heart begins to pound.

"Tell me what I should do!" I call loudly.

I wait for an answer. Hearing none, I get up and walk around the chamber. I study it very carefully, shining my flashlight on every inch of it, even the ceiling. It strongly reminds me of a tomb or burial place. I discover no more apertures, no more tunnels. I shine my flashlight again on the passage at the far end of the chamber. As I stare at it, I recall a hole about the size of my head that gaped from an outside wall of the house in which I grew up on Hopper Hill Road. The hole tunneled under the house and was filled with an old musty smell. I used to think devils lived in that hole and slithered out at night to scare me and my brothers. Whenever I was brave enough, I'd stick my whole face into it and scream like a banshee to shake up all the wicked little demons—then I'd run away into the sunlight, daring them to get me.

I walk to the passage and tell myself that I'm 35 years old. I don't know what this means, but somehow it makes me feel stronger. In order to see where the tunnel leads, I realize I'll have to crawl through the passage on my hands and knees. I tuck my flashlight into my waistband with the light facing out, then crouch down and place my hands into the tunnel. The stone is very cold. I pause... there's something strangely familiar about this. An old dream flashes vividly through my mind: I'm standing in the woods looking at a gigantic turtle made of solid rock. The turtle is positioned in such a way that its hind end is tilted up at an extreme angle to the ground, while it's head touches the earth. Under the turtle's tail is a hole just large enough for a person to tunnel through its body, down to its head. The tunnel continues to go underground.

In the dream I'm with an older man who is some type of investigator. We're after something, but I don't remember what. In order to find what we're looking for, we must enter through the turtle's hindquarters and tunnel our way through its body into the earth. The investigator tells me he'll go first to ward off any danger. He instructs me to follow behind him. I study the hole under the turtle's tail and see that it's very narrow. I don't know how we'll be able to squeeze through and I'm concerned that once we're inside, we may very well get "stuck." I awaken from the dream.

I peer into the dark hole. Remembering the dream gives me reassurance, for it fills me with a vague sense that I've rehearsed the experience in which I'm now enveloped. I draw my knees up into the tunnel and creep along the cold stones at a snail's pace, keeping my sight focused on the glow of the flashlight. All at once I'm seized by a wild urge to shut my eyes. I realize the last thing I want to see in the glare of a flashlight beam is an unfamiliar face in dreadful Technicolor. Without a means of escape, I'd be hopelessly trapped. I stop and fumble at my waistband. Feeling for the flashlight switch, I turn it off.

Personal Notes

Although it's too late in the day to continue, this is not a good place for me to stop. For the rest of the afternoon and evening, I feel I'm living inside a tunnel. Everything is swelling inside of me with no place to go. I sense that I'm carrying a ton of information that is pushing to get out. It's very distracting and claustrophobic. I feel disoriented.

Later in the evening, I share with Ted the incident with my mother. As I read the material aloud, fresh emotions rise to the surface and paralyze my voice. I feel like I'm going to choke. Aware of how painful this is to reveal, I struggle with an acute sense of nakedness while being engulfed by feelings of smallness and humiliation. The feelings are powerful. I want to cry but talk myself out of it.

I reflect on my relationship with my mother today. We've worked hard and with great care over the years to heal old wounds, recreating our relationship with a love that has survived the worst in both of us. I feel so good about where we are together now—the confidences we share, the friendship we enjoy. I worry aloud to Ted that maybe I misperceived her when I was a child. I worry that I've done her an injustice. Ted tells me my love for her is very protective—it wants to "push away the ugly stuff and focus on the good." He tells me to trust my feelings and continue with the work, saying, "The eyes of a five year-old see what we have learned to shut out."

I struggle to believe this but worry anyway.

CHAPTER 3

TUNNELS AND CAVES

June 9 Session

I close my eyes and see that I'm surrounded by darkness. It is cold. Crouched on all fours in the tunnel, I sense the encircling wall of stone pressing about my body. My heart begins to race as I contemplate what I'm doing. I tell myself, "Stay calm... you can do this... don't think about your claustrophobia." It doesn't take hold. Already a sense of entombment is escalating out of control, intensifying my terror of being buried alive. I quickly shift my focus, drawing breath deep into my stomach. I imagine my stomach as a huge bellows, capable of holding great quantities of oxygen. I exhale slowly, pushing the air out with my stomach muscles. They feel very powerful. I tell myself I must concentrate on this power.

I begin to crawl. My eyes are closed and I'm breathing loudly. As I listen to the sound of it, I visualize myself meditating in the safety of my office, surrounded by brilliant morning light. Focusing on this light as a mantle of protection, I begin to feel the blessed reassurance that I'm not alone. I move more deeply inside my breathing, synchronizing my body's movement with its constant rhythm as I crawl steadily over the cool, granite-like stone. Opening my eyes for an instant, I stare into the pitch black before me... how long will I be in this tunnel? I begin to think this tunnel may have no end; that I will be trapped inside it, trapped inside my body, crawling on all fours into infinity. Gasping, I crawl faster. My heartbeat accelerates and I can hear the sound of it pummeling my eardrums.

Suddenly my right hand presses down into air. I stop and draw a breath. I feel the tunnel with both hands and identify an edge. Leaning out of the tunnel at its rim, I dangle my arms, trying to touch a floor, but I can feel nothing. I remember my flashlight, pull it from my waistband and shine it toward the floor. It's about a four foot drop to the ground. I wonder how I'm going to negotiate getting out; the tunnel isn't large enough for me to turn around and drop down on my feet. I realize I'm going to have to spread my hands out and fall face first.

I inch myself out to my navel, then walk my hands down along the outside wall for leverage. All the while I'm thinking there's got to be a better way to do this, knowing I could easily lose my grip and hit the ground with my face. I can now feel the weight of my body crushing down on both my wrists as I hang from the edge at my thighs... I let go. My body slides out and I fall onto my back. Instantly something crashes to the floor—oh God, my flashlight! I grope along the floor, but I can't locate it. Too frightened to venture out any farther without it, I leap up and press my back to the wall, then feel my foot brush against something solid. Reaching down, I quickly probe the object—it's my flashlight.

My eyes are shut tight against the darkness and I'm breathing fast. What now? I feel as though I've been down here forever. A small inner voice tells me to turn back. "Hurry, before it's too late." I consider whether I should go. I've gotten through the tunnel, I'm here, now I can go. "Go! Go!" the inner voice cries. I feel the rim of the tunnel with my right hand, making up my mind to leave. I then hesitate, realizing I haven't investigated where I am.

I quickly raise the flashlight and flip on the switch. The beam reaches clear through to the opposite wall and I'm surprised to see the room is not very large. I lower the flashlight to a crude-looking floor made of mud-colored stone. Sweeping the light slowly over the right wall, I shine it on a far corner of the ceiling. I'm puzzled by the fact that both wall and ceiling appear to be made of concrete. All at once something crosses the beam of light. Thinking I'm imagining it, I aim the flashlight to my left.

Something crosses again, moving fast like a bird. My heart begins to race as I shine my flashlight toward the ceiling. An image freezes in the light: a hand, life-size and deathly white, hovers in midair. I stare at its fleshy palm and fingers, then realize it has no arm, no body. It is attached to nothing.

Gasping, I run for the tunnel, leap up and catch the edge of it with my upper body. Scraping my knees frantically at the wall, I try to climb up far enough to push the rest of my body into the hole. The tunnel explodes with the sound of my panting as voices shriek in my brain, "Get out! Get out!" As I force my body over the rim, I can feel the weight of it pulling me back out. I clutch desperately at the tunnel floor, but I'm sliding too fast. My flashlight crashes to the floor as I plunge backward into the darkness, collapsing on my side. Something brushes across my face and hair. I wave my hands wildly around my face as I inch my way toward the flashlight. I grab it and swing it blindly, when something bumps against my back. Whirling around, I glimpse a leg, ghastly white. I throw my arms over my head and scream shrilly, afraid I'm losing my mind.

"Melina!"

Dionysus' voice penetrates the room.

"I am here. Melina!"

"Where? Where are you?" I cry, reaching out with both hands to find him.

"It is all right. I am here. I am with you. Nothing can hurt you."

I break into tears, crying loudly.

"Help me, Dionysus!"

"Listen to my voice, Melina. The hand is your hand. The leg is your leg. They are the parts of your self."

"No!"

I cover my eyes and press my face to the wall. I want to get out. I want the nightmare to stop.

"Do not fear them," Dionysus continues. "They are the

masculine qualities that stir within your being."

"But how can they move?" I sob. "They're not attached to a body!"

"The power of the Spirit moves them. Of themselves, they can do nothing. The soul you share with the Creator belongs also to them. They are incomplete without it. They seek to reunite with it."

"My soul?" I ask, struggling to comprehend what he means.

"Your soul is espoused to the Spirit," he answers. "She is a vessel for the Spirit's indwelling. Without this vessel, Spirit cannot fully incarnate into flesh."

I turn my face from the wall and stare into the darkness.

"But where is my soul? Why can't they unite with it? Isn't it here?"

"Come," Dionysus urges in a reassuring voice.

My body feels very heavy and I must exert great will to move it. I brace my weight against the wall and stand up slowly. My shoulder is sore and my knees ache. I feel around in the dark, but I can't locate Dionysus.

"Where are you?" I call, groping along the wall.

"Close your eyes and be still," he answers. "I will take you back through the tunnel."

I don't understand how he will do this, but I close my eyes anyway. The engulfing silence presses around me like a fathomless presence. Feeling as though I'm going to dissolve inside of it, I try to focus on my breathing. Suddenly I'm swept off balance by a profoundly disorienting sensation of being pulled rapidly through space. It lasts for an instant. When I open my eyes, I'm standing in the chamber where I found the baby. Breathing deeply, I notice a significant lift in my energy. I look around, but I don't see Dionysus.

"Step over to that far wall," his voice instructs.

I look across the chamber at the wall he must be talking about. I walk over to it, wondering what he means to do.

"Touch the wall," Dionysus prompts. "You will find that it is very soft."

I reach out and scrape the wall with my finger. It gives easily. I can't identify what this wall is made of. I push my hand into it further and see that I've made a dent.

"What is this?" I ask, examining the chalky residue on my hand.

"Dig into the wall, Melina. Do not stop."

I hesitate, then lay my flashlight down. With both hands, I begin scooping the wall away. It is almost effortless and in no time I've made a large hole. I shine my flashlight through it.

"There's something behind this wall, Dionysus. Look!"

Poking my head through the hole, I see a large passageway that winds to the right.

"What's back there?" I ask, scouring the area with the flashlight beam.

"Step into the hole and see," he invites.

Feeling a grave sense of hesitation, I slowly withdraw my flashlight from the hole and take a deep breath.

"I don't know... "

"You have nothing to fear, Melina."

I think about it. Unlike the tunnel, the passageway seems spacious enough to walk through without difficulty. If something should befall me, at least I'll be able to run. I find this last thought enormously reassuring. With Dionysus' presence as an anchor, I feel I'm at little risk for another frightening encounter.

I push one leg through the hole, then the other. Shining my flashlight around the passageway, I see that it is made entirely of small stones that form a high, neatly arched ceiling strongly suggestive of a church. As I walk, the sound of my footsteps echoes loudly. Somehow I don't feel anxious or afraid. This puzzles me. I round the bend which leads to the right. The wall angles abruptly and curves to the left. Peering down the long passageway, I see that it angles once more to the left. Sighing, I stop and lean my back against the wall, too tired to go on.

Personal Notes

I pull back into ordinary awareness feeling as if I'd been slammed by a truck. I'm completely exhausted, body and soul. I proceed with my daily activities and feel strangely irritable. I don't have a lot of energy to invest in the tedious rituals of everyday living.

Ted arrives home from work hungry and itching to fire up the grill for dinner. I gaze disinterestedly at the pork chops he's piling on a platter with great gusto. Somehow they look ridiculous to me. I have no appetite and begin to complain loudly about everything in general. Ted eyes me quietly. Realizing I haven't made the full transition back from the archetypal world, I suggest that I share the material with him in the hope it may help me to "come back." I explain that sharing my journeys with him in the past has provided a reassuring field of gravity—a ground of reality—for my drifting consciousness to return to. He agrees with my assessment and is being positively saintly about my grouchy mood. I make a conscientious effort to snap out of it.

I'm somewhat touchy for the rest of the evening. I try not to drift back in my mind to the experience with the hand, but it's nearly impossible. Again I question the authenticity of my experiences, dreading once more that somehow I'm contriving them. At the same time, I feel "loaded down" with information and experiences yet to come. This dichotomy is excruciating. I plug into a moronic program on television and welcome the ensuing oblivion.

Later in the evening, my brother Joe phones from Ohio. For years we've confided our spiritual odysseys to each other, airing the downside of our private inways to enlightenment: inadequacies of comprehension and application, involuntary leaps into sloth and forgetfulness, frequent bouts with emotional deflation—and how maddeningly convoluted "Know Thyself" can be. I bring him up to date on my archetypal journeys, confessing my feelings of insecurity and frustration. Suspecting a divine hand is at the helm of my experiences, he firmly encourages me to continue with the journeys, suggesting that I trust the inner design of my work. The strength and calm of his voice is deeply comforting and my anxiety begins to lift.

After our conversation, I crawl into bed feeling at peace. Ted strokes my hair as I drift off to sleep. Throughout the night, even as we dream, our hands reach out to touch each other.

June 10 Letter From A Friend

Dear Melina,

As I read your letter, the image surfaced in my memory of a Hindu carving I once saw of the earth goddess, Kali. She was in a squat position giving birth, one arm tugging the head of her emerging offspring, the other arm raised high, readying a sword. What a vivid, honest image of the fragility of our lives, the terror of earthly existence, the ephemeral span of our lifetimes.

The themes of loss and fragility you wrote about so eloquently struck a deep chord within me—the keynote of what my Self seems to be in the process of integrating into wholeness. I, too, have spent hours (years, actually) reflecting upon the treacheries of being human, which you so perfectly expressed in your letter. A sobering perspective to be sure; however, I think it is a necessary one, assuming one's aim is to integrate wholly into the life process. Realizations of this sort are "morbid" only to the extent we allow them to defeat our spirits, sap our courage, and deny us the full experience of what is exquisite about the eternal play of light and shadow as it manifests infinite possibilities of form upon our awareness.

I believe that identifying and facing head-on that core of terror pulsing in our human hearts is the first step toward the awesome task of replacing that terror with courage, thus initiating us into an arena of wholeness, integration and transcendent affirmation of life. Our options remain rather limited, don't they? We see all around us human escape valves for fear. We can do what our postwar generation counterparts have done and retreat into a world of simulated insulation, circumscribed by various collections of niceties—the BMW, the master suite, the boat, the imported tile—all carefully arranged into a fortress against reality. I know a woman who is a highly paid VP in her company, married to a highly paid VP, living in a beautiful home with their adorable adopted daughter (watched over by a full-time nanny who also has dinner waiting every evening), who is able to buy $150.00 shoes at Neiman-Marcus on a whim. This woman is woefully miserable and is currently seeing a psychiatrist in order to find out what she "really" wants. Amazing! Sad.

Another recourse is to become a slave to fear, projecting it upon every challenge, commitment and change that confronts us, until we are paralyzed into a narrow life of constant, intimidating, immobilizing dread. I think of someone like my friend Sara, whose life is stifled by the fact that she fears to tread in so many, many places: elevators, relationships, her past, behind the wheel of a car, on and on and on. The most popular one, of course, is the one you spoke of in your letter—the attempt by vast numbers of us to camouflage fear with an array of distractions: work, religion, family, responsibilities, plans, politics, ad infinitum, until our lives are neatly structured retreats into the sweet sleep of forgetfulness. Finally, at the drastic and truly morbid end of the spectrum, there is the flight into insanity, and more completely, into suicide.

It would seem that neither of us is content with any one of these options, and I see this as very positive. Since, as you've said, our lives operate within a "collective" power and momentum much greater than that of the individual over events, and there is little we can do to prevent the forces of darkness—the demon—from invading our sphere, we are left with no other choice but to confront the terror that lurks in the dark recesses of our souls, our hearts and our minds. I find myself perpetually rotating to the same threshold: the embrace of darkness, its fiery presence in my dreams, its nesting place in my Self. To mobilize what real courage we can, to replace dread with affirmation, is, I believe, the first essential task from which all spiritual lives emanate. Buddha's first Noble Truth: "Life is sorrowful."

Evil, darkness, loss, terror; all these equally are threads of the rich mysterious tapestry that is the experience of being human, alongside the threads of love, compassion, plenty and all that we embrace as "goodness." But how, if we are to become whole, can we allow ourselves the privilege of picking and choosing only those threads we deem acceptable, and attempting to negate the rest? This, in and of itself, constitutes the fragmentation of the soul: our inability, or unwillingness, to embrace the whole, the "suchness" of ourselves; whereas, to do so requires tremendous courage and love of the soul.

The stark reality still remains that "cosmic" or "spiritual" or "philosophic" perspective is of little, if any, comfort when our lives are touched intimately by the sword of loss. All we can do is attempt to live in the full knowledge that one of the perennial faces of life is loss itself, and hope that in our hour of sorrow, our dark night of the soul, reserves of courage and strength will avail themselves to us.

The inescapable truth is this: we live, only to lose everything—youth, health, loved ones, wealth. To fail to come to terms with this verity is to imprison ourselves at the perimeter of experience: fragmentation, spectatorship. The challenge confronting us is that of becoming whole, integrated, a participant, body and soul, in the magnificent tragicomic opera that is the life process. There is something unspeakably divine about this, and at the same time, earthbound. Isn't this what it's all about?

And doesn't it become more and more apparent that truth does appear on the horizon of human consciousness as stone, and not as the flock of great white birds we at one time had hoped for? But how can it be otherwise when we are so of the earth? Stone—whole, complete, at rest, eternal—the Word being made flesh. When our lives resonate with truth, we find so much falling away; our hands "loosen on things that used to feel so important," as you observed. Our minds loosen their grip on old concepts, expectations, attempts at "understanding" and objectifying what is essentially impenetrable. We cannot "have" truth, or "know" truth; rather, we can only be truth. I agree with you—it's not accompanied by anything lofty, and yet it enlarges me, fills me, opens me to the fullness of what I am. What more can I ask for?

Your loving friend and companion,
Marie

June 11 Session

I close my eyes and see that I'm standing in the large passageway with the arched ceiling. I've just climbed through the hole in the wall and I'm shining my flashlight up at the ceiling. Something about the arched stones seems familiar to me. I aim my flashlight down the passageway and see that I must walk again to where it winds to the right and then to the left. Now and then I think I see lighted torches burning from several places along the walls. This is strange. I know they're not here, yet I seem to remember them as once having been here.

I come to the end of the passage. It turns sharply at a right angle and continues a few more yards, leading to a room. I slow my steps, running my fingertips along the cool stones in the wall to my right. I enter the room and see a woman prostrate on a kneeler. Her hands are folded in prayer upon a velvet cushion of deep crimson. A delicate veil adorns her light-colored hair, which falls in waves around her shoulders. Around her neck is a crucifix suspended from a gold chain. She wears a long flowing garment of pale blue, belted at the waist by a thin sash. Her sleeves are turned back at her wrists and her head is bowed. She is crying.

I quickly scan the room and see that it is empty and dimly lit. Behind the woman is a window which opens out onto a garden and large shade tree. I turn my gaze again to the woman. Her crying comes in soft, echoing sobs. Moved with pity, I advance closer. She lifts her head and raises her eyes to something invisible. Her face is pale and sorrowful. Wishing I could console her, I try to think of the appropriate words. I'm beginning to feel a heaviness in my chest and a sensation of being enveloped by an oppressive gloom. I want to leave, disappear, but something holds me there. I gaze at her clothing and realize she is dressed as one living in a medieval age. I sense she is locked inside her past, that it is an imprisonment for her. There's something very haunting about this. I'm feeling more and more uneasy. I want to touch her, relieve her suffering, but I still can't think of what to say.

My lips begin to move soundlessly. I want to call her "Mary." I feel very strange suddenly, and hold the name back. Something presses on my tongue. I open my mouth and hear myself say, "Mary." I say it again, but she doesn't hear me. A force begins to fill my chest cavity, inhabiting my body with a presence. Feeling like someone other than myself, I walk toward her and see that I'm extending my hand. It touches her shoulder. I say, "Mary." She is lost inside herself. All at once I'm gripped by a chill that touches my very bones. Frightened, I step backward toward the doorway, then turn and run down the passageway. Everything is blurring as I run. I see the wall. I slip through the hole.

I pull back into ordinary awareness. I feel very strange and want to stop, afraid of venturing any farther into a realm too deep and unfamiliar to fathom. As I contemplate the woman on the kneeler, an inexplicable feeling of pain gathers around my heart. When I called the woman "Mary," something within me seemed to recognize her. Whatever this is burrows to the very depths of my soul.

I close my eyes and see that I'm standing in the chamber where the primitive altar stands. Lying quietly on the high flat rock is the baby bundled as before. I wonder why I haven't held her more, why I'm not fussing over her. This is unlike me. I pass under the archway that leads out of the chamber and find myself engulfed in dark swirling clouds. I shine my flashlight around, looking for a way out. As I attempt to locate the opening where I first entered, I begin to feel anxious. All I want now is to get out of this place.

Aiming the flashlight to my right, I spot a figure obscured in shadow. I adjust the light and see it is X. The beam freezes on his image and I can't seem to draw it away. He's staring at me with a knowing smirk and walks toward me. I move sideways, holding my flashlight on him. Glancing to my left, I see that I'm nearing a wall. I grope the length of it with my free hand as I walk backward away from X. The wall angles sharply and wedges me into a corner. Panicked, I bolt into the darkness as X intercepts me. His overwhelming presence forces me back against the wall. Swiftly reaching out, he grabs my wrist and wrenches the flashlight out of my hand. He grins fiercely as I struggle to pull away.

"You won't be needing this anymore, now will you?" he asks loudly.

He lifts the flashlight and shines it directly into my eyes. I jerk my head back, feeling a sickening wave of dread.

"You said you can't touch me!" I cry, refusing to gaze into his face.

"Up there I can't touch you. Down here... that's a different story!"

He laughs loudly. I try to pull away even harder. He grabs me by the throat and pushes the back of my head against the wall. His warm breath brushes my face.

"It is useless to resist," he whispers.

He pushes his hand into my stomach and presses hard. Gasping, I strike at his shoulder with my free arm as the flashlight plunges to the floor. X yanks me away from the wall, gripping me tightly by the wrist. My heart pounds wildly as he reaches into his cloak. He raises his arm and I see he is holding the riding crop. He brings it down hard across my shoulder and pain tears at my flesh. Screaming, I try desperately to free myself. He raises it again. Pain rips across my back. He lunges at me and I fall to the ground. Ripping the front of my blouse open, he claws at my breasts. Something savage shoots into my brain. Raw power rages through my body and rises to my throat. Growling and clenching my teeth, I dig my nails into his face. I want to draw blood, I want to tear him apart with my nails and teeth, I want to kill him!

He releases me and draws away. Panting, I look up at my scratch marks on his cheeks. He stares down at me triumphantly, pleased by some apparent victory. He smoothes his cloak with slow deliberate strokes.

"Why seek your redemption in the house of God?" he asks in a mocking tone of voice, placing his riding crop back into his belt. "It's clear you are nothing but a pig."

A madness fills his eyes as his mouth sharpens to a cruel grin. Tilting his head back, he extends his arms as though preparing to rise through the ceiling. Trembling, I watch the dark clouds swirl around him in the dim glow of the flashlight.

"Look, little pig! Watch!"

He lowers his head by degrees until his features come into view; it is the face of Dracula. He raises his arms like powerful wings and roars with laughter.

"I feel as free as a bat!" he cries, his voice filling the cave with echoes.

I cover my face, feeling dread and remorse. The violence, the blood lust, still ebbs in my veins. Tears smart at my eyes as a wretched sense of shame floods by being. Unable to control it, I start to sob, feeling completely trapped.

Some time has passed and I'm still crying. My face is wet and stuck to my hands. Completely withdrawn inside myself, I don't seem to care about anything. Gradually I become aware of faint sounds. I stop crying and listen to them as though in a half-sleep. The sounds grow closer, clearer, and everything around me begins to feel different. Light spills in between my fingers and I look up. Dionysus is sitting across from me. Brilliant green leaves sparkle everywhere. Realizing I'm in the woods, I look down at myself and see the scroll tucked in my waistband. A string of prayer beads rests in my lap. I glance up at Dionysus and see that he's watching me. Aware of how I must look, I touch my face. It is swollen and wet with tears. I quickly bury my face in my hands.

"Just how sick am I?" I ask, my voice stiff and muffled.

I wait for an answer, then raise my head and look at him. Remembering X as Dracula triggers extreme feelings of annoyance.

"What's with all the high drama, anyway?" I demand, feeling my back for a wound. "I mean, do I have to be beat up, shoved around and molested, too?"

Dionysus observes me quietly. I force myself to hold his gaze, then quickly become self-conscious and look away.

"Is there something you want to tell me?" he asks, his manner completely relaxed.

I catch his question in the pit of my stomach. Feelings begin to churn chaotically. I don't know what to say, where to begin. Examining myself, I notice my blouse is still in one piece. I study it closely. It's not even soiled. I look up at Dionysus. His eyes are smiling at me.

"Look, whether this did or did not happen, it was definitely no picnic, believe me."

I want to snap out of this attitude, realizing it won't get me anywhere. I observe my irritation and try to get at its root. Why am I feeling destructive, defensive? Some part of me feels like cowering, while another part is frantically gathering up the remains of my shattered dignity. X comes to mind. I think, "proud bastard." Feeling a fresh wave of irritation, I realize my anger is being fueled by pride.

"Where does pride come from?" I ask, staring dejectedly into my lap.

"Pride is self-love's shadow."

As I contemplate the word "shadow," I realize a shadow cannot be cast without light. I suddenly imagine God as an enormous being filled with Self-Love, looming over the face of creation, casting a huge shadow. I try to imagine Him seeing this shadow and knowing it is related to Himself. What becomes of this knowingness, this awareness? Was pride begotten of God's shadow-relatedness to Himself? Did it take on its own life, become differentiated? I think of Lucifer as a symbol for this life, the "angel of pride who fell from grace," then I remember the scroll given to me by X, "I am sent from heaven to live in the bowels of hell. This is my mission."

I lean back in the grass and sigh wearily. Whether light or dark, demon or angel, everything seems to come full circle, reuniting with the source that begot it. As I gaze into Dionysus' eyes, a quiet voice rises in my heart: "I am the Alpha and Omega."

Personal Notes

For the next few days I rest from my archetypal journeys and fully reenter my own immediate world. The life of the interior realms envelops me in sleep and permeates my dreams. Even though I can't recall the dreams when I awaken, I feel I've been charged with vast amounts of psychic energy and insight. This feeling of insight has no specific object, nor does it spill into my mind as "revelation." I can only define it by saying that I have a sense of "pattern," or a greater feeling of my interrelatedness with the material in my journeys and all things in general. This feeling centers me in a curious way. No mystery has been unveiled, yet the suspended moment in which I live, the one that corrals hours into days and months into years, feels potent and filled with promise.

My thoughts have drifted to the ocean many times these last few days—ocean as mandala: a wordless movement both contained and free; light and dark in perpetual dance; being while ever becoming. A memory surfaces of a sacred communion I once had with the Atlantic Ocean; how my attempt to capture its spirit in the body of a poem became lovemaking—an ecstatic leap into the forms and gestures of soul. Now, five years later, the life of this poem calls to me with the same immediacy, the same urgency. Pulling a book of poetry off a nearby shelf, I locate the poem and read it quietly.

ODE TO THE UNLOUD

I. Ocean

Ah, death in these arms without flesh. Legs, earth-belly,
breasts without vestment. Only. For instance, the Lover
has no mouth, no loud recollection of stories. Recall
ocean, mother, cup. This. The highest degree of Weakness

If story sinks, there's another body. Another story and the body sinks or what the skin calls water. Ancestor. Water like father, brother, the Terrible Eye watching its love back.

II. Mother

Swell of a body floating up high but not bright. Now,
coming down low it has lost a name for itself. Sad hope
for the hidden, the underwater looseness of small animals.
Such a sudden and lovely caution. The Lover. Everything

A journey back and the wail so fragile it is always remembered. No help for the legs swollen with running. Movement. A perpetual distance so hideous. Solemn.

III. Cup

A slim decay of reason as hands recede, waving the absence.
Caves. Light on the mouth poised on its death-call. If only
the Loud, mist and unfamiliar. Motionless as mountain in praise
of consumption. The Lover, singing the Empty

Clearer than itself, an outcome without bone. This. A moment's panic reeling on tongues of water, chant of breath. Itself always, clapping the loss with one hand. Calmly.

June 15 Session

I close my eyes and see that I'm sitting at the base of a tree in the woods, facing Dionysus. A string of prayer beads rests in my lap. I'm menstruating and feel very quiet. The hum of the woods is extremely soothing. I feel as though I'm hearing through my womb; everything is slowed down. Wanting to sleep, I close my eyes. The air fills with the tranquil tone of Dionysus' voice.

"Death's life rouses from its dark slumber and raises its head into the light."

His words move to me quietly as though carried by soft undulating waves of light. The light enters my mind like warm vapor. I reflect on his words dreamily and think, "Death's life? How can death possess life?" I allow the thought to dissipate, breathing deeply. Again the soothing rhythm of Dionysus' voice penetrates the space between us.

"The great bat flies toward the sun."

The image of a large bat flying into the sun gently unfolds upon the screen of my mind. Detachedly gazing at it, I think, "Bats don't fly toward the sun. Their territory is the night." The bat's image is replaced by a dimly lit cave. I imagine walking into it and seeing hundreds of bats; one of them stands out markedly from the others. Gazing at it, I reflect on the experience in my womb with X as vampire. The bat becomes large and statuesque. I think, "He stands sentry at the realm of darkness." At once the bat is transformed into a gargoyle staring from the architecture of a Gothic cathedral. About him, underworld creatures of stone guard the places of the sacred, threatening death to those who would venture into unfamiliar realms. Suddenly I hear the words, "Keeper at the Threshold." My mind begins to reel and I feel as if I'm falling.

I enter a deep valley of darkness. Overhead, the black sky swirls as jagged bolts of lightening crackle over the landscape. I see that I'm standing at a gate. Two immense stone statues loom against the sky; one is posted to my left, the other to my right. Part bat and part dog, they look Egyptian. I sense they are guardians of the Valley of Death. In the distance, luminous balls of light blink off and on like gigantic fireflies and seem to be moving toward me. I want to go and touch them, but I realize I must pass through the gate. I gaze up at the statues and sense their coldness, their lifeless presences of stone. I then focus on the glowing spheres and feel my trepidation dissolving. As the spheres move closer, I sense they are presences of light who have been waiting for me, who will take care of me. I pass through the gate and run into the darkness. The restful sound of Dionysus' voice penetrates my breathing.

"Empty your mind, Melina. Imagine your mind as a large, blank sheet of paper. Together we will draw on it."

My mind goes blank. Suddenly a vague shape appears. It looks like a geometrical figure.

"As you look at this blankness, Melina, focus your awareness from the area of your womb."

The figure becomes clearer and I see that it is diamond-shaped. My awareness of this shape feels as though it is being projected from the life in my womb.

"We are going to draw a map," Dionysus continues. "You are aware of having entered four chambers during your journey into the interior life of your womb. Mark them in your mind as you remember their positions in your womb."

I gaze at the diamond. Four black dots appear at each right angle. They are the four chambers in their respective positions as I journeyed through the womb.

"We are using the womb as microcosm of the Self, Melina. Though not limited to the framework of the womb, the map will serve our purpose as paradigm."

Unsure of what he means, I start to feel befuddled. I don't have a head for math, nor do I have one for maps. I can't even cut a piece of paper in a straight line.

"Connect each point," he directs me.

I see that the points are already connected.

"Now connect the points vertically and horizontally. You will notice the figure divides into equal quadrants. Draw a circle around the figure through its four points."

I draw a vertical and horizontal axis. Then I draw a circle around the figure and screw it up. The circle doesn't connect through the four points. I want to erase it, but I don't know how.

"Focus now on the four points," Dionysus proceeds. "Imagine them as the four chambers through which you journeyed. Find four names that reflect the nature of each of these chambers."

Breathing deeply, I feel myself begin to sink. A fog of darkness slowly lifts and I see the chamber I entered when I first dropped down into the womb. Filled with dark swirling clouds, it is the cave where I confronted X. I reflect on my vision of the dog-bats in the Valley of Death and remember the name, "Keeper at the Threshold." I name this chamber, "Death."

I proceed to the left where I entered the chamber of the child. I must first pass by the wall through which a passageway leads to the weeping woman. I see the whole of her in my mind: her pale hands resting on a crimson cushion, her dress strikingly feminine, her tears glistening in the dim light. I observe her staring at something invisible and remember the name "Mary." I call the chamber, "Feminine."

I continue on through the chamber where the child rests upon a rock. I touch the soft white blanket in which she is bundled and gaze into the child's face. Her eyes are wide and clear, full of acceptance of my presence, and without fear. In them I see light, life, innocence and potentiality. I name this chamber, "Life."

I walk to the right of the chamber and peer through the hole in the wall. My field of perception vanishes inside a long tunnel of darkness. Closing my eyes, I can clearly visualize where it leads: to the small room with empty corners and walls of concrete; to the hand and leg moving eerily through space without connectedness or function. I recall Dionysus explaining these images as representing the masculine qualities of Spirit seeking union with the soul. I name this chamber, "Masculine."

"Let us now contemplate the diagram, Melina. You have placed "Life" at the top of the vertical axis and "Death" at the bottom. On the left of the horizontal axis you have placed "Feminine," and on the right of the axis, "Masculine." Consider now the line which extends from "Death" to "Feminine." This line represents a plane of being. Seek a name for it."

I feel myself sinking more deeply inside my body. Immediately I'm enclosed in what feels like a massive stone cave and dark swirling clouds. I think, "I am spirit conceived in flesh. I have entered the world of form." Realizing I've named this place the chamber of "Death," I'm struck by a sense of irony, for its womb-like enclosure strongly suggests a latent potential to foster life. I then reflect, "I must be birthed into life by a woman in whose body I live." I proceed to the chamber of the Feminine. I see the woman prostrate on a kneeler, her body heavy with the weight of her own life. Around her neck is a cross upon which

Jesus is nailed. She is filled with sorrow and pain. As I gaze at her delicate form upon the kneeler, I notice the latter is made of rich solid wood. Behind her, a window opens out onto a garden, in the midst of which stands a tree, large and heavy with age. I think, "Organic life. Birth. Death." I name this plane of being, "Matter."

"Ascribe to this plane two qualities," Dionysus instructs.

I contemplate matter and organic life, visualizing the earth as a ball of gravitational mass, vulnerable to the elements that surround it in space. At once I sense a correlation between the earth and the woman's body prostrated on the kneeler. I take note of her hands resting against a velvet cushion, its deep burgundy texture exquisitely soft-looking in the pale light. I wonder why these details are so striking. The word "sensation" leaps into my mind. I give to the plane of matter the qualities of "Earth" and "Sensation."

"Descend once again into the chamber of Death, Melina. Seek two qualities by which to name it."

I'm beginning to feel like a Ping-Pong ball and want to get out of this labyrinth. I don't like "constructs" and I'm starting to feel claustrophobic.

"When is this exam going to be over?" I ask impatiently.

I'm pulling at the prayer beads and digging the toes of my right foot into the sole of my left. I open my eyes. Dionysus is looking at me. As I stare into his emerald green eyes, I wonder why I hadn't noticed their color before. Suddenly I feel very small, as though I'm peering out at Dionysus through the eyes of a six year-old. The feeling is extremely uncomfortable. I shut my eyes and burrow down into the chamber of Death. As I do this, I feel my ribcage constrict. I want to hurry and get this over with.

"This is really a lot of information for one mind," I balk, looking around the chamber of Death. "What am I supposed to do with all this stuff? Why do I have to find two qualities? Why not one? Why not 20? How do I know I'm picking the right ones?"

I'm looking for something to kick around down here and almost hope X will show up. The word "duality" comes to mind. As I reflect on its meaning, I recall that every dynamic has a dual nature, a positive and negative current. All at once I find myself standing outside my body. As I watch myself, I wonder why I've become so irritable and dark. My observer-self feels calm, assured, while the me I'm watching is jerky, tight and complaining.

"Okay!" I call loudly. "So this is but another reflection of my duality!"

I reenter myself, feeling disoriented. Peering around the cave for clues to the two qualities, I can't see anything clearly in the darkness. Realizing I'm going to have to work from memory on this one, I try to recall how I came by the other qualities. What did I do? I sit down. Suddenly I'm bewildered. Dionysus' voice explodes around me.

"Melina."

"What!"

"The two qualities."

"Fear and violence!" I reply hurriedly. "Can I get out of here now?"

I'm beginning to think this place is responsible for my state of mind. All at once I feel someone's arms envelop me from behind. Floating up quickly through the top of the cave, I hold my breath as though rising to the surface of a deep lake. Brilliant light spills around me and I see that I'm standing in the woods. The arms release me. I spin around and look into the face of Dionysus, catching my breath.

"I thought you were X!" I exclaim, steadying myself. "You scared me!"

Dionysus says nothing. I study his face, then back away slowly. His eyes seem to be tugging at either side of my abdomen. As I gaze into them, they appear smoky and strangely deep.

"Take off your clothes," Dionysus says quietly.

My skin bristles as an energy races up my spine. I reach up to my already-buttoned blouse and clasp it tight.

"What?"

"Take off your clothes," he repeats, his eyes deepening.

Overwhelmed with self-consciousness, I stare down at the grass. As I do this, my field of vision narrows considerably and my mind becomes saturated with the color green. My gaze moves to my bare legs and lingers on their tanned smoothness. I look back at the grass and unbutton my blouse. It slides easily off my shoulders and falls to the grass. I slip off my shorts. Dionysus does not move near.

I stand there trying to decide if I really want to take my bra and panties off. My dawdling is becoming painfully awkward and I'm beginning to feel that I'm behaving stupidly. This instantly magnifies my sense of self-consciousness. I don't want to cave-in to this feeling while I'm half-clothed.

"Really, Dionysus. I'm a grown woman with children. I don't undress for just anyone, and even if I did, I'd have to have one hell of a good reason."

As I wait for an answer, I feel my face flush. I don't dare look up from the grass. I'm becoming aware of my right hand and want to put it behind my back. Instead, I reach up and unhook my bra. It falls to the ground. I quickly remove my panties. Made of light nylon, they drop like a tiny blue parachute to the grass.

Dionysus walks toward me. Lowering my eyes, I gaze at the hem of his garment as it brushes over the grass. He places his hand under my chin and lifts my face to meet his. It is awesome to be so close, to feel his breath on my skin. I study his mouth framed by a brown beard which looks incredibly soft. Strange feelings begin to balloon in my chest, filling me with confusion. I'm certain he didn't have a beard before now. The image of a garden flashes in my mind, triggering a strong wave of deja vu. Something breaks loose in my body and my knees begin to weaken. Dionysus reaches down and lifts me gently in his arms.

He carries me across a small clearing and lays me down in a sun-warmed patch of grass.

"I want you to drink this," he instructs me, holding out a gourd-shaped flask made of animal skin. Raising myself up on one elbow, I watch him remove the stopper.

"What is it?" I ask.

"Goat's milk."

Dionysus places the gourd to my lips and I sip the beverage slowly. It's very warm and tastes like the body of an animal. I don't like it, but I drink it anyway. As it enters my body, I feel a strange jumpiness in my brain which seems linked to the strong taste and scent of the milk, rife with hormones. I finish the beverage reluctantly.

"Lie back now, Melina. Rest."

Leaning into the grass, I watch Dionysus cap the gourd and place it in a shady area at the base of a nearby tree. Long tendrils of ivy cling to the lower half of the tree like a woman's slender fingers clutching a man's thigh. As my gaze travels up its enormous trunk, I wonder, "What if the tree were being supported merely by the hand that holds it?" Intrigued by this thought, I imagine the grass around the base of the tree as a woman's large hand, her fingers the vines of ivy that hold the tree securely in place. At once I realize how vulnerable the tree is—how trusting. Visualizing the palm of the woman's hand deeply embedded in the earth, I sense how strong it must be to hold so great a weight. Gazing up at the tree's sprawling branches, I realize the woman's hand must also be yielding to counteract the weight at the top. I reach out and retrieve a nearby stick which has fallen to the grass from an overhead branch. Placing one end of it in my outstretched palm, I watch it wobble precariously as my hand darts this way and that, then circles round and round to keep the stick from falling. The word "gravity" comes to mind. The stick tumbles to the ground.

Breathing deeply, I gaze up at a patch of sky peeking through the treetops. It is a dazzling cerulean blue.

Personal Notes

I pull back into ordinary awareness just in time to greet my daughter who has burst excitedly into my office. She's holding something behind her back and is very happy, for today is her last day of school. Suddenly she holds out a beautiful cat she's fashioned out of clay. Its smiling human face and broken tail is held together by a creamy yellow body dotted with large black spots. She places it on my desk and rockets out of the room for the sunny outdoors.

I fall in love with the cat instantly and search for a place to put it among the items that litter a nearby shelf: seashells, stones, a rock with a hole in it, an acorn, a stick, two bird feathers—small gestures of life that keep me whole. As I stare at the cat with its broken tail, I feel its connectedness to my interior life: its primal essence speaks to my roots, to the pool of life which preceded and begot me, while its smiling face hints at something sublime and eternal. I gaze at the cat for a long time. It seems complete. I decide not to mend its tail.

I reflect on the day's material throughout the waning afternoon. By the time Ted arrives home from work, I'm fretting and feel caught in a bind. I can't figure out what's bothering me. I share the session with Ted, then confess that I don't understand what happened to me—I was doing beautifully with the diagram when, out of nowhere, I found myself taking a detour into completely idiotic behavior. I'm lying on my back on the office rug, groaning about it. Ted suggests I'm being too hard on myself; that anyone who spends an entire afternoon in the "chamber of Death" is entitled to feel schizophrenic. This is of small comfort.

Seeing that I've wedged my upper body under a rocking chair, I peek out at Ted sitting across the room and ask him if he thinks I'm anal retentive.

"Sure," he answers, smiling. "You always need to have everything 'just so.'"

I mentally replay the experience in which Dionysus tells me to take off my clothes. I cringe just thinking about how badly I handled this and loudly voice my embarrassment.

"Anyone else would've stripped down in a second and thrown herself on him!" I brood. "I'm 35 years old and still have the body consciousness of a preteen."

I drag myself out from under the rocker and sit cross-legged on the floor.

"What's wrong with being modest?" I ask, struggling to reinvent the scenario. "What if I had thrown myself on him with naked abandon, then what? Just think where I could have steered the experience."

Ted eyes me warily.

"I think you would have discovered that you weren't the one holding the reins," he cautions.

I wonder about this. Envisioning myself in the archetypal world, I imagine behaving completely out of character to my everyday sense of self. No sooner does this thought enter my mind when I realize whatever I choose to do in the archetypal world could be no more "out of character" than my arm could be out of character with my body. This is an enlightening thought and I stretch it. I wonder what it would be like to be extraordinarily wicked. I imagine seducing Dionysus in the most blatant, willful manner—then gulp, realizing I'd be desecrating the foundations of my moral integrity under the seemingly innocent guise of "fantasy." Just the same, the thought is far too compelling to abandon. Unable to shake it, I wonder, "Why don't I do it? What would happen if I did?" This thought makes me feel terrible. I try to banish it, telling myself it would be disastrous. Whether the experience is real or imagined, I'd end up violating what is fundamental and sacred to my deepest sense of self. Then I'd have to wrestle with that dark face of myself—as if my hands weren't full enough. I sigh, feeling hopelessly anal. Ted breaks in.

"Come on, Melina. You know why Dionysus told you to take your clothes off. He certainly didn't have sex on his mind."

I know he didn't. I did. I explain to Ted that I feel Dionysus was attempting to get me out of my head and back into my body rhythms, my instincts, for it was clear I'd lost touch with that part of myself. Taking the goat's milk into my body helped me to regain my connection with nature, myself.

I ruminate on this subject for the rest of the day: instinct, body, nature, earth. The gateway to heaven is a tree, a tunnel through the hindquarters of a turtle hewn from rock.

June 17 Session

I close my eyes and see that I'm sitting in the grass in the woods. I'm alone. On my right is the tree whose lower trunk is entwined in ivy. The earth's gentle hand still holds it as before. Gazing at its branches swaying in the sunlight, I realize I could sit here contentedly for hours. All at once Dionysus is standing before me. I notice he doesn't have a beard. Looking down at myself, I see that I'm fully clothed and my feet are bare. Dionysus seats himself before me. The prayer beads are looped over his belt.

"I see you are yourself," he observes, smiling at me. His manner is pleasant and relaxed.

I reflect on his statement and wonder what he means by my 'self.' As opposed to what? I dismiss it.

"Are you ready to continue with the diagram, Melina?"

"What happened to your beard?" I ask, pointing to his chin. Instantly his eyes light up.

"It comes and goes."

Puzzled by his reply, I don't know where to steer the conversation. I smile at him, aware that I'm stalling.

"Why are you wearing that garment?" I ask.

"You are wasting energy," he states quietly.

"All right, but do I have to go back down there?" I whine.

"Can't I do it in my head?"

No sooner does the question leave my lips when I realize how ridiculous it sounds. This entire journey is happening inside my head. Where am I going but to another place in my mind, triggered by the image of a womb? As I probe this thought more deeply, I have a vague feeling I could be wrong. Where is consciousness? Relaxing my mind, I visualize drinking the goat's milk, its scent, flavor and warmth filling my mouth. As I take the milk deep into my body, I can feel it flooding my cells with its life. I close my eyes and sense this life stirring within my womb in an inexplicable but powerful way. Certainly consciousness is not limited to the region of my cranium. That being so, could parts of the body possess incipient consciousness? If they do, could they also possess their own rudimentary language and symbols? The slimmest chance this could be true excites me. I wonder what stories our organs could tell us if we knew how to connect to their worlds of information. Dionysus' voice scatters my train of thought.

"Melina, quiet your thoughts and relax. You will see the figure clearly in your mind."

I see the diagram filled in on the "Matter" side with two words: "Earth" and "Sensation." I look down to the point marked "Death" and remember the words "Fear" and "Violence." They're not marked.

"Descend into the chamber of Death," Dionysus instructs me. "Seek two qualities by which to name it."

I close my eyes. Yesterday's thought of seducing Dionysus slams into my mind. Gasping, I open my eyes. Dionysus is watching me.

"I'm sorry," I murmur, stiffening with self-consciousness.

I close my eyes and hear my heart pounding in my ears. I feel extremely uncomfortable and wonder if I should abort this whole project for today. I try to concentrate on getting down into my womb, but it's useless. I'm expending all my energy trying to avoid confronting my thought of seducing Dionysus. Flustered, I open my eyes.

"Look, I better get this off my chest," I inform him, pulling myself up on one elbow. "Do I have to watch every thought I think these days? Is it going to boomerang in here and come chasing after me?"

"What thought?" he asks.

"You know what thought," I insist anxiously.

Dionysus is expressionless. I keep staring at him, waiting for some emotion to register on his face. He continues looking at me blankly. I find this aggravating.

"All right," I sigh, sitting upright.

I take a deep breath and stare at my feet.

"I was thinking yesterday what it would be like to... seduce you."

Silence. I keep staring at my feet. A light gust of wind shakes the treetops and an overhead branch starts to creek loudly like an old attic door. I listen to it for what seems an eternity. Suddenly Dionysus begins to laugh. Glancing up at him, I see that his one hand is cupped over his mouth while his other rests against his chest. He begins to sway back and forth as his laughter gets louder. A smile of bewilderment spreads across my face as I watch him bend over and nearly touch the ground with his nose, his entire body consumed by the excruciating bliss of a hard laugh. His merriment is so contagious that I erupt into a gale of laughter, feeling delightfully silly. A huge weight of anxiety lifts from my chest and is replaced by a feeling of elation. It feels so wonderful that I can't stop laughing. The thought of seducing Dionysus makes me double over. It's the purest piece of comedy I've stumbled across in ages. Unable to contain myself, I slap the ground with both my hands, howling.

I collapse in the grass and catch my breath. Turning onto my side, I gaze over at Dionysus sitting in the grass with his arms draped loosely across his knees. Smiling broadly at me, he is the most beautiful, radiant man I've ever seen.

"Are you ready now?" he calls, his voice charged with energy.

"Yes!"

I scoot back to the spot where I was sitting before. Dionysus positions himself in the grass before me. He removes his prayer beads and places them in my lap.

"Quiet your mind now, Melina."

Breathing deeply, I try to relax myself, all the while studying his face.

"Was it really so funny?" I ask.

Dionysus smiles and playfully squeezes my foot. I close my eyes and find that I'm dropping down easily. I try not to think about where I'm going, but already I can sense the darkness, the swirling clouds.

CHAPTER 4

UNEXPECTED MESSENGERS

June 18 Session

I close my eyes and see that I'm standing outside an old building made of cutter's stone. I'm facing a large wooden door with a black wrought-iron handle. I stand back from the door and look around. The building is long. I follow the right outside wall and turn a corner. I can now see that the building is annexed to a church. It is an old structure with a steepled roof and stained glass windows. The grounds around the building are well-kept and simple. A white stone statue of Saint Francis of Assisi graces the center of the main lawn on the church side, while four stone benches stand in an equidistant arrangement around the statue. I stop and stare at it. One stone dove alights on Saint Francis' shoulder. Another is perched on his outstretched hand. It's very quiet here.

I walk back around the corner and follow the wall to the large wooden door where I first arrived. I study it. The door is solid and stoic-looking, tightly sealing the private world behind it. I notice there's no knocker or doorbell. It's just as well. I'm not feeling comfortable with the thought of banging on this door, anyway. I walk around the left side of the building. There are no windows back here. It's too bad, as the landscape on this side is so peaceful. As I walk, I'm looking across a sprawling meadow rippled by gently sloping hills. Clusters of low trees dot the landscape, while sheep graze by twos and threes at a far distance. The scene looks just like a painting.

I've now walked the full length of the wall. Turning a corner, I'm greeted by a lovely courtyard filled with flowers. Narrow walkways crisscross through the neat floral patchwork. Two rows of low stone benches create a border on either side of the courtyard. There are five benches to each row. As I approach one of the benches to seat myself, an older man walks into the courtyard from an open arched doorway leading out from the building. Slight of build, he is wearing a long black cassock fastened around the middle by a red sash. On his head is a small red skullcap framed by thinning gray hair. His sleeves are rolled up to his elbows and he's holding some sort of gardening tool. Noticing me, he smiles happily and heads in my direction with a quick light step. I'm trying to remember what rank of priesthood his clothes suggest. Thinking he may be a cardinal, I struggle to recall the appropriate title. "Eminence" comes to mind. I'm not sure about it and decide to call him "Father."

"Hello!" he calls warmly, extending his hand.

"Hi, Father."

I cordially shake his hand. He's a wiry man with a strong grip. I'm surprised by his strength and energy.

"You have come from the village?" he asks, gesturing at the meadow.

Peering across the rolling landscape, I imagine there's a little town tucked away in one of those sleepy hills. I haven't heard the term "village" used in a long time.

"Yes," I reply, hoping a simple answer will suffice.

"I am so happy you have come to visit us!" he exclaims. "Isn't it beautiful?"

He waves his hands over the garden like an enthusiastic symphony conductor. I suspect he is Italian.

"Yes, it really is lovely," I agree, gazing at the varieties of roses. "What is this place called?"

"La Casa del Madre," he replies.

Surprised, I look around, wondering if I somehow journeyed to Spain.

"The building looks 1930s," I remark. "When was it built?"

We're walking through the garden now. I notice a long arched lattice covered with lush grape vines at the far end of the courtyard.

"La Casa del Madre was built in 1914," he answers proudly.

I reflect on the name, The House of the Mother. I like it.

"Are you Italian?" I ask politely.

"Yes! How did you know?"

He's very excited. I don't know what to say.

"I'm Italian, too," I confess, smiling.

"Ah! So, maybe we are paisano!"

He laughs joyfully. I like this man's energy very much.

"My father and mother, God rest them, are from the Abruzzi region. Do you know it?" he asks, his eyes full of interest.

"Sure," I nod, remembering my travels in Italy when I was a girl.

"And your family?" he inquires.

"Campobasso, near Rome. That's on my mother's side. My father's family is from Palermo."

"Palermo!"

He claps his hands and mentions the name of a church there with an enormous stained glass window of Christ.

"My manners!" he exclaims. "Forgive me! I have not offered you a refreshment. You must be quite thirsty. Tea? We have ice. Father Philip brought it from the village just this morning."

I don't like tea, but I don't want to disappoint him.

"Yes, that would be nice, Father. Thank you."

He motions for me to sit on a bench, then walks briskly across the courtyard and disappears through the arched doorway. Gazing up at the windows on the second floor of the building, I wonder how many priests live here and if any are peeking down through their windows at me. I study the way I'm dressed and see that I'm wearing shorts. I cross my legs. Father reappears carrying a small tray of tea, lemon, sugar and two biscuits. He sets it down on the bench.

"I would offer you grapes, but as you can see, they are not yet ripe."

He points to the arbor. I notice the lattice is filled with clusters of grapes. Most of them are still green. Suddenly I wonder what all this could mean. I gaze at the lemon on the tray and imagine it as a symbol. A stanza from my Freudian poem rushes into my head:

I'm having Mr Smith
with tea. He knows
a lot of songs. I press
a cut lemon to my tongue

"Have you been here long?" I ask casually, sipping the tea. It tastes like hay. I set it down and spoon some sugar into it.

"Oh, 20 years. I have forgotten!" he laughs. "As you can see, I'm getting on in years."

"You look like Pius the XII," I remark, studying his face as if it were a painting.

"Mother of God! Do you know I've been told that before!"

I think about Pius the XII. I can't even remember what he looks like. I wonder if I meant Pius the X, then question whether there ever was a Pius the XII. I look at Father and smile. I'm starting to feel very strange.

"You must see the church," he continues. "My heavens! I have not even asked your name!"

"Melina."

"A beautiful name. Bella! Bella!"

I stare down at my tea. I've never felt too comfortable around Italians.

"Oh yes," he resumes, "I have not finished my story. Years ago, Bishop Augustine from Santa Maria del Mar sent me here to teach. Latin. Theology. Literature. You know!"

He laughs as though somewhat embarrassed.

"You have students here?" I ask.

"Many young men come here seeking to know God, to serve

Him. They want to dedicate themselves to this one love that burns within their souls."

He folds his hands at his chest and breathes deeply, then smiles at me.

"Are you a cardinal?"

"Oh, this?"

He fingers the red sash at his waist and waves his hand.

"It is not important! And you? What is it you do?"

He stands. I think he wants to stroll. I stand up and place my tea on the tray.

"Oh, well, I have two children. I write."

"Two children? And you are a writer? Praise heaven! And what do you write?"

I'm stumped. I think about how I'm recording these very words and wonder how on earth I would even begin to explain this.

"Oh, I do all sorts of things; marketing pieces, editing, poetry."

"Poetry, my dearest love! You will recite for me, no? Do you know Pascoli's work?"

My heart sinks. I can't stand to recite anything. Pascoli? I don't even know Longfellow. He stops and poises his hands in the air as if upon an invisible shelf.

"Assisi, gentle heart, a stone upon your tongue!
God's flowering earth is your Blessed Sacrament.
O, gentle heart, whose eyes behold the moon.
You, her groom, watch! You who know so well
Her Silence! Until the Sun, its glorious light
Proclaims her Holy Name: Mary! Mary!
Mother of Heaven! Mother of the Blessed One!"

I'm staring at him and struggling to keep from laughing. It feels terribly uncomfortable.

"That's lovely," I fib. "Pascoli?"

"Oh, no, no."

He shakes his head and laughs.

"You wrote that?" I ask incredulously.

"Years ago, when I was a much younger man."

He leans over to me and lowers his voice.

"Actually, I wrote it for a young woman. Her name was Mary."

He laughs bashfully and points between his eyes.

"Cupid's arrow got me good! Right here!"

"What happened?" I ask.

"She went off with another man. Oh, this was years ago! He was much more handsome than myself. More intelligent. I didn't blame her. No, indeed. And see? How miraculous are the ways of God! He sent to me another bride."

He walks up to a large red flower and cups its petals fondly in his hand.

"Did you ever get over it?" I ask.

He points to a nearby bush filled with delicate white roses.

"Once I was pruning this bush. She is my favorite!"

He quickly places a finger to his lips and looks around at the other flowers.

"I try not to say such things in front of the others," he confides in a hushed voice.

Caressing a white rose, he traces the outline of its petals with his finger.

"One day I was so lost in the beauty and perfection of this flower that I forgot its thorns. Yes, she got me good. So quick! And such pain!"

He pulls his hand away and wrings it fretfully as though it had just happened. We continue our stroll. He is quiet for a time.

"So you see," he continues, "I am surrounded by God's beauty, His infinite love. This is my life. How happy I am! The joy of heaven is all around, and I forget that I am a man and that I have a body!"

He pokes his belly comically.

"Yes, I must eat, I must sleep, like everyone else! But, I am a dreamer. God knows this better than anyone."

He sighs and shakes his head.

"So, I think He has made His roses with thorns to remind us of our humanity and the purpose for which we were put on this earth."

I think this over carefully.

"Why were we put on this earth?" I ask.

"To love! To love is to know pain, no? Joy? Tears? Even in happiness we cry. So fragile we are! Saint Paul has said, 'In Christ, I die daily.' Ah, death is no fun. But there is no knowing Christ without death. It is through dying that we are born into love. Yes, like a newborn babe! God's love, in here!"

He points emphatically to his heart.

"It is the Path of Jesus. It is our path. The Way, the Truth and the Life."

My old fondness for the Catholic Church begins to flood back. It's a strange feeling mixed with many memories, both good and bad.

"I used to be Catholic," I confess.

"And you are no longer?"

"No."

I want to tell him I sometimes miss it, but I don't want him to misinterpret what I'm saying. I decide to say nothing.

"So, did she leave you, or did you leave her?" he asks.

Struck by the novelty of the question, I want to see where it leads.

"Maybe I felt betrayed, you know?"

"By God?" he inquires. "Or man?"

"Is there a difference?" I ask. "Betrayal is betrayal."

"Of course!" he exclaims. "In the temporal world there is a great difference. If not, we would have long ago realized our heaven, no? Do you think we would have war, hatred and jealousy if this were not so?"

"Yes, I see your point, Father. Well, if that's the case, then I guess I could safely say I felt betrayed by man."

"Ah!" he cries, pausing in midstride. "I want to tell you a story. A fairy tale! I memorized it as a boy from an old book. You will like it!"

He gestures to a bench in the shade.

"Let us rest. Oh! Your tea and biscuits!"

He hastens across the courtyard and retrieves the tray. On his way back, he pulls a handkerchief from his pocket and wipes his forehead.

"A beautiful day, but hot! Are you comfortable?"

"Yes, I'm fine, Father."

He nudges the tray toward me.

"Eat!"

I suddenly realize I'm hungry and reach for a biscuit. Father leans back on the bench and makes himself comfortable.

"Long ago there was a miller. He was an honest, God-fearing man who had worked hard all his life. Now this miller had a daughter, a beautiful daughter, and he cherished her above all else. He had no wife, for she had long ago died and left them to fend for themselves.

"One day the miller was in the forest chopping wood for kindling when he heard a voice. He looked this way and that, but no one was about. The voice told him it was a messenger from heaven. Well, when the miller heard this, he threw down his axe and dropped to his knees. He thought, 'What would a messenger of God want with me, a poor miller?' He trembled in his boots!"

I break into laughter. He's telling the tale with such relish that I begin to feel like a four year-old at storytime.

"The voice then told the miller that his daughter had come of age and would have to be properly wed. When the miller heard this, he buried his face in his hands and groaned.

"'No, Lord. Anything but that!'

"But the voice remained firm.

"'Tomorrow a young man will appear at your door. He will be wearing a plumed hat and will be carrying a bag of coins and a hen under his arm. When you see him, you will know that I have sent him to be your daughter's husband!'

"The poor miller broke into tears.

"'But how can I be sure you are truly a messenger sent from heaven?'

"The voice replied, 'In three years you must come back to this very spot. I will then reveal myself to you.'

"The very next day a young man appeared on the miller's doorstep. He was wearing a plumed hat and carrying a bag of coins and a hen under his arm, just as the voice said he would. The miller welcomed the young man into his home and introduced him to his daughter. The daughter took one look at the stranger and fell head over heels in love. The young man offered the bag of coins and the hen to the miller, then fell on his knees and requested the girl's hand in marriage. The miller was deeply moved. It was clear to him the young man was as struck by the arrow of love as was his own daughter. He consented, and soon thereafter they were married.

"The young man, now the miller's son-in-law, moved in with the miller and his daughter, and for many months there was great peace and accord. The young man, being a tailor by trade, shared his income not only with his wife, but with the miller as well. Never before had the miller and his daughter supped so well, nor had they known such ease in living, for the tailor cheerily performed many tasks about the house and yard. Truly, his kindness and generosity knew no bounds. Every night before the miller went to sleep, he knelt to thank the Lord for his good bounty, the health and happiness of his daughter and the overwhelming kindness of his son-in-law.

"'Truly you are the one and only God!' he exclaimed.

"Three years came and went, as time is wont to do, and the

day of reckoning finally dawned. The miller happily took his axe and journeyed deep into the forest until he came upon the very spot where he heard the voice from heaven. Now he stood with bated breath to meet God's messenger face to face. He did not have to wait long, for out of the deep silence of the wood came the sound of a twig snapping. The miller looked about excitedly. The sound seemed to come from behind a very large tree.

"'Come out, oh messenger from heaven, and reveal yourself!' he cried.

"A handsome young man stepped out from behind the tree and lo! It was the miller's son-in-law!

"'I am he, Father. I am the messenger!'

"When the miller saw that it was but a man, and his very son-in-law, he was deeply angered.

"'I've been betrayed!' he shouted furiously, shaking his fist at the heavens.

"And taking his axe in a blind rage, he threw it high into the air. The heavy blade came down quick and plunged deep into the heart of the son-in-law. The young man was killed instantly."

Father folds his hands on his lap and looks inquiringly at me. I'm halfway through my second biscuit and place it on the tray.

"Is that the end?" I ask.

"No! Of course not. But I like to think a good story has no ending. At least no ending that has been written."

He smiles at me playfully and pats his chest.

"We write our own endings in here, no?"

I grow quiet and turn the story over in my mind. It has a strange effect on me. The more I reflect on it, the more its layers of meaning unfold. I realize I have a great deal to think about.

"Thank you, Father. I enjoyed the story very much."

He tips an invisible hat to me like a jaunty bellhop.

"At your service! And now, you will come and see the church?"

"Yes, I'd love to, Father."

"Let us take the route around the building so that I may show you the grounds along the way," he suggests. "They are lovely!"

He leads me through the courtyard and around the side of the building which faces the meadow. All the while he is talking animatedly about the people in the nearby villages, citing their names and occupations, weaving bits and pieces of their lives into a colorful tapestry. I'm nodding but only half-listening. Something about going into that church is starting to bother me. I imagine being enveloped in its cavernous darkness, surrounded by heavy stone walls and statues of saints clothed in robes of flickering shadow. I don't like what I'm feeling.

We're now rounding the corner of the building and are walking toward the church. Father is gesturing to the statue of Saint Francis in the lawn. As I look at it, I again wonder what all this could mean. Who is this priest? Where is he really taking me? What is the church? I think about my last journey, how I was about to descend into the chamber of Death. Gazing about me, I try to imagine this place as another one of death's faces, only well-concealed. By the time we reach the steps of the church, my feelings of foreboding are overwhelming. I gaze up at the massive door and hesitate.

"Father, wait a minute."

"Yes, child?"

"Look, there's something I need to explain to you. May we sit here for a few moments?"

"Of course!"

We arrange ourselves on one of the stone steps. Father looks at me with an expression of deep concern. I realize I'm behaving nervously and feel badly about the effect it's having on both of us.

"Father, have you ever heard of an archetype?"

"Archetype?"

His brow deepens for a moment.

"Somewhere, yes. A symbol, like the Trinity, no? I once had a student who was very interested in psychology. We would stroll and talk for hours. Brilliant fellow!"

"Well, I don't expect you to really understand this, but right now I'm inside my mind. I mean, this whole place, you, everything—the church—is just an experience I'm having in my mind."

He laughs merrily.

"And here I am thinking all these years that I am a real flesh and blood man, only to find out that I am but an experience inside a woman's mind!"

He slaps his knee. I smile and shake my head, wondering how I'm going to get this to sound serious.

"Okay, Father. Let's pretend. Let's say that I'm having a dream, all right?"

"Sure!"

"Now anything can happen in a dream, right?"

"Ah, one of God's most marvelous inventions!"

"Okay, let's say that I'm dreaming you up, that you aren't real. These stone steps, that lawn out there, that building, are all dream props."

He claps his hands.

"Fascinating!"

"All right, Father, let's say that I go into the church with you and something awful happens."

"In the house of God?" he asks, his expression deepening.

"Now remember this church isn't real—it's a dream prop. It's not really the house of God," I remind him.

"What then is it? If I am dreaming I am in the house of God, I am in the house of God!"

"Well, what if you were dreaming you entered the house of God, only to discover it was inhabited by the devil?"

He slaps his knee.

"Ha! What worry then would I have? Surely I would rather meet Satan on God's own turf than anywhere else!"

I bury my head in my hands, realizing he's not getting this.

"Okay, Father. I understand this is how you would respond if it were your experience. But right now I'm inside my own dream, my own experience! I'm trying to tell you I'm scared of going inside that church, that something horrible might happen to me in there."

"Let us say that it does," he concedes in a tone of seriousness. "Would you not rather meet this horrible thing in a holy place, and with a priest at your side?"

I never thought of it that way. Yes, a priest. What better ally could I have? Suddenly I'm seized by a terrifying thought.

"Yes, but what if you turn out to be the horrible thing?" I ask.

"Me?"

He looks at me incredulously.

"I realize I am far from being a saint, and God forgive me for even thinking such a thought, but the devil? Satan? I am not clever enough!"

I consider he might have a point, although he does seem pretty sharp. What a wonderful disguise he would make for X: a simple priest who gains my trust, then lures me into the chamber of Death through the beckoning doors of a church. I'm appalled at how low my thoughts have sunk. Father taps my knee.

"I will pretend with you. Let us pretend that I am the devil."

He arranges his face into a contorted, hilarious expression. I burst into laughter.

"There! Now tell me, what is your greatest weakness?"

I'm unexpectedly bowled over by the question and ponder it seriously. He waves his hands.

"Come, come! There must be hundreds!"

"Well, I don't know. That's a hard one."

"If you were the devil, what part of yourself would you tempt?"

I think about it. An answer comes quickly.

"My love for God."

"Ha! That is a priest's answer."

"What?"

He leans over to me and lowers his voice.

"You are sure you are not a priest? After all, this is a dream!"

"Well, I might have been a priest in some other dream. Right now, I'm just me."

I look down at myself to make sure.

"Such a serious one you are!" he chides, clucking his tongue at me and shaking his head. "So, you think the devil is trying to steal you away from God?"

I cringe. It sounds so medieval.

"No, it's not like that," I correct him. "I don't even believe in the devil."

"No?"

He gestures toward the church.

"What did you think would be waiting for you in there? Bogeyman?"

"I was just being paranoid!"

"What is at the root of this feeling?"

I'm starting to feel flustered. I don't want to go into the story about X.

"I will tell you something," he says, placing his hand lightly on my arm. "You know what is in there?"

He gazes up at the church and back at me. I look at him blankly.

"Your love for God! Yes! And do you know what's keeping you glued to this step? Yes! The devil!"

"There is no devil!" I protest. "I just got a little frightened, that's all."

"But! What do you think puts the fear in your heart? God? The trees? The flowers? Or maybe it is that bird over there!"

He points to a small gray bird hopping around on the lawn.

"Look, Father, I don't mean to offend you, but I really don't believe in the devil. I gave that up a long time ago."

"Ah, but the devil believes in you! Sure, he is right here! He is as big as your doubt! Can you not feel him?"

As he says this, my flesh begins to crawl. I look around. The feeling of foreboding returns.

"Besides," I argue, "I'm not into the church. I don't choose to worship that way. And it's not because of the devil, either. It's because of what's in here."

I place my hand on my heart. I'm starting to feel touchy and sensitive.

"Yes, and what is your heart but His tabernacle? And your love? It is His living sacrament within you. So what is the difference, this or that, when to God it is all the same?"

I think this over. He does have a way of putting things.

"But that's just my point, Father. God is within. I don't need to seek Him in a church."

"Yes, He is within. And He is also out there."

He points to the trees.

"And in there."

He points to the church. I prop my chin in my hand and fight back a smile.

"Are you trying to convert me?" I ask, throwing him a sidelong glance.

"An ex-Catholic? Mother in heaven, I have not yet learned to perform miracles!"

His face suddenly grows serious. He places his hand again on my arm.

"There are many who seek God on an altar of stone," he explains softly. "They are the hungry ones, no? We must feed them from the supper table of our humanity."

He points to his heart.

"But the real food, the true nourishment, can only come from God. He is wherever we seek Him, and everywhere we have forgotten to look."

He gazes up at the church. His face is filled with tenderness.

"Will you enter with me and receive her blessing?"

I stand and help him to his feet. I take his arm. Together we climb the steps of La Casa del Madre.

June 20 A Dream

I dream that I'm with a young man who is fair and naked from the waist up. I've never seen him before. I keep looking at him, trying to get a feel for who he might be. It seems he is my lover. He holds me close and kisses me. The whole experience feels very strange. I'm trying to adapt myself to him, his "newness."

The dream shifts and I'm gazing at a plane of radiant light in the shape of a large square. The word "consciousness" flashes around it. I'm aware of three persons, including myself, who seem to have something to do with this square. One is a woman; the other is a child. There is a fourth person, but I can't see who it is. The four of us enter the light of the square and become engaged in some sort of activity. It seems I must find or contend with the invisible fourth person. Suddenly there is a death, but I don't know who it is that dies. I then find myself outside the square, relating the death experience to the woman. Worried and confused, I wonder if I had anything to do with it.

The dream shifts and I'm with Ted. We're in bed and he's embracing me. He begins to kiss me around the neck and shoulders. He then kisses me around my navel. Suddenly he stops and says, "Up there you smell like spring flowers, but down here!" He turns his head slightly away and I realize I must have a bad odor. I go into the bathroom and remove my panties. I notice they're filled with thick green discharge the color of moss. Shocked, I inspect it closely and see black specks that look like spores. The green discharge has the appearance of mold, but is very dense like clay. I think, "My God, this stuff must have been inside me for a long time!"

I continue staring at it, wondering what it was inside me that died and was sloughed off. I'm concerned that whatever it was had remained in a long state of decay before it passed out of my body.

Personal Notes

I awaken from the dream and lie very still, allowing the images to pour into my conscious mind. This process is very delicate. The images blur and recede as they respond to a gravitational pull back into the formless. Letting myself drift as though in a half-sleep, I imagine my mind as a large fisher's net resting on the surface of a boundless body of water. The dream images wriggle and squirm like tiny fish. I allow the net to gently gather about them. The images suddenly crystallize. I quickly seal them into my mind.

June 22 A Note Of Interest

For nearly ten months, I had a growth on my right eyelid. I tried to ignore it, hoping it would somehow correct itself in time. As the weeks and months wore on, I noticed it was growing larger. Finally I phoned an ophthalmologist and explained my situation. I was told the growth would have to be surgically removed. This frightened me, as I can't tolerate physical pain of any kind. I called another ophthalmologist and was given the same diagnosis. Discouraged, I stalled making an appointment.

About a week after my initial experience in the archetypal world, I found myself brooding over the situation with my eye. It suddenly occurred to me that I might ask Dionysus to heal it. That night as I lay in bed, I moved into the archetypal world and found Dionysus. I asked him if he would heal my eye. Raising his left hand, he touched my eyelid with his index finger and a brilliant light and burning sensation shot through my eye. I thanked him, fell asleep and forgot about the incident.

Three days later, as I was washing my face at the mirror, I noticed my eyelid looked smooth. I touched it. The growth was gone! I was filled with excitement, but then checked myself. I thought if I rejoiced too prematurely, the growth might come back. I waited.

It's been nearly a month now. It has not returned.

June 22 Session

I close my eyes and see that I'm looking out across a clearing in the woods. At a distance, standing at the edge of the stream, is Dionysus. He is winged. Overwhelmed by his unearthly appearance, I catch my breath and step back. Unaware of my presence, he is looking down at something in the grass and is moving his right foot over it. He seems to be completely absorbed in what he is doing. My eyes are drawn to the hypnotic movement of his wings; how they slowly open and close as if assisting his effort and concentration. Awed by their other-worldly beauty, I barely breathe.

Dionysus suddenly turns his face in my direction. His wings fold up instantly and disappear. He walks toward me. As I watch him approach, I feel breathless and sexually aroused. I don't know what to do with this feeling, as it is overwhelming. Standing before me, he smiles and takes both my hands in his. I seem to hear him ask, "How are you?" but his lips do not move. Transfixed, I don't know how to respond. He releases my hands and walks over to a nearby tree. Placing his arms around its powerful trunk, he begins to move his body, fully clothed, slowly against it in an up-and-down movement. I'm shocked by what he's doing and want to interrupt him.

"What are you doing?" I ask, trying to conceal my disapproval.

"I am having intercourse with the tree."

He doesn't stop. Embarrassed, I lower my eyes, feeling this whole scene is in bad taste. The more I try to avoid looking at Dionysus, the more my body stiffens from a paralyzing sense of alienation from what is taking place. Simultaneously, I'm aware that a part of me envies what he's doing. I want him to either stop or include me. I say nothing.

"If you will come and lean your back against the opposite side of this tree, you will be able to enter into this experience," he invites.

I hesitate, then watch Dionysus' slow, rhythmic movements. A wild current of energy begins to finger its way into my brain. The sexual energy mounting in my womb and stomach leaps into my head like liquid fire. My body becomes loose. I walk to the tree and place my back against it opposite Dionysus.

"Place your arms behind you on either side of the tree," he instructs. "Place your feet apart."

I wrap my arms around the tree behind me and spread my feet apart. I notice my spine straightens considerably and my chest cavity greatly expands. Automatically taking more air into my lungs, I begin to feel more clear. Dionysus reaches around either side of the tree and takes my hands in both of his. His grip is firm.

"Breathe deeply, Melina. Breathe slowly."

As I begin to breathe, I sense my nakedness. The breeze on my skin feels unbelievably wonderful. Deeply inhaling the fragrance of the earth, I become aware of the hardness of the tree at my back; how strong and erect it is; how my body wants to lean into its life and rise like an arrow into its glorious leaves and branches. I breathe more deeply. Behind me, Dionysus is gripping my hands in a rhythmic way, pulling them slightly back toward his side of the tree, releasing gently, then pulling them back again. Allowing the steady rhythm of his movements to penetrate my body, I visualize his pelvis as he rocks against the tree. As I do this, my own body responds instantly. Every cell in my being begins to quake with an exciting alertness. I imagine his phallus. My breathing accelerates. I want to open myself wide to this feeling, the urgency of desire coiling around my body like a large beautiful snake.

I close my eyes and fall more deeply into this feeling, its tightening grip molding me to its will with a devouring need to draw my life into itself. I want this to happen. I want to let go and lose myself utterly inside this feeling. My thoughts are aflame with this one and only desire. The ecstatic face of Dionysus flashes in my mind with a fiery radiance. Heat rises through my nasal cavity as my breathing shifts into quick, shallow gasps. All desire in my body is building to a single point of all-consuming power. All that I am—my life, soul, love and pain—is ascending in a column of pure energy through my body and rushing into the back of my skull. I draw air tightly into my lungs and hold it. Suddenly the power breaks loose and spills its luminous, undulating waves of light into my mind, bathing every cell of my being in a purifying ocean of absolute stillness. In that instant, I am inconceivably whole. One. Baptized. It's more than I can bear. I break hands with Dionysus and slowly drop to my knees in the grass.

I pull back into ordinary awareness, shaken by the experience. I feel very strange and want to lie down. I move to the couch and lie on my back, feeling very tired. I close my eyes. Dionysus' voice permeates the silence like warm mist.

"Pull me close to your heart, Melina."

Energy is collecting in my chest. I feel an odd pressure in my lungs as if a presence were inhabiting the space between my ribs.

"How have you entered me?" I ask.

"I have been inside you all along."

Sinking deeply inside his words, I sense his energy within and all around me. Suddenly I see him hovering over me on my right side, making the sign of the cross over my heart. As he does this, I feel as though a part of me is dying, but I'm too sleepy to feel pain or fear. Afternoon sunlight filters into the room, enfolding each solid shape in a milky radiance. As I gaze dreamily at the shapes, I sense the presences of others standing across the room. I try to make out their forms, but they are hidden in dense swaths of light. All the while my awareness is floating in and out of my body like a vaporous cloud carried by a warm current of air. A sensation of weightlessness balloons inside my body. I feel as if I'm about to be carried somewhere.

"Are we going somewhere?" I ask sleepily.

"No. Rest. We are staying here."

I close my eyes and at once see a large pyramid. I seem to be hovering over it from a great height. From up here it looks as though it has a central point which reaches out in four directions, enclosed by a perfect square. The square begins to slowly rotate. Viewing it now as a diamond shape, I realize it looks exactly like the diagram Dionysus gave to me. Suddenly I'm falling like a leaf. I feel myself drifting down, down. Everything is becoming dark.

"Melina, you are entering your womb."

"Must I?"

"Yes. You will enter the chamber of Death."

"Where is it?"

"It is within you."

I contemplate my body and feel my womb. It is filled with energy. The energy moves upward in an arc, curves around my navel and flows downward. As I follow the downward movement, I can actually feel myself falling as though pulled by gravity. I touch down onto something solid and see that I'm being approached by a large ball of light. I look around. My surroundings are lit up like a wide gully under a full moon.

"Is this the chamber of Death?" I ask, gazing into the soft radiance.

"Yes, Melina. You must walk into the ball of light."

"I will explode."

"No. You will not explode."

"There is a woman in there."

"Yes, she is waiting for you."

"Who is she?"

"She is the ferry angel. She will bring you across the river Styx in her vessel of light."

"Is it the moon?"

"Yes."

The ball of light is very large and softly luminous. An angel-woman with dragonfly wings is seated inside of it, wearing a pale, rose-colored garment. Her face is beautifully delicate, framed by long, honey-colored hair. I walk toward the ball of light.

"Where will she take me, Dionysus?"

"To the other side."

I'm now entering the ball of light. Slipping through easily, I find myself enveloped in a lustrous atmosphere of warmth and softness. Everything looks very translucent. The ball gently rises and begins to glide slowly over the ground. The sensation of moving effortlessly through space is incredibly relaxing and fills me with an unexpected feeling of calm. The woman is now standing opposite me, gazing out through the ball into the darkness. Her expression is one-pointed, noble, and strikes me as very unearthly.

I carefully lean against the ball's inner wall and discover that it can support me. I experiment. Turning around, I push my face into the curve. When I exert pressure, the curve gives. I push a little harder. Suddenly my head is protruding outside the ball and I'm looking down on the river Styx. A sharp night wind rushes through my hair and blows across my face. I catch my breath. Below, the river heaves and churns its black depths under the pale illumination of the moving sphere. I gaze down upon it in awe, perplexed by its movement. I had always imagined the Styx as stagnant and deathlike. I study the water and wonder how deep it is. I'm so close to its surface that if I reach my hand out far enough, I'll be able to touch it. Startled by the thought, I pull my hands in close to my chest. I realize any number of dreadful things might lurk beneath the surface and that I'm completely vulnerable. Frightened, I shut my eyes. I feel as though I'm going to fall.

"Melina."

Dionysus' presence penetrates the stillness within my chest. I'm relieved to hear his voice. The silence here is profound... eternal.

"These are the waters of the unconscious," he says quietly.

"Why does the river move?" I ask. "Isn't it supposed to be still?"

"Its movement is in response to the magnetic energy of the moon, the vessel you ride within."

An image of the ocean rises into my mind: ocean as the great Mother, her body yielding to the sun and heavens—the great Spirit. Visualizing her thundering waves as they pound the shore, I whisper, "Earth-belly, breasts without vestment." The image vanishes. My eyes settle on the deep before me, its dark swells shimmering in the moonlight. A still voice rises from within my heart: "Swell of a body floating up high but not bright. Now, coming down low it has lost a name for itself."

Closing my eyes, I imagine the moon as a symbol for the Feminine, the instinctual side of life, the hidden. The face of the angel-woman appears in my mind, her otherworldly beauty and feminine bearing drawing my full attention. I pull my head back into the glowing ball and gaze at her regal form standing sentry over the realm of the nocturnal. Her strength seems to lie in her waiting, her silence. What is she waiting for? What or whom is she waiting upon? A sudden light spills into my mind. I realize she is waiting upon me.

"The Feminine is a servant," I observe softly.

"She is a carrier, Melina."

"What does she carry?"

"The light of the Spirit."

"Like the Soul?"

"She is Soul. She is the vessel, the mediator between heaven and earth."

I push my head back through the curve of the glowing ball and stare down at the inky waters. A sharp wind whips my face. It's exhilarating.

"Is that her down there, too?" I shout over the wind. "The unconscious?"

"Yes, Melina. She cannot know herself save through the penetration of Spirit."

"But how does that happen?" I ask.

"Through the mediation of the Soul."

"But how can the Feminine be the unconscious and the Soul?"

"Consider the light and dark faces of the moon: Soul is Breath, Shekhinah—the Indwelling. It both holds and carries forth the power of the Spirit into the world of form. This is the moon as Light, Divine Being, the Lamp of Consciousness. Soul is also the carrier for the Unmanifest. Her infinitude of emptiness is the womb out of which Spirit comes forth, the womb in which He conceives Himself. This is the moon as Darkness, Primordial Urge, Unconsciousness. She must surrender her light in order to be impregnated by it. He must penetrate her darkness in order that He may become."

I'm staring into the water, lost inside his words, in awe of their meaning. My whole being is infused with a sense of timelessness and self-erasure. It feels extremely dreamlike. I keep slipping off into something large and unknown. Dionysus' voice pulls my awareness like a magnet. I begin to sink inside of it.

"Christ is Shekhinah, the World Soul. He is the Indwelling Spirit. He is the Feminine. When Jesus manifested the Christ, he brought forth Shekhinah, the World Soul, into flesh. When he died to his flesh, he gave his God-Spirit over to the World Soul, becoming one with Her. The released God-Spirit of Jesus the man, in union with the Feminine World Soul, the Christ, descended into Hell, the realms of the Unconscious, and breathed the living Breath of the Father-Mother Spirit over the dark waters. And as He-She breathed, the seed of AT-ONE-MENT was posited in the womb of All Endings and All Beginnings and the waters stirred unto new life. This is the meaning of the Resurrection: life into death and death into life, Spirit into flesh and flesh into Spirit, the Groom into his Bride and the Bride into her Groom. The divine Child of this union is that which, moment to moment, births you into the everlastingness of your Selfhood; of this one, Christ spoke and named the Holy Spirit. Its fiery breath inflames the human soul and casts its light upon all darkness. Melina, the power of the Christ is within you. Seek through the Child, the Holy Spirit, which shall lead you to all good things. Of its wisdom and counsel, its charity and kindness, all of nature and heaven sing."

I close my eyes and try to imagine the Holy Spirit. It has always been the most difficult aspect of the Trinity for me to visualize. Once again it assumes the shape of a big white bird flapping around inside of me.

"How do I seek the Holy Spirit?" I ask.

"Where am I, Melina?"

"Inside of me."

"Where?"

"Everywhere."

"Close your eyes. Feel me."

I close my eyes and focus inward. I expect to see a light or an image appear in my mind. Instead, all awareness leaves my mind and falls into my chest as though pulled there by a gravitational force. I begin to feel a deep life stirring within my heart. Delicate, expectant and vulnerable, it expands and intensifies, becoming more tender, almost painful. I catch my breath. The pull of gravity continues to grow stronger. I feel as though my inner essence is melting down, liquefying and rushing into the area of my heart. A strange wistfulness, then a sorrow, enfolds my heart. I feel that I'm slowly dying.

"Melina."

Dionysus' voice enters my heart like a flesh and blood

presence through a door. All that am begins to gravitate around his presence as though he were a great sun pulling my life into itself.

"Come to me," he beckons.

My heart begins to race and I feel fear. Energy is rapidly leaving my head. I feel faint.

"No, I can't go yet... "

A brilliant ball of flames appears before me, extending from the horizon to the heavens. Its radiant heat warms my face as I watch its fiery rays stream across the sky. It is glorious, breath-taking. Awed, I whisper the word, "God." Something leaps in my soul: an overwhelming desire for embrace in its all consuming flames. Energy soars in my throat and bursts behind my eyes. At once I hear a voice, my own, then a multitude of voices singing joyously as my feet leave the earth. Rising into the blazing firmament, I extend my arms toward the ball of flames.

Suddenly, winds: powerful gusts. Cloudlike forms are whipping about my body, my hair dancing. I'm being slowed, stopped, turned back in the direction I came. Before me, poised in space: the earth. Its ice-blue immensity fills the whole of my perceptual field. I gaze at it as if for the first time, following the perfect curve of its outer surface with my eyes. An involuntary force deep within my body begins to lean into the curve. The force intensifies. Suddenly I'm pitched forward into a gulf of darkness. I fall fast, my hands and feet wildly clawing the air. All at once, a softness against my back, a shimmering light flooding my eyelids. Everything is still. I open my eyes. I'm lying in the curve of the glowing moon vessel. The angel-woman stands on my left, gazing out beyond the sphere into the darkness.

June 26 Personal Notes

I pull back into ordinary awareness feeling deeply meditative and quiet. Going about the affairs of my everyday world, I find myself revisiting the river Styx as though recalling a surreal dream. Its magnetic life intercepts my every movement, enfolding the most mundane task in an aura of timelessness. Whether I'm preparing dinner or changing my son's diaper, my mind drifts off to gaze at the glowing sphere reflected in the dark waters, while Dionysus' voice melts into the stillness. My sense of self-erasure lingers. I tell myself to snap out of it, to come all the way back. I have work to do and a life to live. The realms of infinity will have to wait.

Later in the evening, I retreat to my office and read over the session. The highly Christocentric flavor of Dionysus' statements about Shekhinah, the World Soul and the Feminine surprise me. Was his choice of language designed to reflect the core of my earliest belief systems, or am I to embrace these ideas as arising from a body of divine truth? In spite of my love and appreciation for the Christian foundations of my faith, the God of conventional religion—replete with Son and Holy Spirit—seems old and hopelessly tired.

As I observe my ambivalence toward these images, I begin to suspect they are symbolic outer garments veiling deeper mysteries buried in the recesses of the soul. I focus again on the words Shekhinah, World Soul and Feminine, sensing their divinely triune nature. Viewing them alchemically, I call to mind the three symbolic chemical substances—sulphur, mercury and salt—to which philosophers added a fourth mysterious life principle: the universal mercury or invisible eternal fire. Is the Christ Spirit this fourth principle, the eternal fire?

I close the notebook and recline on the floor, fixing my gaze on the ceiling. How strange that I should happen upon the river of death in my own womb—a vessel for the inception of life. But then again, how can this be any stranger than possessing a "chamber of death" in an organ of birth? A biblical statement rises into my mind: "Except a man be born again, he cannot see the kingdom of God." I close my eyes, recalling the silvery glow of the moon vessel reflected on the dark waters. As this image imprints itself on the screen of my mind, I gradually lose a sense of distinction between the moonlight's reflection and the water. Moonlight and water become one: an inseparable union—lunar water. I breathe deeply and smile.

In sharp contrast, the brilliant ball of flames appears in my mind's eye, its fiery splendor extinguishing the light of the moon. Gazing at it filling the heavens, I once again whisper the word, "God." I re-experience my body rising into the blazing light to be consumed in its flames like "a bride into her groom"—lunar water into solar fire. How perfectly their contrasting natures and elements complete each other.

Contemplating the idea of God, I think about what appears to be its polarized aspects: the God Feminine and the God Masculine as one, yet differentiated in that they seem to act upon each other as unique energy or life systems possessing a common matrix. I wonder if this differentiation was the effect of a cause divinely intentioned; was itself the genesis of creation as we know it, giving rise to a temporal plane of causality whereby the undifferentiated forces seething in the God Unconscious could be brought into conscious expression through humanity.

We embody this divine paradox: light and dark, male and female, consciousness and unconsciousness. We also possess the divine matrix around which the tension of these opposing forces rotate, churning and pulverizing our egos until we are inevitably forced to turn our inner eyes to them and embrace their wayward trajectories as divinely destined paths toward union and wholeness. Thus we assist in reconciling the chaotic tensions in the God Unconscious as we attempt to reconcile our own.

But the question tugs at my soul: do forces of conflict exist in the God Unconscious? Did we inherit a divine conflict? Was this conflict enacted through our first parents, Adam and Eve, or begotten by them, predisposing the human race to capacities for sin and error? Finally, what are the ramifications of this human-divine conflict beyond the small causal plane of man's existence, nestled in the staggering depths of eternity?

What if original sin were merely an arrhythmic tone in the ongoing creation-harmonics of the cosmos—a magnetically imprinted chord resonating throughout nature and consciousness for neither good nor ill, its dissonant vibration galvanizing our endlessly fragmented perceptions of time and space, good and evil, birth and death. Is this arrhythmic chord the "glitch" in God's original plan of perfection, or the intended flaw in an otherwise perfect work of art?

I cannot conceive that our capacities for reconciliation and integration—the hallmarks of striving after spiritual wholeness—could be realized through staunchly fashioning ourselves after models of flawlessness. On the contrary, a virtuoso's cultivation of musical excellence is shaped by sounding many sour notes that tune his ears to the subtle inner body of which music is comprised: longing, mystery, beauty and shadow. Even Adam and Eve, placed in idyllic conditions under the watchful eye of their divine benefactor, pricked up their ears to the magically guttural voice of the Serpent.

CHAPTER 5

RELEARNING TECHNIQUE

June 30 Session

I close my eyes and see that I'm walking in the woods on a beautiful sunny morning. Everything sparkles and looks fresh. I spot Dionysus sitting on a large rock not far from the stream. He looks up at me as I approach him and seems to have been waiting for me. I sit on the ground next to him and look around. I feel restless.

"You know, Dionysus, I'm getting tired of this place. Can't we meet in another setting? I'm getting to know these woods like the back of my hand."

"Where would you like to go?" Dionysus asks.

I'm struck with the realization that I could go anywhere in my mind I wanted. The notion is extremely tantalizing. I test it.

"How about Shangri-la?"

I look at him expectantly, hoping he'll take me seriously. Suddenly I feel I'm posing the ridiculous.

"Come," he motions, rising from the rock.

Taking my hand, he leads me to the edge of the stream. The water shines like a crystal punch bowl filled with diamonds and is almost too bright for my eyes. Dionysus releases my hand and climbs a large rock which juts over the water. Pulling his long garment up to his waist, he deftly twists it around and tucks it into his belt. I notice his feet are very tan against the light colored stone. His legs are strong and sturdy. He turns to me and smiles.

"It is time to go fishing!" he announces.

"Fishing?"

Peering into the stream, I'm amazed to see schools of silver and gold fish gleaming beneath the water. Their beautiful scales remind me of ancient treasure glistening in a mysterious lagoon.

I wonder how we're going to catch them.

"Are you ready?" Dionysus calls, gesturing broadly with his right arm.

"How are we supposed to catch these things?" I ask. "With our bare hands?"

Dionysus laughs and pulls a large net out of God knows where. He does this so quickly that it looks like sleight of hand.

"Use this," he suggests, offering it to me.

Examining the net, I see that it's sturdily woven from some sort of crude rope and feels quite heavy. Cork bobbers are secured at different places along the edges. Handling it gingerly, I begin to feel very awkward.

"I've never used one of these things before, Dionysus. What am I supposed to do?"

"Cast your net upon the water."

His words strike me as sounding strangely biblical. I dismiss them and reexamine the net. Imagining a drawstring purse, I search the weave for a rope or cord I can hold in order to pull the net out of the water. I don't see anything.

"This is weird. I can't figure out how this thing works."

Dionysus looks over at me and smiles.

"Simply cast it upon the water," he repeats.

I'm struck by how impractical this sounds. How am I'm supposed to draw the net back out? Surely there's got to be a rope or cord I can manipulate. I examine it again. Completely frustrated, I toss the whole mess out over the water and watch it sink slowly, the little cork bobbers rocking to and fro on the water's surface. I can now see schools of bright silver fish collecting in the vicinity of the net. I'm getting excited—if I could just draw the net around them, I'd have a fantastic catch. But how? I look over at Dionysus.

"What do I do now?" I yell.

"Draw your net in."

I look out over the water, stumped.

"How?"

"You will have to wade out into the stream, won't you?"

"But if I do that, I'll scare away the fish!"

Dionysus looks at me with an unbelievably placid expression.

"Do it slowly, quietly," he warns. "One sound, one false move and they're gone."

I hold my breath and enter the water. It's extremely cold. I take very small steps, moving ever so slowly. Holding my arms out above the water, I'm scanning its depths when out of nowhere a ridiculous mental image overtakes my concentration: I'm a towering float of Neptune in the Rose Bowl Parade gliding down a sprawling boulevard into an unknown fate. The image strikes me as so absurd that I nearly burst out laughing. I hold myself in check, knowing how badly I want to catch the fish. Again I'm seized by a nearly uncontrollable urge to laugh. I quickly shift my focus to another subject, recalling a childhood pastime of searching for pennies at the bottom of a swimming pool; how if I was very still and looked through the water at a certain angle, the shiny coins would miraculously appear.

I exhale slowly. I'm moving closer to a line of bobbers and see schools of fish swimming about in the area above the net. Extending my hand in slow motion, I grab one edge of the net, then stand there wondering what I should do next. I decide to gently walk my edge of the net to its opposite side and overlap it like a huge omelet. Suddenly I imagine my father making "garbage egg" to corny Italian music whining from an old Mantovani LP. I see him bobbing his stocky frame to the beat and jerking his head like a rooster as he throws whatever he's unearthed from the refrigerator into a large skillet. The image is so ludicrous that I burst out laughing. The fish begin to scatter like gold and silver torpedoes. I pull at the net, but it's too heavy to manipulate. In seconds the fish are gone.

"Oh no!" I cry. "Look what I've done!"

Dionysus is sitting on the rock, relaxing and enjoying the

scene. I shrug off the whole episode and head toward the bank, dragging the net behind me. It's heavy as hell and I must use all my strength to pull it out of the water. Finally I make it to the bank, drop the net in a heap and clamber up to where Dionysus is sitting. I feel refreshed. The sun feels wonderful on my skin.

"Well, as you can see, I'm no fisherman," I confess, laughing. "Besides, I really wasn't being serious enough. All sorts of ridiculous things kept bombarding my mind out of nowhere. I couldn't help it—it cracked me up!"

"You were wonderful, Melina. I enjoyed every moment of it."

Dionysus is smiling genuinely at me. I toss him a sidelong glance and wrinkle up my nose at him.

"Did you have a good time?" he asks.

"Sure. But I didn't catch any fish!"

"What would you have done with them had you caught them?"

"Oh, I don't know. They're too beautiful to eat. I would've thrown them back, I guess."

"Why catch them in the first place?"

I look at him in surprise.

"You're the one who wanted to go fishing!" I accuse him laughingly.

"And you?"

I think about it.

"Okay, so I wanted to try it out. I don't know why I wanted to catch the fish or what I would've done with them. I didn't even think about that. I just got into the experience."

Suddenly my thoughts are doing somersaults. I'm getting the point to all of this as clearly as if it had been driven home with a sledgehammer. Falling quiet, I gaze into the water.

"You know what I've been thinking lately," I murmur.

"Yes."

"Then you know I've been wondering what to do with all this stuff, why I keep coming back to this place—where all of this is supposed to eventually lead. It's been a real anxiety for me lately."

I look at Dionysus and see that he's all ears. I pause and stare into the water.

"I've been thinking about giving this up, giving you up."

I hesitate and glance over at him. He does not look shocked. My heart is beginning to pound.

"Well?" I ask.

"Well what?"

"Don't you have anything to say?"

"No."

Crestfallen, I bury my chin in my arms folded across my knees.

"Do you mean you wouldn't care?" I ask.

"I did not say that."

"Do you have any idea how hard it is for me to get into something just for the experience? I'm never like that!"

Dionysus flicks a twig into the stream.

"I know," he answers quietly.

"But do you understand what I mean? I've got to have a sense of where I'm going and what I'm doing, a sense of purpose. I'm not a kid!"

Dionysus looks at me somewhat blandly.

"You don't understand!" I exclaim.

"Of course I do."

"If you did, you wouldn't look at me like that."

"Like this?" he asks, twisting his face into an absurd-looking scowl.

I burst out laughing.

"Okay, I'll admit I'm being overly-sensitive, but I'm also very serious about what I'm saying!"

I suddenly feel like a six year-old. We both look at each other with dead serious expressions, then burst into laughter.

"Stop making me laugh!" I protest. "I'm trying to be serious!"

"I know! I know!" he whines in a playfully teasing voice.

Propping my chin on my knees, I wonder how I'm going to get my point across.

"You thought you were trying to catch fish out there, didn't you?" Dionysus asks.

Caught off guard by the question, I feel my spine slightly stiffen.

"Wasn't I supposed to be catching fish?" I ask. "What was the whole point of the net?"

As I listen to the words, "supposed to" and "the whole point of," I wonder how I ever got so anal.

"Why is it I always get tunnel vision in this place?" I complain. "I'm never more thick and stiff-necked than when I'm in here. It's exasperating! I mean, I'm not always like this—I am capable of spontaneity, even an occasional enlightened thought out there!"

I wave my hand at the sky.

"Or wherever it is I roam when I'm not in this place. You should have posted a sign at the entrance of these woods: Warning. Enter at the risk of becoming pitifully ignorant. Not responsible for lost or stolen human qualities of value."

Dionysus raises an eyebrow at me and is not smiling. Regretting my outburst, I gaze moodily into the water. I wonder why I get so easily rattled, even contentious, when I come to this place. I think it must be my amazing resistance. It's become loathsome to me.

"Look, Dionysus, it certainly must be clear to you by now that I've got enough resistance to keep hell burning for the rest of eternity. I'm really beginning to think I'm a hopeless case."

Dionysus is still looking at me with a raised eyebrow.

"This isn't a sympathy trip, either. I'm really discouraged."

Something awful is beginning to twist inside my chest. A terrible pressure is building. I feel that I can't breathe, that I'm going to explode.

"Why do I keep fighting all of this? What is it going to take for me to let down? What is it I really want? Why are you being so infinitely patient with me?"

My thoughts begin to spin: fear, pain, loss. Ego, ego, ego. I'm afraid to hurt and bear loss. My God, how I cling. My rage is the protective garment I wear. Don't take anything else away from me. I've fought hard for what I've got and have the battle scars to prove it. Don't heal them or I might forget the bitter lessons, the precious drops of blood I shed that got me where I am.

A wrenching pain twists in my heart like a knife.

"Oh God, Dionysus, take this sorrow away. Take it out of my heart. I want to love again. I want to truly love... "

I'm beginning to pull out of the experience. My chest aches and I'm breathing heavily. I try to maintain my composure so I can continue with the session, but it's nearly impossible. A large teardrop splatters the ink on my paper.

"It is you who holds and keeps the sorrow there," Dionysus says quietly. "Let it go, Melina. Let it go."

"But I don't know how. I've tried. It just won't leave."

"You do not want to let go of it until you have found something to take its place."

I stop crying and sit up, feeling that I'm getting close to something important.

"Yes, Dionysus, maybe you're right. But what?"

My mind begins to race. I imagine all my "loves" like beautiful hand-dipped chocolates stuffed in a heart-shaped box. What or whom have I excluded? Love of God, love of my parents, love of my brothers and sisters, love of my children, love of my friends, love of my lover. I look over at Dionysus and search his eyes. A flood of images continues to pour through my mind: love of music, flowers, dancing, nature, cemeteries, thunderstorms, Christmas and Thanksgiving. Love of spaghetti on Sundays and the smell of fresh basil and garlic. Love of a good book, of ribbons and wrapping paper, excellent candy, a good movie, a double rainbow, morning light, seashells, sticks. A poem. The ocean.

"My life is good," I acknowledge softly. "I don't know what it lacks."

Dionysus opens my hand and places something inside of it. He then closes it tightly and presses it to my heart. I stare at him for a moment, them peer inside my hand. I look up at him in surprise.

"There's nothing here."

"Look again, Melina."

I stare into my hand and see only a map of my life lines. I rub my other hand over it.

"Just skin," I reply.

"Yours."

"My body?"

"You."

I stare into my hand as if seeing it for the first time.

"There is also something else," he adds, placing his hand beneath mine.

Shaping my fingers and palm to form a cup, he tips it slowly as though pouring something from it into the air.

"What do you see?" he asks.

"A cup?"

"What is in the cup?"

"Air?"

Dionysus pauses and looks at me.

"Emptiness."

He gestures to the net lying on the bank.

"You thought you were trying to catch fish, didn't you?"

He suddenly leaps down from the rock and gathers the net from the bank. Returning to the rock, he seats himself cross-legged and spreads the net over both our laps.

"Look how well made the net is," he points out, running his fingers over the strong weave. "Whoever created it certainly knew a great deal about water and fish."

"Yes, but there are no ropes to pull it up with," I remark.

"Do you assume the net is flawed?" he asks.

I mull over the question, uncertain how to answer him.

"Let's just say that if the net had ropes, catching fish would be made a whole lot easier."

"Perhaps, but the experience would not be nearly as interesting."

"I don't understand."

"Let us imagine the creator of this net knew exactly what he was doing when he fashioned it," Dionysus explains. "He did not include ropes because they were not an intended part of its design. As a result, those who wish to use the net are faced with a unique challenge. They must completely relearn technique. Perhaps this is what the creator intended all along."

"I think that's stretching things a bit, Dionysus. It suggests that catching fish is merely a sport or game. What about the poor slob who needs to catch fish for his dinner, who's not interested in the challenge?"

"It hardly matters if he is interested in the challenge. If he is hungry enough, he will have to relearn his technique, won't he? The challenge is built-in whether or not he chooses to enjoy it. In the end, relearning his technique will reshape his thinking. Reshaping his thinking will bring to light new skills he did not know he had. Using these new skills will bring enjoyment into the experience. Enjoyment will ease the necessity of effort. When this takes place, he will no longer be a slave to his hunger."

I slowly turn his words over in my mind. Yes, I enjoyed my experience, but it seemed by accident, hardly related to the task at hand. My laughter caused the fish to scatter.

Dionysus continues.

"Because you had your mind set on achieving a result when you entered the water, your purpose being to catch fish, you focused all your energy and control to that end. When joy swam into your net, you saw it as an intrusion to your goal and tried to resist it. Your resistance to your own mirth required effort. Your effort severed your relationship to the experience. When your mirth finally overtook you, it scattered the fish only because you had set that outcome into motion the moment you entered the water with your network of controls. This network of controls you mistakenly blamed on your fisher's net."

I gaze down at the net spread over our laps. I'm struck with how utterly simple it is: unadorned, uncomplicated. I run my fingers over its coarse weave and think of Peter the apostle, the "fisher of men." I shake my head.

"Saint Peter was like that poor slob I mentioned earlier. He toiled with those huge nets each day just to put supper on his table. His survival needs consumed him, formed the basis of his entire livelihood. Then along came what's-his-name... "

I wave my hand in the air and burst out laughing.

"You know, the guy dressed in robes with the white dove hovering over his head. Peter's life was irrevocably changed thereafter."

Dionysus breaks into a wide grin. Rising from the rock, he extends his hand to help me up, then gathers the net and drapes it loosely over my shoulders, straightening the cork bobbers.

"Melina, Peter relearned his technique."

July 3 A Dream

I dream that I'm sitting in the cocktail lounge of a restaurant in an old city like Chicago. It is nighttime. I'm gazing out of some very large windows at a magnificent, ancient-looking structure across the street, which is the exact likeness of the Roman Coliseum. Large, beautifully carved statues of Greek and Roman male figures, angels and gods stand atop the immense rounded wall. They are mysterious-looking against the night sky.

Suddenly I float up through the ceiling of the restaurant and find myself hovering over rooftops of the downtown area. From this heightened view, the city looks like an archeological find;

centuries-old roofs and chimneys made of intricately carved stone shimmer like a mythical city in the moonlight. Amazed, I wonder how many people have ever seen the breathtaking world that's up here. I'm convinced the city's origins and early history lie in these stones, now forgotten by modern man.

As I slowly descend, I pass by the large beautiful statues on top of the coliseum. I notice one of the statues is the exact likeness of the bartender in the restaurant in which I was sitting. I'm perplexed as to why a statue of a contemporary, living, and ordinary man was added to the ring of ancient gods.

I find myself in the restaurant again and question the bartender about the statue. Friendly and unassuming, he smiles and seems a bit embarrassed talking about himself as an art form preserved in stone for posterity. Nevertheless, he tells me a sculptor asked him to pose for it.

"Don't you feel kind of funny having a naked statue of yourself looming in full view for the whole city to see?" I ask.

He laughs and says no, it doesn't bother him because "it is too high for people to see."

July 4 A Dream

I dream that Ted and I are in a rambling, four story house which was built around the turn of the 20th century. Within the house is a very aged-looking, wide wooden staircase that leads up to the fourth floor of the house.

As Ted and I climb the staircase, we become spooked by a growing sense that the house is inhabited by an invisible malevolent presence. Ted suddenly stops me on the staircase and points to the ceiling, calling for me to look at a design or pattern in the plaster. It seems he is seeing something ominous and terrible. I shout at Ted not to feed his energy into such things, for it will only frighten us more and bring about some ill fate. Swept up in whatever he's seeing, he keeps insisting I look at it. I get very upset and scream at him that I absolutely refuse to look, that it would be the worst thing I could possibly do.

We start racing up the last flight of stairs, hounded by a mounting sense of urgency. We're running so fast that when we reach the top floor, we're catapulted across the landing into a powerful energy field. It instantly invades our bodies and minds, paralyzing us in its grip. I realize to my complete horror that this is the malevolent presence from which we were trying to escape. Ted and I are now suspended in this force field and can't move of our own volition. I can feel my brain being taken over by the evil presence, which is threatening to extinguish not only my identity and consciousness, but the very life of my soul. To save both our souls from this spiritual death, I realize I must call on God for help.

I begin to loudly recite The Lord's Prayer and have great difficulty exerting my will upon my vocal chords. I struggle desperately to focus the power of my will through the force field in order to break through its suffocating hold on my voice. The struggle feels similar to drowning. Suddenly my voice breaks free. Filled with wild terror, it sounds as if it were coming from a deep warp in space. I'm now slowly waking up from the dream and realize I'm reciting The Lord's Prayer out loud.

Ted awakens and calls my name. Extremely frightened, I bolt upright and grab onto him. I'm afraid of going back to sleep, thinking I may reenter the dream. I talk Ted into going downstairs with me for a glass of juice so I can fully awaken and shake the dream from my mind. I realize it's been several years since I've had a nightmare of such frightening proportions.

July 5 A Dream

I dream that Ted and I are lying in bed. Looking down at the floor, I notice that water is gathering at the furthermost edges of the room and the floor-length curtains at the windows are getting soaked at the bottom. More water floods into the room and begins to create a whirlpool effect. I get up on all fours on the bed to see what is happening. Everything in the room seems to be moving in the water, including the curtains at the windows, which are being swished to and fro. The whirlpool surrounds our bed but doesn't touch it. Ted says the main drainpipe must be clogged.

I jump out of bed and locate the main drainpipe, then take the end of a broom handle and push it down the pipe to loosen whatever is in there. Spotting the corner of a large terrycloth towel sticking up through the pipe, I tug at it and pull it out. I peer down the pipe and see a woman's left hand reaching up to me. It is a beautiful, delicate hand with lovely rings on two fingers. I pull the hand hard until I've moved the woman up the pipe to her shoulder. Her head is turned toward her shoulder and I can now see the crown of her dark tousled hair. All at once she tilts her head back and looks directly at me. I see that the woman is me.

July 11 A Dream

I dream that Ted and I, as well as my two small children, are living in an unfamiliar house. The house is haunted by a group of invisible presences who seem fairly harmless. We put up with them and go about our daily lives as though they're not there. Gradually their activities become more boisterous. Growing increasingly spooked by all the poltergeists, I wonder if I can continue to ignore them. I'm afraid if I openly acknowledge the presences, they'll invade our lives in a more intimate, disturbing way.

Tucking the children into bed one evening, I feel the presences very strongly. I leave the room. My children suddenly cry out in distress and I return quickly. The presences are shaking the beds and yanking off the covers. I realize they've gotten out of control and we can't stop them. Ted and I gather the children into the kitchen. We huddle together and someone cries, "Here they come!" Looking toward the doorway, I feel them enter the kitchen. I clutch the children to me and recite The Lord's Prayer out loud. As I say the prayer, my fear begins to vanish. A feeling of security falls over me and I sense we're no longer in danger.

The spirits suddenly materialize as they walk in a single file through the kitchen and out into the hall. At the front of the line is a little boy holding a huge stuffed animal. He's accompanied by his parents who look young, quiet and serious. Behind them are several teenage girls dressed in brightly colored party dresses, laughing and talking to each other as though they're school chums. Behind them stands a young teenage boy who is in deep anguish. His mouth is open as though he's wailing loudly, but I can't hear him. Disturbed by whatever is causing his suffering, I feel a deep sense of compassion for him. None of the other spirits seem to notice him. He's utterly alone.

I walk out into the hallway and observe three elevators taking the spirits "up" in small groups. When I see this, I realize the spirits are leaving the earth and returning to a plane of formless being. As I watch them, I'm deeply stirred by many emotions. The finality of their departure, as well as their complete surrender to a higher power which seems to be orchestrating their exodus, is awesome to me. I realize these individuals will never again be as they are, but must surrender all they deeply cherish: their autonomy, their relationships with those they love, their most private hopes and dreams and all that is known and familiar to them.

A strange wave of melancholy fills my heart for them, accompanied by an inexplicable sense of relief and hope—a recognition and acceptance of the irrevocable terms of life that "you can't take it with you," which lifts the burden of striving from the human soul. I'm deeply moved by these realizations as I peek through an elevator window at the people inside. They seem insulated within their final moments together, untouched by anxiety or feelings of loss. I'm completely awed by their composure and brightness of disposition. Wishing I could be close with them, I long to embrace and speak with each one before they leave. I know I could easily love them, if only there was time.

July 22 A Dream

I dream that I'm standing in the dining room of a large house. The room is dark and feels very oppressive. In the center of the room is an oblong table set elaborately for dinner. My parents, brothers and sisters are gathered in the room and as I observe them, I sense something strange about their behavior. They return my glances in a disapproving, covert way as though they're attempting to conceal something from me. I begin to feel anxious.

Suddenly a loud explosion issues through the floor. A monstrous apparition appears amidst us, roaring and spewing smoke and vile fluids. Its head is bestial and enormous. My family glares at me with knowing smiles as though they've pledged themselves to this unholy entity and plan to use its power against me. I panic and run.

Racing for a doorway at the other end of the room, I glimpse the dark silhouette of a man outside the window. He's wearing a fedora and carrying a machine gun. He aims the gun into the room and plasters the table with rounds of bullets. Fragments of china and crystal fly everywhere. Terrified, I drop to the floor under the table for safety. I'm certain the man's intention is to kill me. I watch his silhouette at the window as he surveys the damage. I sense he's aware that I'm hiding beneath the table. He points his gun low and begins spraying the floor with bullets. I'm sure I'll be hit as the bullets explode around me.

Frightened out of my mind, I crawl frantically across the floor to an open doorway that leads out to a hall. Once out of the room, I jump up and run down the hall, looking for an exit. I feel the odds are completely stacked against me and that I won't be able to escape in time. Glancing behind me, I see that a gang of mobsters carrying machine guns are running after me. I turn a corner in the hallway and run into Ted. Nearly leaping on him in panic, I scream that I'm in danger and desperately need his help. He stares coldly at me, unaffected by my pleas. Instantly I know he's "one of them" and is conspiring against me.

I back away from him in horror, only to find myself surrounded by mobsters holding machine guns. One of the mobsters lifts his machine gun and aims it at my face. I know the gun is filled with acid and that I'll die a slow death as my flesh is burnt away bit by bit. He pulls the trigger. The acid hits the left side of my face and eye and begins to eat a large hole in my skull. I stand there paralyzed with dread, knowing the acid is slowly eating its way to my brain.

August 2 A Dream

I dream that I'm with members of my family and their young children. Observing the children as they play, I begin to notice something strange about their behavior. I soon realize they're victims of some sort of possession.

The dream shifts and I'm talking anxiously with a group of women about whatever it is that has possessed the children. No one else seems to notice something strange is about. Somewhere in the house, religious rites are being performed.

The dream shifts and I'm with members of my family. On the wall is a picture of my brother Mike guarded by what appears to be Saint Michael the Archangel. Mike knows about the possession and has placed the picture on the wall for his own protection. When I inquire about it, he tells me the devil is trying to invade us and has already invaded some of our children. I'm very frightened, for now that I know what's going on, I feel more vulnerable to the vile influence.

All at once I feel something enter my body through my back. It leaps up my spine to my head. The back of my head bursts into flames and I realize my hair is on fire. I fall to the ground on my back and try to smolder the flames. Once I've accomplished this, the presence within me leaves.

The dream shifts and I find myself seated in a room, relating my experience to my brother Dominic. He's very frightened and doesn't want to listen. I know we must all make a collective effort to protect ourselves and our children. I contemplate ways of invoking divine protection. I also realize I must place a picture of myself, guarded by an angel, up on the wall.

Personal Notes

I awaken from this dream feeling heavy and anxious. The image of the "devil" invading innocent and unknowing human beings, particularly children, is one I find both terrifying and loathsome. Nonetheless, I reflect on its possible symbolic implications to my life and process.

As I contemplate the recent dreams I've recorded over the last few weeks, I'm drawn to their repetitive motifs: fear of possession, intense feelings of vulnerability, fear of being overwhelmed by powers beyond the scope of human reason, fear of psychic disfigurement, loss of identity, loss of soul, death.

It's clear I've journeyed deeply into an enigmatic realm from which I may never be able to return—the underworld of the soul and its plethora of disturbing images: mobsters wielding machine guns, houses haunted by ominous presences, the Self being birthed through a drain pipe tunneling underground. What stamina it takes to be assaulted night after night with the ghastly and terrifying, waking to days of grave reconsideration of what I'm doing. My faculties of discernment are being taxed as never before: when are the dream images signposts of real psychic danger? When are they regenerative forces wearing the masks and costumes of my fear and distortion? When are they fragmented representations of the ego in the death throes, begging my intervention in its painful dissolution?

Pulling on memories of my initial psychic awakening many

years ago, I derive comfort from the knowledge of having survived a similar baptism by fire. The birthing of unconscious forces through psychic layers of resistance, denial and fear cooked up cinemascopic dreams of unimaginable violence and terror. I must continually remind myself that when the forces of truth burn their way into consciousness, they come as a conflagration filled with the tremendous and awful.

As the morning wears on, I find myself gravitating to thoughts about X. No matter how I try to objectively view him as my own personal demon with collective overtones, I experience a resurgence of anxiety as I contemplate him alongside the dream of having been invaded by the "devil." Filled with confusion, I hunt for Ted and find him flipping through the paper at the dining room table. Pulling up a chair, I carefully feel my way into a conversation about X, hoping Ted will be a sounding board for my blind spots.

A Dialogue With Ted

T: Why do you need to project your passion onto this being—X—that you can condemn later through the eyes of "victim"? It's a way of not accepting your own passion.

M: Maybe it's all a part of my own psychodynamics.

T: You're defending the structure. You can choose any other structure. Your whole religious make-up says if you have a strong sexual nature laden with passion and lust, you're innately bad, morally flawed—a spiritual degenerate. So you create X, the personification of evil, who can act out to the max all your dark inclinations, as well as your guilty feelings about yourself. Then you get to vicariously live out all your "badness" through X as his victim, while denying the monster in yourself, that is, "This isn't really me."

M: Christ, I must be more screwed up than I thought. How am I going to come to terms with X?

T: X is an agent.

M: Yes, I know you're suggesting X as a transformative agent, but I'm still stuck down here in the dung heap phase of this. In other words, before he turns into the Buddha and whisks me off to nirvanaland, I want to get inside his dirt, my dirt. I mean, if my passion is tied up with "dirt"—and you realize I'm speaking figuratively—then I don't know if I want to give him up because right now he serves me. It comes down to this: if all my passion is tied up in X, how do I know I can experience the intensity of my sexual drives and appetites without him? You realize, of course, that I'm not talking about X as the twisted tormentor in my archetypal journeys, but X as an unconsciously rooted dynamic that energizes my sexual experiences. If I'm cold, he's hot, which is to say when our worlds encounter each other, *steam happens*.

T: You're trying to transform his energy, not obliterate your passion.

M: That's easy for you to say since you assume one can exist independently of the other. Well I don't know that, do I? And it's a hell of a risk to "transform" X's energy when I could be sterilizing my soul of all its color and smells, its shabby roof lines and day-old fish—you know, the stuff of myself that makes me see or experience something differently than Joe Shmoe down on the corner. I'm not trying to glamorize this "stuff"; I'm strongly suggesting that it's like salt and pepper—it enhances the flavor of experience.

T: That's fear of change talking, a defense.

M: I don't want to become a sterile being! I don't want "divine sex"!

T: As long as you're flesh and blood, you're going to have flesh and blood sex.

M: Not without X.

T: The ego will struggle unto death to maintain itself.

M: The forbidden quality of X is the passion I experience.

T: You're afraid of taking responsibility for your passion. You fear that without this elaborate system, you won't be able to experience the intensity of your own drives and desires. In fairy tales, the shadow is an autonomous complex working at apparent odds against the hero. At the end of the tale, we find out this seemingly autonomous, opposing force is working for and with the hero to accomplish his goals. These goals can only be reached by the hero's acceptance of the force which seems to be working against him. In other words, the hero accepts the ugly, menacing dwarf as his companion. Then the dwarf with his bagful of miracles can help the hero accomplish his goal. When the dwarf is rejected, split off, the hero's fate is doomed.

M: Okay, let's see if I've got this. My realization of X as a transformative agent is the first step toward integration. The way X images himself to me is my own unconscious creation. But if I can see that he inevitably leads me to my divinity, why should I change him?

T: You have to see beneath X's facade. Why do you need a Nazi living inside of you? Are you afraid of power? Yes! So all your personal power and fear of it gets transferred onto this other thing in yourself as a corrupting influence: power is a Nazi with a riding crop.

M: I see what you're saying, but I don't know how to get around this construct. It's very formidable. All I know is I don't want to banish darkness in myself and elevate everything to "goodness" and "light" because that would be a denial of my basic humanity, as though one is real and the other is an illusion.

T: Light is real. Darkness is an illusion.

M: Oh right, God forbid we should tolerate the notion that darkness might have a legitimate place alongside "light" in the intimate affairs of the human psyche. No, that's getting back into that religious hierarchical bullshit that birthed the bloodbath of the Inquisition. That kind of mindset engenders conflict, and I know because I've lived with it for years. For the first time in my life I'd like to think I don't have to reconcile the opposites. God and X can be. Separate but one. What I really want to know, and this is the question we should be looking long and hard at because its answer is the beginning and end of this whole conversation: in the Garden of Eden, where do the lies of the Serpent come from?

August 3 X As Archetype: A Private Meditation

He approaches me with his rage and his riding crop, his disdain and willful pride. I submit to his torment, conscious of my choice to surrender, conscious of how this excites him. I do not feel shame. I know his excitement is threaded into my own desire. Falling deeply inside myself, I feel his energy charge my body with an urgent rawness. It is stripping me. I hear him growl obscenities and feel them burn into my brain, my flesh, peeling away images I hold of myself—the sacrosanct identity forms I wear tightly around my being like impenetrable armor. I feel these forms being rent, torn away from me, and as I become more naked, a powerful vulnerability rises in my body, holding my fragile life inside of it. It unfolds and a rare clarity emerges, an awareness which is no longer the effect of mentally manipulating an idea about myself. I experience myself as instinctive life rooted in blood and bone: breathing, feeling, sensing. I feel "clean," real.

I'm beginning to realize my participation in X's world is a deep chthonic ritual, a psychic rite of passage through my body into the dark and profound chaos of my unconscious self, which breathes me more fully into physical and spiritual life. I observe X and see his anger as the wrath of the Old Testament, his moral judgment the punishment for being human. He delights in his wrath, his unyielding authority, which fuels his need to victimize, punish and humiliate. I wonder if the impulses of X arise from deeply possessive urges of the unconscious—the

Devouring Mother, who is compelled to swallow her children, returning them to the womb of utter darkness.

It is a strange and awful face of God that churns within me.

CHAPTER 6

THE SOUL'S KEEPERS

The richest events occur in us long before the soul perceives them. And, when we begin to open our eyes to the visible, we have long since committed ourselves to the invisible.

— Gabriele D'Annunzio

September 11 Session

I close my eyes and see that I'm standing in the woods near a narrow creek. A thin trickle of water winds its way through dead twigs and small boughs that have fallen from the trees overhead. Gazing at my surroundings, I realize I'm in a completely unfamiliar area of the woods. Enmeshed in overgrowth, many of the trees appear far younger and less stately than the ones in my previous journeys, while others are stooped and bear sparse foliage. A forlorn feeling exudes from this place; nature seems to be in a suspended state of dormancy, looking messy and forgotten.

I want to relocate myself, but I'm not sure how to do it. On the other side of the creek is a steep slope. I cross over and begin to climb it. As I labor up the hill, dead twigs creak and snap under my weight. Tangled weeds tug around my ankles, arresting my movement with a strange deliberateness. As my dislike for this place increases, I climb more quickly and determinedly.

I reach the top of the slope and look out over a rolling landscape filled with ornate monuments to the dead. It's clear I've come upon a cemetery. Immense trees stand magnificently across acres of tranquil earth. Beneath them, angels stare fixedly into the infinite, their heavenly forms postured tenderly in granite. The tranquility of this place is overwhelming, almost euphoric. I take a deep breath. My mind feels free here, free to explore, postulate, meander where it will. I like this feeling very much.

I walk across the grass toward a rose-colored marble monument. At the base of the monument are three tarnished brass plaques set neatly in a horizontal row. I try to make out the inscriptions, but I can't seem to get a clear focus on the letters. The effort begins to make me feel sleepy. I abandon the endeavor and drink in the serenity of the landscape. My gaze settles on a nearby grove of trees draped in shadows of cool green. The longer I gaze at it, the more I want to close my eyes and drift off to sleep.

Stooping, I run my hands over the cool grass, then lean into it and turn onto my back. As my limbs and trunk sink into the grass, I close my eyes and relax, breathing deeply. A dense concentration of energy disengages at the base of my skull and a wonderful sensation of floating fills my brain, as though each of its cells had become a tiny helium balloon. The feeling is delightful and extremely restful. As I sink more deeply inside of it, a familiar voice rises from the interior of my mind. Focusing on the voice, I notice I'm using what seems to be the backside of my eyes to do this. It's as if I'm hearing through a function of my inner sight. I quietly observe what is happening.

"Melina, I am here now," Dionysus states quietly.

I want to answer him, but I can't generate the energy to respond. I try to nod in acknowledgment, but my head feels as heavy and immovable as a boulder. With my eyes closed I can see a thin line of energy moving at an angle from each of my eyeballs to a point somewhere above the roof of my mouth. As I continue breathing slowly and deeply, I can feel a slight "popping" sensation in my sinus cavities. The screen of my mind suddenly becomes a fine mist of soft light. It's very soothing. Attempting once more to respond, I discover that I can project my thoughts without disturbing the interior tranquility of this experience.

"I can hear you, Dionysus. Where am I now? Where am I going?"

My chest cavity feels as if it were inflating with helium and seems to be rising just inches above my body. The sensation is extremely weird and is beginning to affect my breathing. My heartbeat accelerates. Simultaneously, I'm seized by a disorienting sensation of falling through my back between my shoulder blades toward an inexplicable point of gravity in the earth. My breathing comes faster. The tiny helium balloons in my brain and chest begin to "pop," setting off microscopic explosions like miniature firecrackers. Memories of this phenomenon occurring during past meditations help me to maintain equilibrium, for I know the sensation level of this experience is now reaching a peak and will soon level off the way an automatic transmission downshifts into lower gear. I wait. The electrical flurry in my brain, chest and back begins to diminish. A soothing calm spills through my body and consciousness, filling me with a sense of relief.

"Melina."

Dionysus' voice fills my consciousness like a great eye turned inward upon itself. It seems my whole awareness has become the eye. I try to connect to the voice from somewhere deep inside my stomach, but I can't feel my body. I'm a floating eye with no umbilical cord.

"Melina, why have you come here?"

I search for an answer, but I can't seem to connect into anything intelligible enough to articulate. Oddly, I don't feel a sense of anxiety. The question continues to resonate inside of me, sending ripples of energy moving in ever widening arcs across the screen of my mind. I'm strongly compelled to follow the arcs by projecting my awareness along their progressions. As I do this, I experience a sensation of movement as though I'm bodily traveling through space. I see that I'm moving into darkness. Everything is becoming still, so very still. I can't determine whether the darkness is expanding or I'm becoming very small. I still don't feel a sense of anxiety. However, I'm beginning to experience a slight wave of nausea in the pit of my stomach.

"Melina, breathe calmly and deeply," Dionysus instructs me, his voice penetrating the interior of my brain like warm vapor.

I take a deep breath and slowly exhale, feeling more and more disoriented. A highly concentrated point of energy deep within my body begins to rock back and forth as if it were being shaken loose. Instantly I experience a need for more oxygen and feel that I'm going to hyperventilate. I try to focus on my breathing but my body is pumping signals of distress to my brain. I want to cry or wail as a powerful force inside of me struggles to break free of all constraint and form. I'm now searching for my voice. I don't know how or where to focus in order to activate my vocal chords.

"Melina, you must use your mind to communicate."

"I'm not feeling well, Dionysus. I don't know what's happening to me."

"Be calm. You will know."

As he speaks, I sense what appears to be thick dark curtains being draped over the left and right hemispheres of my brain. They're pressing in and feel horrible. I want to push them off, but I can't use my hands. I gaze down at my body and notice my arms look small and stumpy. My hands appear gnarled. I feel an instinct to pull them in close to my body, close to my chest. My body seems to be turning in a slow revolution towards something, as if I'm being twisted.

"Dionysus, I'm going into a funnel."

My head is pointed downward at an aperture in the funnel. Seeing through the top of my head, I'm watching the aperture as it opens and closes, opens and closes. I feel a terrible pressure on all sides of my head and at the base of my skull. Waves of darkness press against me, pushing at my back and ribcage. All at once I can see my body as though my eyes and consciousness were located outside of my head I study my back and behind. My legs are tucked under my behind; my left foot is crossed over my right. It is a baby's body. My spine looks very curved.

"You must go back in now, Melina. Reenter your body."

Something strong tugs inside my chest. It feels like emotion, but I can't identify it. I realize I'm about to be birthed and wonder how long I can stay outside my body like this, watching. Suddenly I'm overwhelmed by a powerful need to be inside my body, as if in response to the sheer force of my mother's will enveloping me.

"Melina, I want you to stay with this feeling. You are capable of slowing down your experience and focusing within this one moment. Will you do this?"

"Yes."

I'm confused that I've said "yes." I'm aware that some part of myself doesn't want to do this, but this part seems to be standing outside the experience, yelling behind a soundproof door.

"I feel like a turtle," I observe, experiencing an odd sense of detachment. "I want to be shut up safe inside my shell, my home. I want to pull in and close everything out. Look at my body. See how I don't want to come out? I'm a little turtle."

"You must reenter your body now, Melina."

I'm beginning to feel a sense of sadness. I can still see my back and behind, my two little feet crossed, but now the right foot is showing and the left one is not. For a moment I feel like a great gust of wind hovering over a landscape. I like the heightened vantage point and don't want to give it up. Yet even as I think these thoughts, they're fading. I'm drifting down, slowly. Darkness is coming in. I want to pull oxygen through my nose but I can't. Something is tightening across my brain, my forehead.

"Melina, you can breathe through your nose now. Relax. You are deep in your body. Breathe."

I inhale through my nose, yet some part of me can't inhale through my nose. There's an obstruction. I'm getting stuck here.

My eyeballs are turning inward toward my nose. I hear a sound: a woman's voice as though she's bearing down. I sense her energy around my body and feel distress. The distress is coming at me like black hands pulling and pushing. I feel disoriented—in a stupor or somewhat numb. I don't like what's happening, but I can do nothing. What a helpless, vulnerable feeling.

"Are you feeling helpless and vulnerable as an infant?" Dionysus asks.

"No."

"What are you feeling as an infant?"

"Something in my chest is pulling and churning. I think it's fear."

"What are you afraid of?"

"I really don't know. I'm not even sure it's fear. I'm having difficulty identifying it."

"You must burrow more deeply inside of it."

More layers of darkness press across my brain. I feel as if I'm suffocating. My awareness seems to be diminishing, shrinking to the size of a pea. The pea disperses and is no longer inside my head. My awareness is in my body. My awareness is my body.

"Pain. Discomfort. Distress," I pant, my ribcage tightening like an elastic band around my lungs.

"What do you feel in your chest?" Dionysus asks.

"Anxiety. Levels of distress piling up on itself."

"What do you need, Melina?"

"Stillness, comfort, protection, sleep."

"What do you want, Melina?"

"Mother. She lives inside my body. I feel her in my genitals. I am rooted to her."

"You live inside her body. You are being birthed through her genitals. She is the root through which you, the fruit, are nourished."

My anxiety increases and with it, my confusion. I have no identity. I am mother. Body is mother. There is no other awareness.

"I'm ready to disengage from this experience," I respond wearily.

Already the pressure around my head is abating and my breathing is coming easier. A soft light spills into my mind like gentle mist. I'm beginning to sense proximity between my immediate awareness and the birth experience. The impression of something sinking through the top of my skull instantly relieves the sensation of being suspended in space. I feel as if I'm being "dropped" into my normal awareness like a ship's anchor into a familiar and safe harbor.

"I'd like to wake up now, Dionysus. My back is stiff."

"Be still," he answers. "You have only just begun."

Physically uncomfortable, I'm beginning to feel like an effigy. Once again I sense the cemetery splayed out around me with all its glorious monuments to the dead. I want to open my eyes and look around, but my eyes are glued shut. I'm growing restless and impatient.

"I think I've had enough for now," I repeat, my voice tightly controlled.

"You have had nothing. You are merely orbiting."

Jagged energy streaks through my brain. My chest tightens as a flood of pent-up emotions pushes at my diaphragm. I think about how I will answer him.

"Can't you appreciate how emotionally disorienting it is to be confronted with your own birth experience?" I exclaim. "How can I possibly be objective when I have no way of knowing if what I just experienced ever really happened? How do I know I'm not borrowing collected data stored in my memory from books I've read or stories I've heard? This whole birth scenario makes me extremely uncomfortable!"

Feeling I've said too much, I take a deep breath. The quiet around me is becoming deafening. I want to clear my throat, but I can't seem to coordinate my body functions with my will. The more I focus on it, the more I feel a coughing jag coming on. I try to repress it.

"You are dealing with heart energy, Melina. Coughing will not dislodge what is interfering with your breathing. You have little choice but to return and complete what you started."

"I'm really getting tired of all this trauma, Dionysus. Doesn't it make you suspicious?"

"Suspicious of what?"

"That I might be manufacturing these experiences from some deep unconscious warp where I store my most profound misconceptions about myself."

"And what if you are?"

Tongue-tied, I don't know where to go with this.

"But how do I know?" I ask. "Isn't there an easier, more reliable way to approach the truth about myself?"

"A way in which you can circumvent your own pain, Melina? Your pain maintains you. It is your point of gravity, your locus of control. You can go nowhere but to journey its trajectories."

A feeling of gloom falls over me. What a dismal portrayal: a dog on a leash. Sighing heavily, I envision my body as a cage in which I flit from one side to the other. Peering through its bars to the strange world beyond, I'm both relieved and burdened by the boundaries around me, the roof over my head. Yet all I ever think about is the world outside the cage, the sky over my head. I internalize it, bring it inside and make-believe I'm out there, free and unrestrained.

"Let's face it, Dionysus. There's no way I'm ever going to reconcile my contradictions. Paradox is a fact of life."

Someone nearby breaks into laughter. Startled, I try to see who it is but I still can't open my eyes. I know it is not Dionysus.

"Melina, Melina. You do take yourself so seriously," Dionysus remarks softly, his voice filled with amusement.

I'm still recoiling from the laughter which has put me on alert. I can feel my body sending out psychic probes along the grass to identify the nearby intruder. I feel very vulnerable.

"All right," I call out blindly. "I know I'm going to stay glued here unless I go back, so let's get this over with."

Someone laughs again, but now the sound is some distance away to my right.

"Who is that?" I ask.

"Mirth."

"I asked who, Dionysus, not what."

"Mirth."

"Don't you think Mirth's timing is a bit inappropriate? I mean, I am about to be birthed."

As I think over what I just said, I feel a wave of sadness. Why shouldn't my birth be joyful? Why do I expect it to be frightening and traumatic? Banishing these thoughts, I refocus my awareness deep inside my body and experience a momentary sense of insulation from my fear. Just the same, I encounter a wall of hesitation.

"Dionysus, I'd like to tell you something."

"I am listening."

"I'm scared to go back there."

"I know, Melina. Now relax. Breathe deeply and calmly."

I take a deep breath and at once experience an inexplicable feeling of wistfulness balling-up in my chest. Tears involuntarily well up in my eyes and spill down the sides of my face. I don't understand why I'm feeling so sad or where the tears are coming from. The tears are very quiet and feel clear and pure. I don't know how I know this or why it makes any difference.

"Dionysus."

"Do not speak now, Melina. Rest."

I begin to float. My thoughts become weightless points of light and drift up and out of the top of my head into a soothing ocean of nothingness. Tension I didn't know was in my back suddenly dissolves. I seem to be floating in a thick swath of cotton, a wonderful blanket of warmth. In this cradle of peace and softness, I think of the word "credo" and wonder what it is I truly believe.

As the lulling stillness deepens, I sink further inside a pocket of absolute peace and warmth. Within it I feel indescribably secure, completely trusting. My body is totally at rest as though held in the hand of a powerful protector. I mentally intone the word, "God." Instantly a soft yellow radiance fills my stomach and bathes the inside of my chest and throat with a delightful warmth. The source of this radiance seems to be anchored behind my navel.

I'm becoming more aware of my limbs; they feel loose and watery. From my waist down, my body feels extremely fluid-like. This sensation makes me want to urinate. It also makes me want to move my legs around. I have a strange tickly sensation in my groin area and upper thighs. I want to shake this sensation down through my calves, but I can't seem to negotiate this movement at all. It's as if my will isn't making the right connection to my body.

"Melina, do not use your will," Dionysus instructs me.

"What should I use?"

"Use nothing. Surrender your will-to-respond over to your body. What you are seeking is reflex."

Turning in slow revolutions as though suspended in an antigravity chamber, I think about how to activate reflex. All I can feel now is the urge to urinate. I'm getting tired.

"Melina, inhale slowly and deeply. As you exhale, allow your awareness to drop down into your body along your spine. Release your awareness at the point just below your navel."

I take a deep breath and slowly exhale. The energy in my head feels as if it were being pulled backwards to the base of my skull and funneled down a long narrow chute. As the energy intensifies, I feel that I'm falling down an elevator shaft inside my own body. All at once I plunge into a pool of warm yellow radiance. Thousands of phosphorescent ripples encircle me and sweep down my legs like small electrical charges. Suddenly my legs jerk and my spine arches. What a grand sensation! I kick around vigorously and find I can do this easily as long as I stay completely focused inside the physical sensations in my lower body. Images spill into my mind, increasing the physical pleasure of kicking: I imagine I'm a sea horse locomoting through water as my body jerks, thrusts and revels in movement. The image shifts and I see myself perched on my tricycle as a small child, furiously pedaling around in crazy circles.

"This is great!" I exclaim, laughing. "I'm really getting into it!"

It seems my body is suspended in a vaporous or fluid-like state. The fluid appears somewhat milky or gauzy. I'm kicking my legs and making a racket but even so, there's a soundlessness to my movements that I can't quite figure out. It's very strange.

"Melina, are you aware that you are inside your mother's uterus?"

"I can't explain what I'm really experiencing because I don't understand it. I feel as if I'm not fully tuning into all the levels of this experience. Some part of me is shut off like an engine with only one or two pistons working; I'm not functioning at full capacity. All I want to do is kick and pee and turn. I don't care about experiencing anything else."

"Are you able to touch your face?"

"I'm really not interested in my face."

"What about your hands?"

"No."

"What are you doing now, Melina?"

"I don't know. Something is going on, but I... you know, it isn't dark in here. Everything is strangely illuminated in a pale light. I can see fine."

"Are you surprised?"

"Yes. It's as if a little night-light is on in here. I'm no longer in an upside-down position like I was before. I feel as though I'm moving along in a capsule, or I'm being carried around in a bag somewhere in space. It's very weird. I can see the sun in the western sky to my right. It looks like a big shimmering orange."

"What do you want to do now, Melina?"

"I'm not sure. My toes are pressing into something squishy. I'm getting tired."

"I want you to rest now. Close your eyes. Sleep is coming. Can you feel it?"

"Yes."

My awareness is collapsing fast into a powerful need for rest. A quiet floating sensation is overtaking my body and I can no longer keep my eyes open. Everything is becoming dark. It seems I'm dipping or moving downward very slowly. It's very dreamlike.

"Melina, are you asleep?"

"Yes, falling softly."

"Where are you going?"

"Into the dark funnel."

"What do you feel?"

"Nothing. I'm descending. The funnel seems so far away, as if I were dreaming it."

"Are you alone?

Alone. The word echoes and falls in gentle ripples into the funnel.

"Alone, yes," I answer.

"Melina, listen to my voice. Slowly shift your awareness to the area of your back between your shoulder blades."

I see the funnel below. It seems to be made up of dark swirling clouds moving in a counterclockwise direction. I feel as though I'm looking down at it from a very great height. I slowly shift my awareness to a point between my shoulder blades just above my chest. Instantly I feel a sensation there as if this part of my body were connected to a string. The string is being gently tugged from somewhere above me.

"Melina, what do you feel?"

"Spider. I feel like a spider dangling from a string."

"I want you to gather your awareness into a ball of light and focus it between your shoulder blades. You are going to roll the ball slowly up the string. Will you do this?"

"I'll try."

My chest and lungs are expanding as if they were filling with helium. My heartbeat is becoming more rapid. Everything is swirling around and becoming white—waves of white mist. Breathless and overwhelmed, I try to maintain my focus as the energy in my chest condenses into a magnetic ball of light. As its radiance intensifies, the ball begins to emit heat. My spine between my shoulder blades is becoming tender as the ball presses against it. Waves of anxiety balloon in my chest.

"Take a very deep breath, Melina. Hold it for a few moments, then release it quickly and forcefully."

Everywhere, white light becoming more brilliant, burning behind my eyes, in my nostrils. Energy is rising fast, seems to be pressurizing in my upper body. I feel as if I'm going to explode.

"Dionysus, I... I'm losing touch, can't focus."

"Breathe, Melina."

My heart is pounding wildly. I can't breathe. I gasp for air and pull it deep into my lungs and stomach. The ball shifts, feels as though it's pushing through my back.

"Release, Melina. Release!"

The ball is splitting my back, my skull. I let go, collapse into a torrent of brilliant heat ascending in a white column at intense speed. My cells are pulling apart, spinning, evaporating. Everywhere, a roaring, deafening sound as energy erupts from my eyes, ears, mouth, nose, guts. It is raw, strangling, all-powerful. I'm spun out of the column at a right angle and swept into an immense arc or band of light—a magnetic ring of sound comprised of thousands of resonant layers merging together in one deafening tone. Its penetrating vibration seems to be splitting the inside of my skull near the top of my head. I'm flailing about in the ring while being pulled along from left to right. My head is tilted directly at whatever the ring is orbiting.

The tone now seems to be resonating from the interior of my body, as if I were an immense tuning fork. My mouth is open and I'm making a loud wailing sound from somewhere deep under my diaphragm. The urge to wail is completely beyond my power to control and feels both electrifying and terrifying. I sense at any moment I'm going to split apart from vibrational force. As I wail, my body stiffens as if it were being electrically charged at an ever accelerating rate. My body and consciousness feel like a vertical rod of teeming energy particles tilted at an angle toward the center of the magnetic ring.

"Melina, you can travel to the center of the ring. You can penetrate and merge with its innermost point. Do you desire this?"

The energy begins to charge around my heart. Instantly my inner sight sharpens and expands as though an obstruction were freed from the faculty of second sight. My wailing ceases. I feel unbelievably clearheaded and can now see the center of the magnetic ring. It is an immense, pitch black void filled with pinpoints of light: celestial bodies that seem millions of light-years away. Sensing my consciousness as an arrow waiting to be sprung into the darkness, I feel an overpowering urge to penetrate the void. At the same time, an electrical movement or acceleration of energy is building at the very base of my spine, practically in my rectum. My whole rear end rises involuntarily as though it can scarcely contain the force. I feel my entire essence is becoming the moment which precedes volition.

Heat is moving up my throat, causing my breathing to become more rapid. No longer moving along the magnetic ring, I'm now suspended in a boundless gulf of emptiness. My God, such stillness... utter frozen silence. My sight penetrates deep into the blackness, a void made perceptible by infinitesimal points of silver light.

All at once I begin to tilt forward. The sensation is awesome, as if I were being maneuvered by a powerful, invisible machine. I can no longer feel the heat in my throat, nor can I sense my own breathing. I try to inhale, but I can't feel my lungs or my chest; there are no signs of respiration whatsoever. The sudden absence of a need to breathe creates an explosion of light in my forehead, followed by a sensation of movement. I'm moving forward at a very slight, downward angle into the void and notice my body has become formless, a nonsolid mass. I don't know how to describe this. My body feels like gas or ether—a moving mass of icy vapor. I feel simultaneously solid and invisible.

"Melina, you are preparing to merge. Do you wish to proceed?"

Staring into the void, I concentrate on the word, "proceed."

"Yes."

Movement increases. I feel that I'm rushing through space, but I can't feel any wind or pressure. Volition continues to accelerate. I can't tell how fast I'm going, but I sense I'm moving speedily. I'm amazed I don't feel fear. My predisposition toward anxiety seems to be replaced by an extraordinarily acute awareness which is dominating all of my other reflexes.

I'm now seeing an object in the distance which is becoming more distinct as I rapidly approach it—a great disc suspended horizontally in the void. It's difficult to determine how large it is. I see what looks like winged beings standing on the disc. Some are jumping off the disc into the void; others seem to be flying toward the disc from somewhere overhead.

My speed is decreasing and I'm now viewing the disc from a distance of about 200 yards. The object looks like a huge sun dial or a device to mark the passage of time. The winged beings appear to be completely preoccupied in their endeavors. As I watch their unearthly forms moving about in the pale illumination of the disc, I wonder who they are and where they are going. Suddenly an enormous beam of radiant, red-orange light flashes at me from the disc and hits me squarely in the heart. Stunned, I reel backward.

"Melina, you are being contacted by the Keepers of the disc and asked to communicate your desire."

Still stunned, I try to focus on Dionysus' voice. Everything is spinning, dissolving. I keep expecting to feel fear. Instead, I'm experiencing an unexplainable, vacuous feeling which is very powerful. My awareness is still extremely alert. I'm groping around in a circle, not knowing how to channel or direct this awareness.

"Melina, what is your desire?" Dionysus asks again.

The question reverberates inside the expanding vacuity of my awareness. I'm at a loss to articulate thought or emotion and feel the most urgent need to reorient myself sufficiently to answer the question. I try to focus on my desire, but I can't seem to locate it in my body or awareness. As I continue to search for it, I encounter a peculiar wave of self-consciousness which gives rise to an acute sense of displacement. All at once I find myself questioning my motives for being in the void; whether I inadvertently trespassed upon a private, sacred realm merely to satisfy my own curiosity, my thirst for knowledge. This thought magnifies my sense of having entered a hallowed place with superficial intentions and a selfish heart. Feeling guilty of a violation, I resolve to reconcile my error and return to my normal awareness immediately.

"I desire forgiveness for my intrusion," I firmly answer.

I'm beginning to move and see that I'm slowly heading for the disc. One of the winged beings stands near the edge of the disc on the side I'm approaching. He is watching me. I'm coming in very close now; the Keeper's eyes are enormous and dark against the milky-gray pallor of his face. I have the impression he's made of an etheric substance. His countenance is extremely serious.

Having come to a standstill, I'm now hovering in the void only a few feet from the disc and the being. As I stare into his eyes, I experience a strange sensation of vertigo. I'm becoming increasingly more disoriented as I attempt to telepath my intention to him, exerting enormous effort into keeping myself focused. Finally, through repetition of the same thought, I sense I'm beginning to make contact.

I desire your forgiveness. I desire your forgiveness. I desire your forgiveness.

The being reaches out with his right arm and clasps me firmly by the neck. He pulls me toward him and begins to apply pressure to my throat. Panicked, I gasp for air, struggling wildly to free myself. I can think of nothing but keeping myself from choking to death. Rays of blue light rush from my throat where his hand is applying pressure. I feel my essence is diminishing, is being squeezed out of me. Terrified, I stare into the being's luminous dark eyes and feel myself growing limp. I'm losing all strength to resist. My body is beginning to sag.

The being lays me down on the disc and removes his hands. I lie there on my back in a stupor. The disc begins to slowly tilt in the direction my feet are pointed and I realize I'm going to slide off. I want to hold on to something, but I can't move; all energy has gone out of my body, leaving me only with my awareness.

The disc is now tilting at a deeper angle. As I stare into the pitch black gulf, I wonder how long it will take before I slide off into the void. I'm no longer feeling fear. I'm experiencing a sense of resignation, a lack of will to save myself.

Personal Notes

I pull out of the session feeling completely wiped-out, down to the marrow in my bones. I'm extremely quiet for the remainder of the afternoon. I feel oddly hollow, with no reserves of energy to make contact with my feelings.

As I go about my afternoon tasks, a debilitating image keeps appearing in my mind's eye: I see the disc, with me lying on it, as a gigantic griddle tilting in space. I see myself, or rather, feel myself as a sausage about to roll off the edge into the void. No matter what I do, I can't banish this ludicrous image from my mind. Over and over I feel myself rolling off the edge of a cosmic-sized griddle—a link sausage plummeting into space.

The effect of this repeated image saps my energy even further. I feel strangely listless and apathetic. I wonder if the apathy I'm experiencing is a result of having had my "awareness" or cognition squeezed out of my body by the winged being. Without dynamic interaction with cognition, what is the body but a hunk of mass, a "piece of meat"?

Arresting images of the void and ring of sound, as well as images of my in utero experience, linger hauntingly for the rest of the afternoon. I find myself absorbing the images from within a deeply introspective, quiet awareness. I feel their profound impact in an inexplicable way, yet I don't know what to make of the experience as a whole. Over and over I find myself gravitating to the state of being inside the body of a fetus, realizing that my body—a vulnerable mass of developing cells maintained by a larger body—is the totality of my awareness. This realization feels distinctly alien and uncomfortable. I then juxtapose it against my experience of feeling like a link sausage about to roll into space: in the womb, I experience my body as my only organ of awareness—self in toto; on the disc, I experience my body disconnected from awareness—as meat.

Later in the evening I receive a phone call from my brother Joe, who is curious to know how I'm coming along with my session work. I relate to him my experience with the Keeper of the disc; how my desire for forgiveness was met with near strangulation. True to his style, he tells me in no uncertain terms that I really blew it.

"What an ass!" he exclaims, attempting to snap me out of my stupor. "Can't you see your request for forgiveness was simply a way to avoid the whole encounter? In a true stroke of cowardice, you masked your evasion with a plea for forgiveness so you could appear noble and further avoid facing your fear. It's no wonder you were met with near strangulation. Maybe what the Keeper was really after as he squeezed your throat was the truth."

I sigh into the phone, too tired to counter his remarks with reasoning I know would prove lame. Besides, on the face of it, his observations seem perfectly sound. I admit that had I exercised more temperance and circumspection, I might have intuited the magic words that would have yielded a completely different response from the winged being—one far more revelatory and personally satisfying. Perhaps then I could have circumvented the humiliation of feeling like a link sausage, a sad outcome to what could have been a highly promising experience.

I mull this over as I wearily climb the stairs for bed. Perfection is for the saint—that just wouldn't be me, now would it, brother?

October 13 Session

I close my eyes and see that I'm seated on a large rock in the woods, facing the stream. Above, the sky is a clear turquoise blue flecked with small fleecy clouds. I'm very drawn to it. The air is cool, almost chilly. A gusty wind blows through the trees. I think of Fall and feel melancholy, quiet.

Sensing movement, I gaze to my right. A half-naked man approaches at a distance. His sun-bleached hair shimmers in the light. As he advances, I see that he's wearing a flimsy white garment tied loosely around his loins. As his face becomes more visible, I study his a strong jaw and unbelievably green eyes. I think it's Dionysus, but I'm not sure.

"Dionysus?" I call, squinting into the sunlight.

He smiles and seats himself next to me on the rock. I'm suddenly aware of his physicality, his nearness to my body, and feel somewhat uncomfortable. I get up and sit tailor-fashion on the ground facing him. I stare into my lap, feeling strangely vulnerable.

"Why do you present yourself to me that way?" I ask him quietly.

"In what way?"

I pause. I don't want to make a big deal about the way he's dressed.

"Half-naked," I answer.

"I can remove my clothing if you'd like."

"No!" I object loudly. "That's not what I mean."

I gaze into my lap. Overwhelmed by curiosity, I wonder what he'd look like naked and if his pubic hair matches his golden tresses. The thought makes me feel awkward and ashamed. Unable to find a middle ground amidst the onslaught of my emotions, I begin to feel sorry for myself.

"I really don't know what I mean, Dionysus."

I look up from my lap and gaze directly into his face. It is breathtaking. I feel overwhelmingly attracted to him and uncomfortably susceptible to the effect he's having on me.

"You know, I'm sitting here having all of these intense reactions to you, and you haven't even done or said anything," I remark.

"What are you feeling?" he asks, his eyes betraying mild amusement.

"What are *you* feeling?" I toss back.

Dionysus looks at me steadily with a calm and open expression, then leans forward and digs up a small clump of dirt with his fingers. Taking my left hand, he presses the moist soil into my palm, closing my fingers around it.

"The earth," he answers.

I look at him. I do not open my hand.

"You're feeling the earth?" I ask.

"Yes. You are, too."

Smiling, he leans back and gazes at me. I say nothing for awhile.

"What does that mean, Dionysus?"

"Ask the earth."

I look at him blankly and feel very stupid. Glancing away, I stare at a patch of grass between my knees.

"Melina."

"What?"

"Did you receive your answer?"

"I really don't understand this labyrinth we're in," I snap. "I don't want to ask the earth—I want to ask you. Why do I have to take all of these circuitous routes? You come here half-naked, knowing full well I'm going to be affected by your powerful male energy, then when I get pulled in by it, you tell me to take my confusion to a clump of dirt. That's frustrating!"

My face feels hot. I can't believe I've worked myself up like this in such a short time, and over nothing. I know I'm making a jackass out of myself, but I can't seem to exert any control over my behavior.

Dionysus rises from the rock, kneels down next to me and takes the clump of dirt from my clenched fist. He reaches out and firmly grabs my jaw, then pushes me backward. Startled, I flail at the air as my head hits the grass. Dionysus throws his weight over me and begins to apply pressure to my jaw. I clench my teeth against the pain as I push with all my strength against his wrist. Fearing my jaw is going to break, I open my mouth to relieve the pressure. Dionysus pushes the clump of dirt hard against the roof of my mouth and releases me. The taste and texture of the dirt instantly floods my mouth. I hold my breath, feeling paralyzed and embarrassed. I want to spit the dirt out and think about spitting it at Dionysus. The thought frightens me. I realize I'm afraid to spit the dirt out at all, not knowing what this may incite him to do next.

"Taste your answer, Melina. Swallow it all and allow your hunger to be quelled."

His words strike to the very core of my body, dislodging feelings of sadness and fear. The dirt is mixing with my saliva. I feel tears coming and know they'll make me salivate more. I gulp. As a portion of the dirt slides down my throat, I feel I'm being invaded. My teeth are filled with mud; I'm hideous and feel like an animal. An image of the grotesque tree stump I encountered in a past meditation fixes itself boldly in my mind's eye. I stare at it, remembering how it said it was going to grind up my flesh and bones, swallow me and shit me out the other end.

"How long has it been since you've made love?" Dionysus asks in a clinical-sounding voice.

Leaning forward, he places his hand on my stomach and presses a spot just above my navel. It feels uncomfortable. I try to recall the last time Ted and I made love and realize I've lost track of the weeks. I want to tell Dionysus I sometimes like celibacy, I even prefer it, but I'm afraid to move my tongue.

"Do you fear that engaging more fully in physical life will weaken your spirit?" he asks.

I resent this question and its implications to my sexual life. It smacks of a stunted Catholic upbringing and makes me squirm. I do not answer him. Dionysus continues to press an area of my stomach just above my navel. A strange pressure is gathering at my temples. Unable to bear it, I lean over and spit the dirt out of my mouth, then pull myself up onto my elbows.

"What's your point?" I ask sourly.

I want Dionysus to move his hand away, but I don't know how to ask him to stop poking my stomach. I slowly probe my mouth with my tongue, prying the last of the mud off my teeth.

"Lie back down," he says quietly.

I want to argue but relent. I lie down and stare up at the treetops rocking in the afternoon breeze. Resting my gaze on their languid movement, I can feel the tension draining from my body.

"Why did you ask me about making love, Dionysus?"

"Because you wanted me to ask."

I think about this carefully.

"Is that all?" I ask.

"What else need there be?"

"But you implied something."

"I implied nothing."

Falling quiet, I reflect on the passions of the flesh, knowing the path to Self is through the temple of the body. Yet it is through the body I encounter X, whatever dark part of me he represents. I do not encounter X unless I embrace my humanity—my frailty and physicality. When I encounter X I feel shame and guilt, lust, violence, chaos, sloth and self-loathing. When I experience these things, it weakens my spirit. It divides me, conquers me. I look over at Dionysus, feeling troubled.

"You are the one who asks to be conquered," he remarks softly.

"What? Conquered by X?"

"That which you call darkness is the Great Emptiness," Dionysus explains. "You have fashioned X from the fragments of your many selves and lives, and placed him at the threshold of the Great Emptiness. He is resonance where there is none. He is light where there is only darkness. He is life, the container in which All Is Not."

My thoughts are paralyzed with confusion. I lie quietly for several moments, trying to digest the meaning of his words.

"Did I create X?" I ask.

"You have created the way you perceive and experience X."

"Hatred, lust and avarice don't belong to X?"

"X is a container," Dionysus replies. "He possesses everything and he also possesses nothing."

"He possesses love and hate?"

"He possesses both the capacity to love and the capacity to hate, as you do."

I reflect on the word, "capacity": the ability to hold, receive or contain.

"Why have I not experienced X as other than evil?" I ask.

"Your experience of X has been largely a state of mind, Melina."

The impact of this statement causes me to feel simultaneously freed and imprisoned. I'm tempted to chastise myself for all of my negative projections, but I'm overcome by a strange sense of weariness. It is not a physical weariness, but a weariness of the soul, as though I've been walking around in the same circles for centuries, donning various faces to hash out the same old dilemmas.

"My brain is wiped-out, Dionysus. My soul is overburdened and my body is in adrenaline overdrive, a fight-or-flight mode. I'm a mess."

I drag myself over to a nearby rock and prop my shoulder against it. I notice a strange "yawing" sensation to the way I feel, as if I'm poised precariously on the rim of a big hole or gap in the "world net." Gazing overhead at a collage of branches and leaves against the blue backdrop of space, I sense this net as an immense weave of resilient, invisible fibers that hold together all that is visible. I'm connected to this net by a psychic cord at my navel. If I shift my awareness of this net to include notions of reality that are unfamiliar to me, I experience a "tugging" at my solar plexus and a sickening sense of disorientation which registers as nausea. I hate this feeling, but I'm helpless to control it. Experiencing it often, I recognize it to be the herald of a shift in consciousness, an eddy in the life force which leaves in its wake some unpleasant side effects. I sigh heavily.

"I just want to get to a place in myself where I won't care about X: what he or it is, what he represents and how that bears upon me. I want to be rid of this obsessive concern—just free."

I look over at Dionysus gazing absentmindedly at something in the treetops. His arms are crossed relaxedly behind his head as he leans against the trunk of a tree. As I stare at him, I wonder what in the world he is, what he represents in me. If X is largely a state of mind, it stands to reason that Dionysus is, too. I now wonder to what extent my overly eager "willing suspension of disbelief" has endowed Dionysus with greater autonomy, deity and color than what would otherwise arise from the nascent stuff of one's "state of mind."

I stare more fixedly at Dionysus and tell myself that what I'm seeing is a projection; the "man-god" image is my unconscious creation. If it were possible to take away the image, the seductive appearance of form, what would be there? If I've fashioned X out of the fragments of my many selves and lives, and placed him at the threshold of the Great Emptiness, then surely I've done the same with what I call "Dionysus." Who or what is X and Dionysus, sans my projections? If X represents what I think to be evil, which is a state of my own mind, then Dionysus represents what I think to be good and sacred, a state of my own mind as well. If I could take away my projections of good and evil, what is the essence that would be left? Are X and Dionysus intrinsically the same? Do they even exist? Without the personas my unconscious has given to them, would they dissolve into the Great Emptiness, and me along with them? Is this the bottom line of what I'm really resisting--ultimate dissolution?

The shocking effect of this line of thought hurls me to my feet. I quickly walk over to Dionysus and plunk myself down at his side. I'm compelled to squeeze as many answers out of him before he dissipates forever into the realm of nothingness I'm afraid of most.

"Dionysus, may I ask you something?"

He looks at me relaxedly. I hesitate, wanting to choose my words carefully.

"First of all, I'd like to share with you why I think you're here," I begin.

He smiles broadly, apparently amused by what I've just said.

"I am afraid you will only be wasting energy, Melina."

Unprepared for this remark, I mentally backtrack over my

statement.

"Perhaps you didn't understand what I meant," I explain.

"I do understand. You cannot tell me why you think I am here. You can only tell me why you think you are here."

"In other words, I can only relate my thoughts and feelings about you in regard to myself?" I ask.

"Any thoughts and feelings you have about me are about yourself," he replies.

"Then what difference does it make if I share with you why I think you're here, when we both know I'm really talking about myself?"

"I have already told you, Melina. It is a waste of energy."

Falling silent, I brood over what to do with my recent insights. I wonder if my desire to discuss them with Dionysus is once again moving into "projection."

"Dionysus, if I asked you to leave this place, would you?"

He gazes upward. As I watch him, I try to see what he is seeing. I spot a large open space in the treetops where the sky seems poised like an oval blue doily embroidered with leaves.

"In your world, would you ask the sky to leave? Could you, Melina?"

He looks at me dreamily. The idea of asking the sky to leave is obviously absurd. I examine why I even asked him if he would leave, then realize I was looking for a way not to have anything on which to project.

"What is behind your form, Dionysus? I know your form will change as it already has many times. What is behind your form? What is its essence?"

"That which is behind yours."

"So, to know what you are behind your form is to journey into what is behind mine?"

"That is a way of putting it."

"Isn't God behind all form?" I ask.

Dionysus pulls a large red apple seemingly out of thin air and begins to munch it. As I watch him, I wonder what the apple tastes like. Cupping the fruit in both his hands, he raises it to his nose and inhales its fragrance. A look of deep pleasure sweeps across his face. Observing his enjoyment fills me with an old and inexplicable ache, a longing for something I have no capacity to name. I close my eyes as if to evoke it into my mind's eye. All I can see is the image of Dionysus consumed in the joy of eating, the apple like Eucharistic food in his adoring hands.

Breathing deeply, I open my eyes. Dionysus is chewing the apple slowly, his eyes half-closed as if in prayer. As I watch him, I wonder how one can realize union with God, while also embracing the desires of the flesh.

"I don't want to lose my appetites," I murmur, unable to draw my eyes away from the glistening fruit.

Dionysus pauses over his apple and gazes at it thoughtfully.

"It is not hunger you fear. Or lust. Or desire. Is it?" he asks.

For a moment I feel as if someone took a veil from my eyes. I imagine myself fully centered in my desire, acting in perfect attunement with my deepest yearnings. Instantly I feel a sense of wholeness, as though my capacity to be in this world and participate in its life more fully had been immensely expanded. I also sense I've been waiting for some higher authority to give me permission to do this. I look at Dionysus without knowing what to say.

"I'm confused about how to handle or channel my desire, Dionysus. When desire becomes lust, I'm afraid."

He places the half-eaten apple in his lap and studies me.

"What is lust, Melina?"

A definition forms quickly.

"Lust is a tight coil in the body that draws one's life force into animal consciousness. It is a seductive prison and its jailkeepers are chaos, violence and pain. Lust can never be satisfied and is consequently obsessive. It is destructive because it can lead nowhere but to gluttony and self-loathing. Lust is sitting in your own vomit after too many meals, too much sex."

"Have you ever experienced lust?" Dionysus asks.

"Yes."

"When?"

"I lusted after a guy once. I was married."

I gaze into my lap and stroke the ring finger of my left hand.

"Had you not been married, would you have called this experience lust?"

"All right. So lust has to have a counterpoint, a taboo or it's not lust," I concede. "Is that what you're saying?"

"It is what you are saying."

Dionysus picks up his apple and takes a large bite.

"What is lust in and of itself, without the taboo?" he asks.

I think about this for awhile.

"I suppose it's wanting something very badly and setting out to get it no matter how that is accomplished, including self-violation."

"Again, the counterpoint."

Dionysus looks at me steadily. The words, "self-violation" ring in my head.

"Maybe the question should go something like this," I offer. "Can someone lust without violating self?"

"Melina, what is self? If self is one with lust and lust one with self, what can be violated?"

"That's completely decadent! Come on, history books are filled with examples of how lust for power brought nothing but misery and destruction. Look at Nero's Rome or Hitler's Germany."

"You do not understand lust."

Dionysus resumes munching his apple, gazing intently at the fruit as if scrutinizing its core and seeds.

"You're telling me that having insatiable cravings that drive a person to do terrible things is okay?" I ask incredulously.

"He who is truly one with his lust knows only joy."

"You must be talking about some alchemic transformation," I scoff, waving it off as impossibly abstract. "I suppose once you've been plowed under by the bitter lessons of lust's abuses, you inevitably rise to the top of the heap in an exclamation of joy."

Dionysus gazes at me drolly.

"You said you wished to share with me why you think I am here," he states in a more serious tone. "You realize now this cannot be done. You can share only why you think you are here, and you have done that."

I look at him in disbelief.

"I have?"

"You are here to experience your lust."

A chill grips my heart, leaving me feeling weak.

"But... I'm afraid, Dionysus."

"You said you do not want to lose your appetites."

"Yes, but what I really meant was I don't want to lose touch with my humanity. I wasn't implying that I want to dive into a sea of lust."

Dionysus places his apple down and gazes at me. His look is very penetrating.

"You cannot lose touch with what you have never possessed. You possess nothing, yet you are possessed by everything. It is not desire and lust you fear, but the not having of desire and lust. You fear not having the hunger and the pain, the Great Awakeners."

I stare into my lap, overwhelmed by his observations. I close my eyes, allowing his words to sink deep inside my body.

"Yes, some part of me recognizes what you're saying," I admit quietly. "It's as though pain is a goad which continually shocks one out of his stupor, or keeps one from falling into a deep ambivalence about his own life. I suppose it can serve to be an agent of awakening."

"Do you see this awakening aspect to be pain's function?" Dionysus asks.

"Do you mean its purpose? I don't know if pain has any specific 'function.' I see it more as an effect rather than a cause. To me, pain's language indicates some sort of healing is imminent."

Dionysus gazes at me. I begin to doubt what I've just said and wonder if I actually know anything at all.

"I suppose pain is a result of misperception," I conclude.

"Are you saying that without misperception, there is no pain?" he asks.

I mull this over for awhile. I realize the naked truth can be very painful. Maybe misperception is the way we narrow our lens so as not to have to confront the naked truth about ourselves.

"This is a catch-22, isn't it, Dionysus? Either way you go, you run into pain. There's pain in misperceiving and there's pain in confronting the truth. So what difference does it make?"

"Pain itself is the difference."

I look at him blankly.

"The difference between what?" I ask.

"There is no difference between anything."

"But you just said pain is the difference."

"I did."

I stop and reflect on the meaning of the word, "difference": that which is unlike something else; that which is unique; that which is greater or lesser, better or worse than something else. I realize such a definition is filled with qualifiers and value judgments. If I take the judgments and qualifiers away from the meaning of the word, "difference," there's nothing left. I wonder what is the "nothing" that is left.

"So, pain is one of the effects of being self-conscious, or perceiving oneself to be a unique unit of consciousness, a separate entity," I deduce.

"Pain is not the effect of anything. Nor does one have a self."

Anxiety is beginning to gnaw in the center of my chest.

"I don't understand."

"What is self, Melina?"

"I really don't know, Dionysus."

I fold my arms across my chest and stare at him.

"Now if I knew that, I probably wouldn't be here. Besides, how can you say there is no self when earlier you told me X is a fragmented representation of my former selves... or whatever it was you said?"

A sinking feeling is building in the pit of my stomach. I sense a huge contradiction coming and I do not want this to happen.

"Look, Dionysus, one of the problems with a discussion like this is it can never go anywhere. Everything we say goes out like a boomerang, journeys its limited path and returns to its starting point. I'm no closer to understanding anything than when I started."

"Do you see this as a problem?"

"Yes, particularly in that I don't seem to have the heightened vantage point you do."

"You then see us as different from each other?" he asks, raising an eyebrow at me.

I stare at him mutely. The word "different" bangs around in my head with all of its accompanying qualifiers: better, worse, less, more, higher, lower, smarter, dumber. I wait for the noise in my head to abate.

"I really do want to understand this," I persist.

"You can understand nothing."

"Then why are we even having this conversation?"

I'm now pacing back and forth at his feet, agitated beyond belief and thoroughly convinced he must have dropped to earth from the planet Neptune. I'm trying to figure out how I got so stuck inside this exasperating jigsaw puzzle. I don't know where to go from here.

"Come, Melina."

Dionysus pats the ground at his side, inviting me to sit next to him. I realize I'm sulking and I'm not ready to stop pacing.

"What do you mean I can understand nothing?" I groan. "I've come here to try to understand a lot of things that have eluded me all my life."

A feeling of anguish is beginning to burn in my chest. I sense at any second I'm going to burst into tears. I do not want this to happen. I walk over to Dionysus and kneel down at his side. I'm very close to his face. As I gaze into his eyes, their open, undisturbed depths perplex me.

"Dionysus, this is scary for me. Sometimes I get so confused, I think I might be losing my mind. I don't know where all this is taking me. Sometimes I think I'm preparing to die. I look in the mirror and wonder if my face is changing. Sometimes I have the sense I'm aging rapidly. My own mortality seems to be sitting on my shoulders like a heavy old man gumming a senseless, toothless grin. Each day I live inside an edgy awareness that something is slipping away from me, but I don't know what it is. I look around at what could comfort me and everything feels transient, as though it will all come unhinged at any moment like flimsy paper objects held loosely together with cellophane tape.

"I've felt this way for the last five years, ever since I turned 30. Something seems to have gone out of my life then, and it's never returned. Nothing has replaced it. At first I thought it was due to my divorce, the loss and pain of an ended marriage. But time and mending has shown me this is not the sense of loss that has endured these five years. I want to find out what it is, what has become for me a void where once a sense of peace and trust dwelled. I was warmed and comforted at that inner hearth; it was a place in myself I could always return to, a place from which I could gather nourishment, courage and vision without fear of depleting its resources. What has happened to it? Why did I lose it? What is this hole that's left in me in which there are no echoes, no familiar forms of life? I feel I have nothing left but a huge labyrinthine mind which can do little else but strangle all that I was once able to intuit freely and without question. My heart feels like a cold furnace waiting for the right spark, a match—anything—so it can burst into flames and warm the innermost corners of my soul.

"So now I'm here in this place because it's the only place I can be. When I first encountered this realm, I thought my experiences here would show me the way back to my inner hearth; that somehow the fire would be reignited with hope, surrender and waiting on the Will of whatever it is that has guided me thus far. But now I'm beginning to sense I'm being led into inner realms of my being that require an even greater emptying, more than I thought could be possible on top of previous losses, whose painful effects still endure.

"So something within me is fighting this, saying no to the requirements for further emptying, no to the painful episodes I know will inevitably accompany my journeys here. I don't know how strong I am. I've long since forgotten why the pursuit of fortitude was a requisite I deemed vital for undertaking a journey into myself. At this point, I figure I'm going wherever I'm going with or without strength, with or without light, with or without the inner hearth."

As I gaze into Dionysus' eyes, they seem somehow larger than before: clearer, greener. My tension has slipped away and I feel clear and steady. For a moment I wonder if this feeling is coming to me from staring deeply into Dionysus' eyes. Is it Dionysus who is clear and steady, or is it me? Suddenly I feel exhausted. I lie down and nestle my head in the curve of Dionysus' lap. It is warm and unbelievably soothing. I wish I could stay like this forever, my head cradled in the lap of a loving presence while above, the treetops swaying like a heavenly canopy. Long moments of silence pass. Everything begins to look as if it were floating under water.

"Dionysus?"

"Hmm?"

"What did you mean before when you said there is no self?"

"There is only the One."

I think about this for awhile.

"Do you mean One as All?"

"One. All. There is no difference."

"One as the whole, the whole not necessarily being the sum of its parts?" I ask.

Dionysus looks down at me. I'm twirling a leaf in the palm of my hand. I smile at him.

"There are no parts, Melina."

I think this over carefully. If I'm not a part, I must be the whole. Yet I'm not the whole, obviously, or I wouldn't be asking these questions.

"Dionysus?"

He looks down at me again. The afternoon sunlight frames his hair in a shimmering corona.

"What did you mean when you said that pain is not the effect of anything?"

"Pain is a state of mind."

"Surely it must be more than that," I insist. "Even Christ suffered pain."

"So He did."

I look at him questioningly.

"Animals feel pain. Is that also a state of mind?"

"Yes."

I'm bewildered. I think he must be talking about "mind" in a context unfamiliar to me.

"Whose mind, Dionysus? What mind?"

"There is no more I can tell you. If you want to know, you will have to experience it for yourself."

I contemplate entering the feeling realm of an animal in pain. A goat comes to mind and I think of Pan. I imagine him bleeding to death under a heap of leaves somewhere in the forest. Pangs of distress and worry begin to build in the pit of my stomach. I want to distract myself, move my focus somewhere else.

"What other qualities, virtues and vices do you relegate to a state of mind?" I ask.

I glance up at Dionysus gazing ahead at something in the distance. Thinking he may not have heard me, I wonder if I should repeat myself.

"It is time for you to close your eyes," he says quietly.

I close my eyes, grateful for a respite from my mental clamor.

"Go to sleep, Melina. Rest."

CHAPTER 7

FALLING AND FLYING

October 26 Session

I close my eyes and see that I'm lying in the woods with my head resting in Dionysus' lap. Everything looks and feels as it did on my previous journey. I'm staring up at the treetops, lulled into dreaminess by the languorous movement of all that breathes and sways about me. I seem to be without a care in the world. My body feels like warm dough laid out to rise.

"This reminds me of my childhood," I murmur, looking up at Dionysus.

Resting comfortably against the trunk of a profoundly large tree, he looks as though he has all the time in the world.

"Everything seems to be slowed down here," I continue. "I can almost feel the planet moving beneath my body."

"It is you who are slowed down, Melina."

"Yes, the way I used to be when I was little."

"What was it like when you were little?" Dionysus asks, gazing down at me.

I shield my eyes against the afternoon sunlight as I study his features. His eyes are clear and very alert.

"Oh, like this place mostly. I grew up around woods. Everything was very big then—the sky was big, the trees, the grass, the clouds. I always felt as though I was going to fall through something invisible if I wasn't careful."

"Invisible?" Dionysus asks, breaking into a grin.

"Yes, you know, like a huge hole where God forgot to sew everything together. I used to think this was the same hole the sun fell through in the evenings when the sky got dark. Then scary things would creep into the world through the hole and frighten people, make things ugly, kill flowers and cause bad things to happen."

"What happened to this hole by day? Where did it go?" Dionysus asks.

"Oh, it was around."

"Where?"

"No place special and everywhere at the same time. That's why it was so scary. You never knew when you might walk into it."

"Is the hole here?"

Surprised by the question, I look around and try to "feel" the hole.

"Maybe I'm in the hole," I reply.

"This?" Dionysus asks, gesturing at the trees and grass, the sky overhead.

"Well, I don't know, Dionysus. What else could the hole be but a metaphor for the unknown, the unconscious?"

"Metaphor has nothing to do with it."

I think this over quietly.

"Do you mean the hole I imagined as a child was real?"

"You did not imagine it, Melina. However, your imagination intercepted your awareness of it."

His statement strikes me as incredibly strange. I play with this concept for awhile, turning it over in my mind like a noisy bag of marbles.

"I've never heard of anything like that before," I confess. "It throws a different slant on things, doesn't it?"

"Does it?"

Dionysus smiles broadly. Suspecting he's playing devil's advocate, I check my tendency toward gullibility.

"This hole that is nowhere in particular and everywhere at the same time is what you call the Great Emptiness, isn't it?" I ask.

"Yes."

"And it isn't necessarily filled with creepy things," I continue, pausing to think this through carefully. "That's where my imagination intercepted my awareness of it?"

"The imagination creates to fill in what is otherwise empty," Dionysus answers.

"Creates what?" I ask.

"Creates. This implies an object when there is none. This also implies a subject. There is none."

"But you just said, 'imagination creates.' Imagination is the subject," I point out.

"Imagination is the reflector."

"Then the 'reflector' creates, whatever that means."

"The reflector creates by bringing into being that which is already created," Dionysus explains.

"But if the reflector brings into being that which is already created, then the reflector isn't creating at all," I contend. "It's merely reflecting the already-created."

"Which is the essence of how things are created."

I throw him a sidelong glance.

"You know I can't stand it when we do these full circle, back to point 'A' discussions. Everything inevitably gets swallowed up by the big zero. How can we possibly get anywhere?"

What I'm really thinking is I'm simply too dense to follow this. I stare up at the trees and start counting the leaves. All the while, a chatter is going on in the back of my mind.

"So what or who is the reflector?" I ask.

"I have already told you, Melina. The reflector is the imagination."

"Are you saying that without an imagination, I would be unable to focus on creation as a viable, tenable reality?"

"Without imagination, a tenable reality does not exist."

I sit up with a start and turn about to face him.

"Do you mean I'm imagining all this?" I ask, making large swooping arcs with my arms to take in the whole of creation.

"Yes."

Falling quiet, I examine the idea that imagination intercepts awareness. Awareness of what? Can one be aware without being aware of anything? Who in the world would want to live in such a colorless, vacuous state?

"What is it that imagines or reflects, Dionysus?"

"Mind."

"Why does mind do this?"

"The doing is a function of being. Trees respirate. Again, the doing is a function of being."

I lean back in the grass and think over the implications of this statement. It seems oversimplified.

"Dionysus, to say that mind imagines as a function of being is to imply that imagination is an inherent dynamic of beingness and possesses a deeply sacred—if not divine—relationship with both spirit and soul."

I shake my head, dismissing the idea with a toss of my hand.

"Maybe for angels and gods it works that way, but for much of earthbound humanity, it isn't nearly so mystical. Sure, the imagination is an extraordinary faculty. Thank heaven its wealth of inspiration keeps us from falling prey to apathy and stagnation as we go about tending to our highly mechanized lives. But whatever else the imagination may be, it functions primarily as a coping mechanism to insulate us from too much psychic shock. Let's face it, Dionysus. We live in a world filled with poverty, disease, heartbreak, war and death. We need something to mitigate these frightening realities, don't we?

"You see, it is just because of this sorry state of human affairs that imagination is like a crutch," I continue. "We don't know how to live in the Great Emptiness, so with the help of a reflector, we populate it with images for our own security, learning, and perhaps, even our own entertainment. What's sacred or divine about that? It seems to me true being has no function other than to be what it is, for as a whole and nondependent system, it is complete unto itself, while not truly being gives rise to the necessity of function—ergo, imagination."

My brain feels like pancake batter. Dionysus has been watching me with a steady unbroken gaze. Suddenly he breaks into a smile.

"What is 'not truly being,' Melina?"

"Getting loaded down with distractions of our own making. Getting sucked in by the reflector and the reflected. Chasing one's tail like a squirrel in a round cage."

"You are guessing."

Perplexed, I think over what I just said.

"Are you suggesting that unless I know what 'truly being' is, I cannot know what 'not truly being' is?" I ask.

Dionysus shakes his head.

"I am suggesting nothing."

I realize I'm still flip-flopping between extremes: "this" as opposed to "not this." I know this is not the state he's talking about. Perhaps he really is talking about and suggesting "nothing."

"Tell me more about your childhood," Dionysus invites as he leans back against the tree.

My mind is still percolating with questions. I wonder if the power of imagination gives form or substance to that which already exists in the unmanifest or invisible states.

"Where does imagination get its power?" I ask.

Dionysus reaches into the air as if waiting for a leaf to fall into his hand.

"Will and desire, bridged by intellect."

The three giants. I suddenly want to back away from this subject, sensing its enormity. I lean into the grass and allow my thoughts to meander into the world of my childhood. Imagining my mind as a huge magnet, I wonder what cluster of memories it will draw to itself. Dionysus turns his gaze from the treetops and quietly observes me. His voice breaks the stillness.

"The reflector borrows images stored in the memory of the World Soul."

I wonder if he is referring to the collective unconscious. I really don't want to pursue this, but I'm compelled by curiosity.

"What do you mean by, 'The reflector borrows images'?" I ask. "Where do these images come from?"

"I have just told you. The images are borrowed by the reflector from the memory of the World Soul."

"Borrowed?"

"Yes."

I prop myself up on one elbow and gaze at him.

"If I'm to grasp what you're saying in its most absolute sense, Dionysus, then I have to ask, what is a 'World Soul'? What world? Whose world? And why one world? Why not hundreds of worlds—thousands, millions?"

I wave my hand around in large circles as if to encompass the entire cosmos, certain we're not the only life forms spinning on a planet through infinity. Dionysus reaches out and lightly strokes my forehead with his index finger.

"You are an impatient one, aren't you? The World Soul is Shekhinah."

I release a sigh. This is hardly the response I was looking for. I lie back in the grass and stare at the tree limbs overhead, allowing my gaze to wander into the soothing shadows between the leaves. Contemplating Shekhinah as the feminine presence of God in the soul, I imagine it as a veil which conceals divine mysteries resting in the quiescence of eternity. In that quiescence, I also imagine the most profound chaos churning soundlessly, an immense vortex drawing into itself all that is known and all that is knowable. I sense this chaos as an arrhythmic movement of yearning—tumultuous life in the body of God, simultaneously contracting from, and expanding into, conscious being.

"You say the World Soul has a memory?" I ask, turning over onto my stomach.

"Yes, as you do."

"And the reflector, the imagination, borrows images from that memory?"

"Yes."

"Does the World Soul have a reflector?"

"The World Soul is a reflector."

"What? The World Soul is imagination?" I ask in disbelief.

"The World Soul intercepts awareness," Dionysus explains. "When you gaze into the World Soul, you gaze into a mirror. What you see are images. Yet the images are held within, and conceived by, the World Soul."

"So the World Soul, which is also the reflector, borrows images from itself?"

"Yes."

"For what purpose, Dionysus?"

"For what purpose does the wind rustle the leaves?"

He waves his hand in the air, then allows it to fall slowly to the earth. I look at him in amazement.

"Let me see if I grasp this, Dionysus. The images one perceives as he gazes into the World Soul manifest to the perceiver by means of the reflector or imagination."

"Yes."

"My reflector or the World Soul's reflector?"

"They are one and the same."

"Is my memory and the memory of the World Soul one and the same as well?"

"Yes."

"Then what is the difference between my soul and the World Soul?"

"There is no difference."

"But if the World Soul is a reflector, then my soul is also a reflector?"

"Yes."

"Is this to say that my soul intercepts my awareness?"

"Yes."

"Why? For what purpose does the soul do this?"

"The doing is a function of being."

"Agh!"

I roll backward in the grass and clasp my beleaguered skull.

"It's no wonder humanity was blessed with a sense of humor! How else could we cope with this endless labyrinth of existence?"

Dionysus looks at me placidly. As always, he seems quite undisturbed. I wonder how he can hold all this information without losing some screws in the process.

"Just give me a bed, a pillow and a warm blanket," I moan.

Rolling over in the grass, I collapse on my face. The earth beneath my nose smells positively wonderful. I inhale it fully as though it were an aphrodisiac. Still, in the back of my mind, thoughts are squirming around like a tangle of mad worms.

"Dionysus, you say the World Soul conceives images that are brought to bear on awareness through the interception of the reflector or imagination, which is itself the World Soul. To me, this is a vicious circle."

"Why vicious?" he asks.

For a second I go blank. Yes, why vicious? I remove the qualifier. All I have left is a circle, alpha and omega. The sudden simplicity of this idea hits me squarely between the eyes, yet I can't comprehend it at all.

"I suppose what is 'conceived' comes from that which is already created, a paradox in itself," I reflect aloud. "But how does the World Soul have access to the unknowable essence of that which is already created before it is conceived and comes forward as image? How can one have access to the unknowable?"

"The World Soul is the unknowable essence," Dionysus replies.

I prop myself up on one elbow and gaze at him, trying to comprehend his last statement.

"Am I to understand that the World Soul is the unknowable essence of that which is already created, as well as the agent by which the already-created is conceived and comes forward as image?"

"Yes."

"But how can that which is unknowable be known, Dionysus?"

He stretches like a cat, then smiles.

"Through dreaming."

I sit up in the grass and pick at my big toe, intrigued and bothered by his answer. Dreaming? What is dreaming? Who are the dreamers? What is that which is dreamt?

"Dreams we take least seriously, you know. I mean, come on, Dionysus. Dreams? What is the difference between dreaming and imagining?"

"There is no difference."

"Certainly there's a difference!" I laugh. "When I'm dreaming, I'm not consciously controlling the pace, message or content of what's spilling forth into my dreamscapes from wherever dreams come from. When I'm imagining, I can consciously control what I'm seeing and experiencing in my mind. I can alter the pace, change the content and manipulate the message according to my desire."

Dionysus begins to chuckle. He seems truly delighted by what I've just said. I stare at him in bewilderment.

"The doing is being done through you, not by you," he explains. "The doing is acting upon you. You are not acting upon it."

"Well... "

"Here," he demonstrates, handing me an empty bowl.

"What is in the bowl, Melina?"

I stare into the bowl. It is pink and plastic.

"This is stupid-looking."

"What is in the bowl?"

"Nothing!"

"Look into the bowl."

Already I'm seeing strawberries. The strawberries appear first in my mind, then in the bowl. The movement of thought into form is so swift and subtle, I'm amazed that I'm aware of the transition. I look up at Dionysus.

"Are you hungry?" he asks, nodding invitingly at the fruit.

I realize I want very much to taste these strawberries. They're exquisitely plump and red, nearly perfect.

"Yes," I answer, unable to think of anything else.

"Have one."

I pick up a strawberry and hold it in the light. It glistens like a large ruby and looks lustrous. I take a small bite. The warm juice spills over my tongue, filling my mouth with a flavor so luscious and sweet I'm tempted to call it rapture. I close my eyes and breathe its perfume, then push the rest of its succulent flesh into my mouth.

"Ha! You're teaching me a bad habit," I laugh, smacking my lips.

"What has happened here?" Dionysus asks.

"I don't know. What has happened?" I echo, going for my second strawberry.

There are five strawberries altogether in the bowl. I take note of the number, realizing five is the number of the senses.

"Where did the strawberries come from, Melina?"

"I tell you, Holmes, I don't bloody know."

I burst out laughing and feel a silly mood coming on fast. I think it must have something to do with these damned strawberries.

"Okay, okay," I reply, trying to control myself. "I imagined them, obviously."

"Were they in the bowl before you imagined them?"

I dump the strawberries onto the grass and turn the bowl upside-down.

"Well if they were, I've sure figured out the riddle of the loaves and fishes, haven't I?"

I wail with laughter. Dionysus is smiling at me. I start kicking my feet back and forth in the grass.

"Let's see how long you can tolerate this, O god of joy!"

I pick up a strawberry, bite it daintily and dab the sweet red juice to my lips.

"Kiss me, you fool!" I loudly command, giggling and puckering my lips.

Dionysus looks positively delighted. He leans close to my face and stares into my eyes. He kisses me. I feel his lips and do not breathe. The woods fill with a sudden stillness. I hear only the sound of my heart thumping in my ears.

October 28 Session

I close my eyes and see that I'm sitting in the grass in the woods, facing the western sky. It's late afternoon. Dionysus is seated two or three feet to my right and is no longer leaning against the tree. I look down at my bare feet and see that I'm playing with the toes of my right foot. Nearby on the grass is the pink bowl. I do not see the strawberries.

I'm remembering having been kissed by Dionysus and feel extremely good. I reach up and lightly touch my lips, then explore my mouth with my tongue to see if any hint of strawberry remains. I taste nothing. Suddenly I wonder if I had been kissed at all. I even wonder whether I really ate the strawberries. Surely I imagined it. Aren't I imagining all of this? I look over at Dionysus. He's quietly watching me.

"I know you're going to tell me there's no difference," I warn him, "but I'm going to ask you anyway."

I pause and study his face, trying to detect a change in his expression. Seeing none, I continue.

"Remember when I told you I thought creepy things crawled through that big hole that God forgot to sew up?"

I wait for a response.

"You know, when I was little?"

Dionysus is caressing the arch of his left foot and looks quite immersed in what he's doing. I imagine I'm talking to the air and go right on.

"You told me I didn't imagine the hole, but my imagination intercepted my awareness of it. It seems to me what we're dealing with are two sets of realities: one in which awareness is intercepted by imagination, the other in which awareness is not intercepted by imagination."

I pause to make sure I'm really saying what I mean.

"I don't suppose there's anyone walking around in a body who has experienced awareness without the interception of the imagination, especially if it's a built-in function of being, as you say."

I realize I'm starting to lose the thread of where I want this to go. Dionysus looks up from his foot and studies me.

"What I'm getting at is you and I and a lot of other people know the world we live in is highly illusory. This illusory quality is the very net we get entangled in and blinded by. We flop around in this net like so many fish yanked out of our natural home.

"If there's no difference between dreaming and imagining, and, as you say, through dreaming the unknowable can be known, then it seems to me we can never escape the net of illusion. Dreams are full of illusions. The imagination or reflector is loaded with illusions. Even memory is limited to the extent that it can reveal only that which registers upon awareness as 'picture' or 'symbol,' and what are these but kaleidoscopic images that change according to the feelings and moods in which we evoke them? What can ever really be 'known' when everything we dream, imagine and remember, by its very nature, is in a constant state of flux, highly interpretive and subject to the play of illusion?"

I pause and stare at him.

"Furthermore, if image already exists in the memory of the

World Soul, I fail to see how the reflector or imagination is responsible for bringing it 'into being.'"

Dionysus slowly stands up, grabs my two hands and pulls me to my feet. He walks me over to a profoundly large tree, takes me by the shoulders and presses the front of my body against it. He then positions my nose against the bark. It feels terribly awkward.

"What are you doing?" I object loudly.

"What do you see?" he asks.

I stare straight ahead. I'm so close to the tree that I must pull my head back slightly to make out what I'm seeing.

"I see a tree," I answer.

"You do not see a tree."

"I'm looking at a tree!"

"You are remembering the moment of having dreamt the tree, Melina. You are bringing into being an image held in your memory through the function of your reflector. Your reflector is manifesting an image of a tree to your awareness. Without memory, you cannot identify that which you see."

I'm reminded of the strawberries in the pink bowl; how I saw them first in my mind, then in the bowl.

"So I'm seeing an image in my mind of a tree through the function of both memory and the reflector?" I ask.

"Yes. The image is not only in your mind, but in the mind of the World Soul."

"But what about this tree I have my body pressed against? I can even see ants trailing up and down its bark."

I circle the trunk with my arms, emphasizing its girth.

"The tree does not exist."

I abruptly turn around and face Dionysus.

"Well of course it doesn't exist inside this surreal experience I'm having. I mean, I AM inside my mind right now. So are you. So is all of this."

"You are missing my meaning."

"Do you mean trees—the plum tree in my backyard, the redwoods up in La Honda, the lemon tree in Mickey and Merle's front yard I can see from my office window? They don't exist?"

"No."

I sit down in the grass and cross my legs.

"Okay. They don't exist. Real or not, if one falls on my house, I'm in big trouble."

I grab a handful of grass and start twisting it around my fingers. A strange sadness is welling up inside of me. I feel as if I'm shrinking.

"I love trees, Dionysus."

I look up at him beseechingly.

"But they do exist! They exist within the reality I operate from and that's enough for me. Look, I don't care about all this Zen stuff. You can have it."

I wave my hand to include the entire realm of woods, sky—even Dionysus.

"I'll keep the raunchy life, thank you. I happen to like it."

A tangle of strong emotions is tugging at my heart. I can't seem to unravel them, nor can I understand why I've sunk into this mood. Why do I suddenly feel compelled to defend the earth? All I've ever done is blame my problems on being banished from Paradise to eke out an existence in a world filled with wasps and snakes. I feel like my baby son, distraught that my most cherished possession, the one I most abuse, might be snatched right out from under my nose. I glance over at Dionysus.

"Why are you telling me all this?" I ask.

"It is what you have asked me to do."

Scowling, I tug at a blade of grass between my knees.

"Do you always do what I ask?"

"Yes."

I stare at him. Suddenly I feel a sense of remorse.

"I'm sorry," I murmur, hanging my head. "I've really been an ass. Forgive me."

I close my eyes and concentrate on the sound of the wind rustling through the treetops. Thousands of leaves laugh and chatter like a party of tongues in happy dialogue. I breathe the sound deep into my body, then gaze up at Dionysus. He is pointing to something in my lap, his eyes shining with amusement. Looking down at my hands, I see that I've tied several long blades of grass into huge knots.

October 31 Session

I close my eyes and see that I'm sitting in the woods in the exact spot as on my last journey. Dionysus is seated to my right. His legs are stretched out comfortably and crossed at the ankles. Gazing at my surroundings, I notice everything seems suspended like dream-shapes in a gigantic glass bowl of very still water. Imagining I'm looking into a huge crystal ball, I quietly tell myself that all I'm seeing is a reflection of my own mind.

I gaze over at Dionysus. He's looking straight at me, yet appears to be dreaming with his eyes open. For a moment I wonder what he's dreaming. I'm struck with the thought that he is dreaming me—dreaming me here in this world, dreaming me watching him dreaming. A lovely, fuzzy sensation expands in my head and makes me smile. Dionysus smiles back at me, still looking as if he were dreaming with his eyes open.

"I've done some soul searching over the last few days since we last talked," I confide.

Dionysus arranges his hands on his lap. I see that I have his full attention.

"You always seem to give me your undivided attention," I continue. "This is something I can't seem to do completely with anything or anyone. No matter who or what I'm focusing on, my inner gaze is always distracted by something else, yet that something eludes me, is driven out of my reach by an internal restlessness. I feel like a kid hopping around with a glass jar trying to catch fireflies, seduced by the 'many' and never satisfied with the 'one.' Yet I know deep in my heart I'm looking for the one."

I pause and reflect on this last thought. I don't want what I'm saying to sound sappy and self-indulgent. While I'm thinking this, I realize I'm trying to edit my feelings. I decide that confronting emotions that seem mawkish is inevitable if I'm ever going to find a place of inner clarity. I look at this last thought and wonder if it's just another face in my long parade of rationalizations.

"See what I'm doing?" I exclaim, throwing up my hands. "I'm always stopping in midstream and playing arbitrator between me and myself. I'm beginning to think this is the hand that held the dagger in that Dracula dream I had several months ago. All I'm doing is dismembering myself through constant mental dissection."

An image of the chamber in the womb, the one that looked like an underground cell made of concrete, looms in my mind's eye. I remember the floating leg, the hand. It makes me shudder.

"This is the castrator, the mutilator, the brutalizer; this is X. What makes him so inhuman, so cruel, is his absence of feelings—except for hatred."

I instantly see the contradiction in this thought.

"If X is capable of hatred," I muse, "then he must be capable of love. They're two faces of the same coin."

I stare at Dionysus. I want him to say something, but he remains silent. I gaze into my lap, realizing my statements about X only allude to myself.

"The split is in me," I continue quietly. "At some point, the One became shattered, split in half. It's as though I salvaged the pieces of the one half and glued it back together like a broken statue, but it was never the same after that. Whenever I gazed upon it, I knew it to be flawed."

"What is this 'one half'?" Dionysus asks.

"I don't know. Perhaps it encompasses all that I hold sacred. I could not say it is one thing."

I'm beginning to feel a sense of sorrow. As it deepens, it registers as brokenheartedness. I take a deep breath and proceed.

"Maybe it's love... my idea of love and how that's wrapped up in my private experiences and conceptions of God. I turn inward and contemplate Him with a sorrowing heart, as if some part of me is asking, 'Did I betray God? Or did He betray me?'"

I pause, disbelieving what I'm hearing from my own mouth. Despite the endowments of a thoroughly modern life—education, reason and alternative spirituality—my statements betray a religious sensibility that is uncomfortably archaic. I realize I'm no different from any number of Old Testament characters who, having made the all too human mistake of personalizing deity, spent the rest of their lives paying dearly for it. I shake my head and sigh heavily.

"All I know is the themes of betrayal and guilt have lingered around my heart since childhood. My Catholic upbringing provided a neat moral container, a spiritual paradigm for coping with these feelings in myself. When I grew old enough to carry the weight of my existence with all of its paradoxes, my Catholic support system collapsed. Something huge moved in to replace it. Within this 'hugeness' was a new hope, a brighter lamp to light the way, and a smile which seemed to be eternity itself."

I lean back in the grass, remembering clearly the day this all happened.

"I was 19 years old and standing barefoot in a Georgia cornfield, watching the sunset," I continue. "I don't know how or why, but of its own accord, a screw loosened in the way I normally perceived reality. The effect was an explosion of awareness: I saw that my existence was not a static point of consciousness situated upon a straight line which extended into infinity, but my existence was the line itself. I realized my consciousness had access to the line by means of the moment, which was itself both past and future happening simultaneously. This blow-out of perception opened up unbelievable possibilities for me. My joy was boundless."

Remembering this experience has made me very animated. I've been talking with my hands, painting scenes in the air. Dionysus is nodding thoughtfully. A smile is playing around his mouth.

"That sure is a lot of beans for a 19 year-old," he remarks, his smile widening to a grin.

Leaning back against the tree, he tucks his arms behind his head and stares at me languidly. I don't know what to think and gaze down at my hands.

"Yes, a lot of beans," I admit softly. "It fueled me for quite a number of years."

Oddly, I begin to think of the tale, "Jack and the Beanstalk"; how Jack sold his mother's cow for a handful of beans. Intrigued with this image, I mentally play with it: the beans take root in the soil of the mind while Jack is sleeping, then grow into a massive tree which reaches nearly to heaven. Jack climbs the tree which leads to his higher mind, whereupon he discovers certain treasures—the singing harp, the hen that lays the golden eggs—all in possession of a man-eating giant. Jack outwits the giant merely by waiting for him to fall asleep. He grabs the treasures and slides down the beanstalk to the earth below, which is the only place the treasures can have any practical use. Ah, but then he has to destroy his stairway to heaven lest the giant descend on him and tear him asunder. So he chops down the very means by which he gained entrance to the treasures of the higher mind. Yet what does it matter, since now he has "below" what he took from "above", sans the man-eating giant?

Given the fairy tale as metaphor, I wonder what the beanstalk symbolizes. Slowing the story down in my mind, I try to gather its symbols frame by frame: the beanstalk grows by night... from a handful of silly beans... which Jack purchases via the trade of a cow... in a moment of mindlessness.

"Dionysus, what does the cow represent in 'Jack and the Beanstalk'?"

"Milk."

I think this over. It seems too simple.

"What does milk represent?"

"Mother."

"What does mother represent?"

"Earth."

"And the earth?"

"Body."

"The body?"

"Bondage."

"Bondage to what?"

"Poverty."

I reflect on the word, "poverty," a pivotal word with many shades of meaning. I wonder if Dionysus means spiritual, emotional or physical poverty. I decide he's talking about any state in which dire need gives rise to the necessity of relief. This thought instantly dislodges the memory of a prayer I recited as a child in parochial school, which outstripped all supplications arising from grave privation: "Hail, Holy Queen, Mother of Mercy, our life, our sweetness and our hope, to thee do we cry, poor banished children of Eve; to thee do we send up our sighs, mourning and weeping in this vale of tears..."

"Yechh!" I exclaim, turning a sour face to Dionysus. "Imagine the collective effect of this desperate wail reiterated over centuries by thousands of souls envisioning earthly existence as something out of a Hieronymus Bosch painting. It's no wonder the words, 'mother,' 'earth,' 'body,' 'bondage,' and 'poverty' are all bound together like a barbed wire fence!"

I grab a stick and poke it into the dirt.

"So, maybe Jack's beans are the seed-thoughts of change.

Think so, Dionysus?"

"No."

I eye him carefully.

"What, then?"

"Desire. Fascination. Play. Magic."

His words evoke a host of mental images: Puck in *A Midsummer Night's Dream,* Peter Pan, imps, elves, Pan, faeries, and the delighted face of a naked baby boy playing with his penis during a bath.

"You are imagining innocence," Dionysus remarks, reading my thoughts.

I nod quietly. Dionysus leans forward and plucks a blade of grass near his foot. Settling back against the tree, he slowly twirls it between his thumb and forefinger, absorbed in thought.

"When Jack traded the family cow for a handful of magic beans in a moment of mindlessness," he explains, "this is to say he was empty of all self-consciousness, as is a small child. In this state, the doing is a function of being. There is no blame, no guilt, no sense of having wronged. There is no perceptual transition between 'this' and 'that,' and consequently, no voice to arbitrate difference. When one is without guilt, he is free to truly dream."

"Is it through this 'dreaming' that the unknowable can be known?" I ask.

"Yes."

I wonder if it's any coincidence that Jack's stairway to heaven should take root and grow by night when he's fast asleep and dreaming. I reflect on the biblical story of Jacob who, having fallen asleep, dreamt of angels ascending and descending a ladder reaching from heaven to earth. I'm struck by the similarities between these stories and my experience with the winged beings jumping off the disc into the void. How did I get to the disc but through focusing my awareness upwards along a thread of light? Was this thread of light the "beanstalk," the "ladder"? Was I dreaming? I remember Dionysus asking me, "Are you asleep?" I answered, "Yes, falling softly." Even though I was dreaming, could I also have been remembering? My experience of fetal awareness may have arisen from genuine memories sealed in my subconscious preceding birth, yet it seemed as if I was encountering intrauterine life for the first time. Could dreaming be another term for "remembering"? Is imagining the same as remembering? Remembering what? The unknowable? How can one "remember" the unknowable?

I think back to my experience with the disc and the struggle that ensued between myself and the being with saucer-like eyes. Prior to my struggle, I had been asked, "What is your desire?" I went blank, didn't know—is it because I had stopped remembering? What replaced remembering? Self-consciousness, confusion, embarrassment: a feeling I had done something wrong, followed by a need to make amends. Was this the very reason for my struggle with the being?

"Dionysus, what does desire have to do with all of this? And what does Jack's giant represent?"

"I cannot tell you what the giant represents, Melina. You will have to experience this yourself."

"Surely I don't have to stick my finger in the fire to discover it's hot," I reason. "Can't I make an educated guess?"

Dionysus looks at me blandly.

"The giant is death," I continue, "self-annihilation. That's got to be it. What else could it be?"

I'm pacing back and forth, taking long strides in the cool grass. I glance over at Dionysus. His expression is unchanged.

"What, am I boring you?" I ask.

"You are wasting energy."

I plop myself down in the grass, bewildered as to how I could be wasting energy. A moment ago I was doing just fine—when did I cross the line between using energy wisely and squandering it? I cross my legs and prop my chin in my hand. I'm trying to untangle the mess in my mind when a loud "crunch" splits the air. I glance over at Dionysus munching an apple as if it were his last meal on earth, oblivious to the noise it's making. This grates on my nerves.

"Doesn't your mother feed you?" I ask glibly, staring at him.

He's chewing the apple with obvious enjoyment, unaware that he's annoying me.

"I've lost my whole train of thought about the beanstalk theory," I mutter, pulling disinterestedly at a blade of grass.

Another loud "crunch" punctuates the stillness. It goes right through me. I close my eyes and grit my teeth.

"Don't you know that having to endure another's noisy eating habits is my all-time pet peeve?" I ask in an irritated voice. "Why do you keep eating? Why are you eating those stupid apples?"

I throw him a hard stare. Dionysus places the apple in his lap and looks up at me.

"I am hungry."

He picks up the apple again and takes a huge bite. It makes an ear-splitting, snapping sound. I jump to my feet, walk over to where he's sitting and place my hands on my hips.

"You're doing that on purpose," I accuse.

"Eating?"

"No, it's how you're doing it. You're teasing me."

Dionysus slowly places down the apple.

"When is the last time you made love?" he asks.

My jaw drops. Blood is rushing to my face.

"What's that got to do with this?"

"It has everything to do with this."

My eyes are bulging. I open my mouth to say something, but nothing comes out. I turn on my heel and head for a tree several yards across a small clearing. All the while I'm thinking how typical it is for a man to insinuate that a woman's irritability is nothing more than masked horniness.

"Why are you so concerned about how often I make love?" I yell, concealing myself behind a tree. "Do you experience my orgasms vicariously, or what?"

I turn my face to the tree, regretting what I just said. I realize the only thing I can do now is march back over to Dionysus and try to straighten out this mess. I take a deep breath and pace back across the clearing to where he's propped comfortably against the tree. Seating myself at a distance, I fold my hands in my lap and look into his eyes. They're completely without guile or judgment.

"Can you tell me what's going on?" I ask.

My voice sounds strangely small, as though I were talking into a tin cup. I shift the weight of my body slightly forward and lower my head.

"When your body is undernourished, it sabotages the soul and takes its energy," Dionysus explains.

"I'm eating," I correct him, confused by his words.

"That is not my meaning."

"Are you saying I should jump in the sack with Ted?"

"When the body takes energy from the soul, the mind gets very tight. It will not give up its energy for anything."

I think this over, weighing its implications.

"Do you mean my mind will fight against my body?" I ask.

"Yes."

I find this thought somewhat strange. I'd always assumed my body's conflicts were with my soul, not my mind. I now see how senseless this really is.

"But if the mind won't give up its energy, Dionysus, how does the whole system come into balance again?"

"The body's language is filled with nuance," he explains. "It tells you what it desires each and every moment. It sings to you, dances, cries, pokes, whispers to your cells, your flesh, your eyes, hair and mouth. The body lives, breathes and sustains itself through desire.

"You perceive the body's desire as 'necessity': a network of needs in order to function. Consequently, you give it only that which it needs, not what it desires. If you gave your baby son only what he needed and not what he desired, he would have starved months ago. You do not remember the meaning of the hymns your body sings, nor the melodies and rhythms that comprise its ongoing dance. You give it breadcrumbs when it would have the whole supper, droplets of water when it would have the full cup of wine."

Dionysus takes the half-eaten apple and raises it to his lips. Holding my gaze, he slowly bites into the apple. It makes a soft, crunching sound. As I watch him, I can almost taste the apple. I swallow.

"When the body's desire is ignored, it goes blind. It cries. It wails. It senses absence of response as abandonment. Your body is a child; it ages, yet it never grows old. In its desire, it is and will remain as a child, even in death."

He pauses and gazes up at the trees. A quiet has fallen over me like a weightless blanket. I look around and notice the sunlight is beginning to wane.

"In its abandonment, the body turns to the soul," Dionysus continues. "The soul has no light of its own save the light of the mind which beholds it. It is through this light that the soul is wed to the body. Yet as long as the body seeks its energy from the soul, the soul cannot fully inhabit the body, for the body cannot contain the soul while also being administered by it."

"What is the body administered by if not the soul?" I ask.

"The spirit. The indwelling spirit comes forth from the light of the mind as it beholds itself in the reflection of the soul. When the wailing body intercepts this union in order to replenish itself, it disturbs the Lover's gaze. It breaks the spell."

"The spell?" I ask, disbelieving my ears. "You say that as if the spirit and soul are bound up in some sort of enchantment with each other, like a man and woman in love."

Dionysus smiles at me.

"They are."

I turn away and gaze into a network of nearby branches, telling myself there's something wrong with this explanation. It's all too human. Too fragile. Too neurotic. He must be reflecting to me my own definitions, my own concepts.

"Dionysus, we're talking about the divine here. We're talking about spirit, about soul. How can you ascribe such human qualities to the numinous, the inconceivable? That's ridiculous."

"What is 'human,' Melina?'

For a moment I go blank. Who knows? Who really knows? Where does "human" let off and "divine" begin? Is there a "letting off"? What is the origin of all this?

"I have no idea, Dionysus. All I know is you're mixing up terms and states, interchanging definitions and behavior, shuffling the cards so fast that everything is becoming a blur."

I reflect on my body and try to visualize it as a blind wailing child who senses my absence of response to its desires as abandonment.

"You said when the body is undernourished, it sabotages the soul and takes its energy. This implies a sort of willful, destructive behavior. Is that what you meant?" I ask.

"I am speaking of interference, Melina. Interference precedes and gives rise to dissonance, disharmony. The body's interference is blind. When blind, it cannot act from will."

"Does this also mean when I don't respond to my body's desires, I'm somehow interfering with its life, its well-being?"

"Yes. Your life. Your well-being."

Something about this logic is screwy. If I caved-in to all of my body's desires, I'd be nothing more than a hedonist.

"Look, Dionysus, a lot of my body's desires are dark. If I were to live out that darkness, I'd be a criminal, an animal. I'd regress to primate consciousness—body survival, dog-eat-dog."

Dionysus studies me. I try to think if there are any gaping holes in what I've just said.

"Where is the regression, Melina? You cannot fall into what

you already are."

"Do you mean an animal?" I ask.

"Yes."

My whole body tenses. I feel trapped.

"All right," I concede in a matter of fact voice. "I can handle that intellectually—you know, as an irrefutable fact of life. Sure, I'm an animal. I poke myself and I bleed. I eat meat and I possess a killer instinct. And yes, I fantasize sexually about all sorts of things that would curl the devil's horns. But I can't handle this part of my nature emotionally. I mean, it goes beyond merely offending my sensibilities, my aesthetics. It contradicts my aesthetics."

"Melina, the contradiction is in your mind, not in your body, nor does the contradiction exist in your soul, spirit or emotions, yet it is causing great interference, great dissonance in and among them."

I grow quiet and try to digest what Dionysus has just said. It's becoming clear to me how I parade my "light" face to the world, while X gets to carry the baggage of my confusion, darkness and contempt for the body. No wonder he's such a sadist.

"Well, I think we're hitting bottom here," I sigh.

"Bottom?" Dionysus asks.

"Yes. I feel as if I'm sitting at the bottom of a deep empty well. There's no rope. The sides are too steep to climb. I can't get out."

"You are right."

I look at him in shock.

"What?"

"The well in which you are sitting is your own body. You cannot get out."

Personal Notes

I reflect on my session with Dionysus for the rest of the day and find myself mesmerized by the dialogue about the body and its desires. I feel as though I'm walking a very precarious edge in myself, an edge where virtue and vice blurs, beckoning me into a vast gray world ever more perilous for its ambiguity. I wonder, just for a moment, if this could be the "hell" I used to think about as a child—not a fiery abyss inhabited by pitchfork-wielding goblins, but a pastoral landscape filled with large restful trees and a seductive Greek god who whispers in my ear, "Forget it all and go for the apple."

Isn't this the very seduction Lord Henry employed to snag the unsuspecting soul of Dorian Gray in Oscar Wilde's *The Picture of Dorian Gray*? Curious about it, I scan my office shelves and find the book. I know exactly which passage I'm looking for, having marked it years ago out of astonishment. Finding it, I read it over carefully. The precision of Lord Henry's mind and the seeming impeccability of his rationale make his statements all the more hypnotic.

I believe that if one man were to live out his life fully and completely, were to give form to every feeling, expression to every thought, reality to every dream—I believe that the world would gain such a fresh impulse of joy that we would forget all the maladies of medievalism, and return to the Hellenic ideal—to something finer, richer, than the Hellenic ideal, it may be. But the bravest man among us is afraid of himself. The mutilation of the savage has its tragic survival in the self-denial that mars our lives. We are punished for our refusals. Every impulse that we strive to strangle broods in the mind and poisons us. The body sins once and has done with its sin, for action is a mode of purification. Nothing remains then but the recollection of a pleasure or the luxury of a regret. The only way to get rid of a temptation is to yield to it. Resist it, and your soul grows sick with longing for the things it has forbidden to itself, with desire for what its monstrous laws have made monstrous and unlawful... Nothing can cure the soul but the senses, just as nothing can cure the senses but the soul... that is one of the great secrets of life—to cure the soul by means of the senses, and the senses by means of the soul.

CHAPTER 8

THEATER OF DREAMS

November 3 A Dream

I dream that I live in a one-story wooden house on the bank of a huge river. The house is old and very rustic. I live there with Ted, my two children and a grandfatherly old man who is a river rat. Knowing a great deal about river life, he instructs me about fishing and the rigors of living in an unsophisticated environment. One afternoon we're down at the bank on a windy gray day, watching the waves bang up the dock. The water is very moody and choppy. The old man is talking to me about it, but I now can't remember what he said.

The dream shifts and we must move from the rustic house for reasons that are irrevocable and unknown. It seems we must vacate in a hurry, as though our time there "is up." I'm aware another family is moving to the riverbank who will live in our house. Because they are waiting for us to leave, I'm running around like a distraught chicken, trying to organize my affairs. There is simply not enough time.

The dream shifts and I'm standing on the balcony of a building thousands of feet high. Leaning over the railing, I'm looking down upon the sprawling river below and have a great view of everything. A young woman is standing on the other side of the balcony with her husband, mother and child. I realize this is the family who has been waiting for us to vacate our house. Searching the riverbank for the rustic house, I locate the exact spot but see no dwelling. Shocked, I keep looking. I suddenly realize the house was torn down, piled onto a truck board by board and junked. No shred of the house remains.

As I try to understand why this was done, I sense that all traces of my family's life and identity were deliberately blotted out—wiped clean from the bank as if we had never existed. I stare down at the river, feeling desolate and displaced. Gazing once again at the new family, I make a remark to the young woman, suggesting "You'd better beware lest the same fate should befall you." She is impervious to my warning, my feelings and the helpless state of my affairs.

The dream shifts and I'm standing in a large old boarding house which is run by a matronly woman. Many of the boarders are women and children and the atmosphere is somewhat chaotic. Suddenly a middle-aged woman I've never seen before shows up and demands to search the place. It seems she's looking for "smuggled babies." Everyone is curious and follows her as she ransacks the place. We all enter a large bedroom filled with many bunk beds. The woman begins lifting up the mattresses one by one. As she does this, I wonder how babies could possibly breathe stowed under mattresses.

Finally we get to the last bunk bed. The woman lifts the mattress. There, tucked this way and that in an uncovered box spring, are a dozen or more sleeping babies. I'm amazed. I look up at the matronly woman who runs the boarding house and realize she is the one responsible for the smuggling. I then bend over the babies and examine them. I know a cat lives in the house and cry, "The poor things! They've been bitten up by fleas!"

November 4 Session

I close my eyes and see that I'm strolling in the woods with Dionysus on a clear sunny day. At a distance to my right, the stream sparkles like silver icicles on a Christmas tree. Feeling very relaxed, I'm walking slowly, casually. I glance over at Dionysus and see that he's wearing a long robe. Prayer beads hang from a belt of rope fastened loosely around his waist. While this bothers me, it doesn't interfere with the evenness of my mood.

"May I ask you something, Dionysus?"

He gazes pleasantly at me. His eyes are alert and clear, his manner calm. I hesitate, trying to find a clear way to put this.

"For the last few weeks I've been bothered by a nagging thought. I could be wrong, but I have the impression you're reflecting a deep pattern of mine, an unconscious system which organizes all I'm seeing and experiencing with you before it registers upon my awareness. It's as though the dynamics of this realm and our exchanges together have been set up in advance. I'm not talking about this system in a deified sense, either. It's not like something mystical or even spiritual, nor is it coming from a theological, philosophical or psychological superstructure, although often it seems as if it is. It carries those qualities but doesn't seem to belong to those qualities. You can't escape the system or pattern and neither can I."

I'm studying the grass as we stroll, aware that what I'm trying to articulate feels very strong.

"I really don't know what this system or pattern is," I continue. "It seems to be a neutral thing and has no sex, no identity, no particular persuasion, no emotion, no specific ideology, no soul. It is of God and yet it is Godless. It doesn't think, it merely 'is' and runs like a huge machine for its own sake without an 'on' or 'off' button. It just keeps on going and you and I are stuck in it. I can tell. The whole pattern is being reflected in you or by you, I can't tell which. You're becoming predictable."

"In what way?" Dionysus asks curiously.

"Oh, I don't know. It's hard to put my finger on. Why don't you ever get angry? Why is it I'm always the one acting out anger while you're the one observing calmly, keeping your senses intact, never losing it? I'll tell you. It's because the system, my system, is setting it up that way. You know I can't bear contradiction, even though I'm riddled with it. How could I endure you acting out rage when I need you to be the benevolent shoulder for me to lean on? How could I trust you if you're always inconsistent, flying off the handle, smacking me one moment and embracing me the next?

"Well, the simple truth is, I couldn't handle it. I'd fall apart. I couldn't keep coming here, nor would I learn anything about myself. I'd merely be in a constant state of turmoil and fear. So, this helps me to understand what's happening in a way, why you're always the way you are. But I also realize that keeping you this way can be a trap. You can't grow, exfoliate who or what you really are. The persona my system has given you is one dimensional. In other words, if this keeps up, I'll stop growing and exfoliating, too. Not only that, but all of this keeps X as menacing as he was the first day I ran into him in the forest months ago. He's the carrier for my darkness; you're the carrier for my light. I go spinning back and forth between the two of you until I'm whirled into paste. Then what? All I'm doing is running laps around the cause and effect loop of my own subjectivity. I mean, really! Shelve the discussions about the unknowable. I've got my hands full right here."

I glance over at Dionysus. He's gazing ahead into the grass as we walk and seems immersed in thought. I continue.

"For instance, see that get-up you're wearing? I know what that's all about."

"What is it about?" he asks, his voice even and relaxed.

"It's part of a huge complex I have. It's the Christianity thing around my neck like an albatross. The Church, Catholicism. The ascetic life: suffering, guilt, redemption. Holy Moses, you name it and it's in my complex."

Dionysus looks over at me and smiles.

"What is a complex, Melina?"

I think about this. I'm not really sure.

"I guess it's whatever I'm extremely hung-up on deep down inside. It's a huge tangle in my ball of yarn that's blocking up the works. I really don't know what the accepted psychological definition of a 'complex' is. I don't even know if complex is the right word, but I'm sure you catch my drift."

"Would you prefer that I take the robe off?" he offers.

"No, no, I couldn't handle that either. See? Look how tied up we are in this ridiculous drama! Doesn't it make you want to do something really far-fetched, really outlandish so we can blow out of this thing?"

"Like what?"

"Anything! Let's mess up the gears of this huge contraption we're inside of. Let's think of ways we can do that."

Dionysus stops and looks at me. His expression is far from playful.

"Melina, all you can do is observe what is here, what you feel, all that you experience. Do not try to change anything. You can change nothing."

My enthusiasm is fading like a withered balloon. We resume our stroll in silence. Gazing at the glittering stream spread out in the sunlight, I imagine it to be a long sequined scarf dropped from heaven by an immense goddess. The absurd image makes me laugh out loud. Dionysus stops and gazes at me, then places his arms around my waist and hugs me. As I hold him, an indescribable feeling of tenderness floods my heart. I close my eyes to seal this feeling deep in my soul.

"Thank you, Dionysus. Thank you for everything."

Smiling down at me, Dionysus gently lifts me off the ground. Trees and clouds begin to move around us like the view from a carousel as he slowly spins me in a circle. Laughing and growing dizzier by the second, I release myself from his arms and fall into the grass, feeling refreshed. Dionysus lies next to me and props his head in his hand. I gaze into his face. At this moment he feels exactly like a brother I've known all my life.

"It would be wonderful if things could always be this way," I yearn softly.

"They are this way, Melina."

I hesitate. I really do want to believe this, but I encounter barriers of doubt.

"Maybe life is like this somewhere else," I conjecture, gesturing at the clouds, "but not in this crazy world we live in. As long as pain, poverty, sickness and death remain with us, we'll have to dream of our Shangri-La out there."

I lean back in the grass and gaze at the western sky silhouetted with hills. Just beyond the stream is a nest of small slopes that roll and lean for a great distance. My gaze lingers on those hills for a long time. I notice a shape like that of a man standing on one of the hills. I think it's a tree but imagine it to be a farmer looking out over his acres, or even a shepherd watching after an invisible flock of sheep.

"Do you know what I've been thinking of lately?" I ask, a world of images converging in my head.

I pull a blade of grass and twirl it softly on the tip of my nose. The sun is deliciously warm on my face.

"I keep seeing this wonderful old neighborhood. It's a neighborhood I've never been to before, yet I seem to know exactly what it's like. It's old and well-lived in. It has a lot of smells—smells of people working and playing, people eating, sleeping and loving. Do you know those smells?"

Dionysus smiles at me. I'm grateful he's being so sweet.

"Someone lives in this neighborhood who loves these smells very much. She even likes the look of the beat-up garbage cans packed to overflowing, clustered on the curb every Friday morning like a group of fat happy school kids waiting for the bus."

I look over whimsically at Dionysus.

"Are you enjoying my story?"

He nods, smiling.

"This woman is Italian," I continue. "She's heavy-set and wears a dark polka-dot dress that reaches nearly to her ankles. It has small rhinestone buttons down the front and lace trim around the collar."

Dionysus breaks into laughter.

"Really!" I insist, trying to keep a straight face. "She also wears support hose that are rolled up just above the knees. No one knows this except her sister's babies who play under her dress while she's cooking the family meal on Sundays.

"Anyway, this woman has seven children. Three of them are in high school and one is about to graduate. His name is Vincenzo and she's more proud of him than anything in the world, except the statue of Saint Joseph her uncle bought for her in Rome. Her youngest, the baby, is six years old. His name is Dominic. He has short choppy bangs and fat legs. She grabs him all the time, either to straighten out his pants, smack his pudgy hands or squeeze him heartily against her oversized breasts."

I burst out laughing.

"Dionysus, you know this woman doesn't really exist, don't you? I'm making all this up. I mean, this whole scenario has been hanging around in my head for the past few weeks."

"Go on," Dionysus prompts, nodding at me.

I gaze up at the clouds, trying to get a fix on this imaginary woman who has been haunting my daydreams.

"Anyway, this woman just loves Mario Lanza. She thinks he's the next best thing to God's only-begotten Son. Every Saturday afternoon after she's hung out the wash and pinned her hair up in curls for Sunday Mass, she grabs a big basket piled high with linens, sets up her ironing board and places a 78 LP Mario Lanza record on the phonograph. For the next three hours she's sailing in paradise as her iron hisses and hums over the tablecloths, the sheets, the hand-embroidered doilies. Now and then she dabs at her misty eyes with one of her husband's big handkerchiefs she keeps tucked in her apron. Yes, that Mario Lanza... he really gets to her, you know?"

I thump my chest with a fist and sigh. Dionysus is grinning at me. His eyes are alive and sparkly.

"Oh, what this woman puts up with. She listens to everyone's problems: the butcher's wife has cystitis, the pastor needs more money, Mrs Gradicci lost out to Carla Menduzzi's cousin in the Knights of Columbus Annual Women's Bake-off. Yet she doesn't complain. Oh, she yells a lot and bangs pots and ladles around her kitchen, but for the most part she's a good-hearted soul. She tosses pasta out her kitchen window to stray dogs and even lets Vincenzo eat grated Romano cheese right out of the bowl with his fingers. Not even my grandmother would let me do that!"

I pause and think about my grandmother. She passed away just six weeks ago. I miss her a great deal, yet I haven't cried. I gently shake her memory from my mind and look deeply into Dionysus' eyes.

"You know what this woman thinks when she walks through town on her way to evening Mass? She thinks about how rich her life is. She looks up at all the shady elms and sycamores and smiles about the button she sewed on Dominic's shirt. She can still smell the loaves of bread she pulled out of the oven before she slipped out the door for Mass. And as she crosses Henry Street—yes, at this very moment she's somewhere crossing Henry Street, maybe in Boston, maybe in Milwaukee—she thanks God for her life, thanks Him every day at the same exact spot. This is her private moment with Him, a moment she can savor which is hers alone. Each day when she comes upon it, a feeling floods over her that makes her so terribly happy at being alive that she nearly weeps! She thinks, 'Right here is God, on this very corner. He waits for me every moment, every day of my life.'

"This is the reason she walks to Mass every evening: it is the stroll, the street corner, the shady elms and the smell of bread, the moon hanging low in the sky and the sound of her worn black shoes tapping softly along the sidewalk... "

I sit up and stare into the grass. I'm not sure what I'm feeling, but it's pretty strong.

"How small and safe her life is, how terribly uncomplicated," I observe softly. "Her needs are so simple. How free she is to love."

I cross my legs and prop my chin in my hand. I look Dionysus square in the face.

"I don't understand it, Dionysus. Some part of me envies this woman. Can you believe it? I gag at the mere thought of Mario Lanza. And ironing? It has to be my most despised chore. What do I envy? A life that revolves around statues of saints and attending Mass? A husband who puts on his best bowling shirt and shuffles down to the corner bar on Saturday nights to drink wine with the neighborhood cronies?"

I toss a handful of grass into the air and groan.

"That kind of life represents all the things I rebel against most."

"What does it serve to rebel against yourself?" Dionysus asks.

I cock my head at him.

"If that Italian woman represents myself, she's an anachronism. What do I do with her? I can show her off in a display case of Old World artifacts or shove her in a cedar chest, pressed flat like a corsage in a post World War I flying manual. Or I can dust her off every Easter and introduce her to my kids, but she's scared to death of the modern world. Can you imagine how intimidated she'd be by a food processor, to say nothing of a microwave oven!"

Aware of how corny this is sounding, I search for a way to shift off this subject.

"Why don't you talk to her?" Dionysus suggests.

"I told you. I made her up. Besides, she speaks Italian. *Non la capisco.*"

I rub my hands together and stretch my legs out in the grass. I'm beginning to feel restless.

"This woman has a name, Melina. She has a life, a story. She has a heart, a soul, a mind. She has her memories, her children, her ancestors."

I look at him blankly.

"So? Talking to her would be like talking to my dad. It's the same old stuff, the same record, the same song. I know it all by heart."

A sudden realization smacks me between the eyes—my God, maybe she is my dad. Maybe she represents the way I've internalized my own father, his world of ideas.

"It's a beautiful day, Dionysus. Let's not waste it. Let's go find an apple tree or an interesting rock. Come on."

Raring to go, I stand up and brush off the seat of my pants. I hold out my hand to Dionysus. He lies there and looks at me.

"Now who's being stubborn?" I tease.

"Sit down, Melina."

I fold my arms across my chest, regretting I ever opened my big mouth about the Italian woman and her fat kids. I can see now where all this is going.

"Can we do this another time, Dionysus? Please?"

I'm really pleading. I don't want to get tangled up inside the Old World figures—the patriarch, the matriarch and their passel of kids marked by the twisted jealousies and power struggles of their forebears. Dionysus is studying me quietly.

"You can talk to this Italian woman," he suggests, "or you can talk to the person who stands over on that hill."

He gestures to the low rolling hills across the stream that dip and bend into the horizon. Again I see a figure like that of a man. It's the one I imagined to be a farmer or shepherd.

"I thought that was a tree," I remark.

"Too narrow. Not enough branches at the top."

Dionysus winks playfully. I get the feeling I'm being set-up.

"Who is it?" I ask, knowing full well he's not going to tell me.

I realize if I want to know, I'm going to have to ford that stream and find out. I stare at the stream for a long time and remember when Pan threw me in and yelled, "Eels!" I smile. It seems that happened years ago, maybe even in another life.

"Will you come with me, Dionysus?"

"I will walk with you to the stream."

A flutter of nervousness steals through my stomach. For a moment I wonder if the figure on the hill might be X. I suddenly feel I should be wearing a sword and shield, a helmet and God only knows what else. I look down at my shorts and bare feet, wishing I had more clothes on.

"May I run home and get dressed first?"

Dionysus laughs. I realize how ridiculous this must have sounded—I keep forgetting where I am.

"You are fine as you are, Melina. You must travel light. There is a stream you must cross to get to the other side. The water is deep in the middle."

I stare at him, wondering if I should read warnings into what he's just said.

"There really aren't any eels in there, are there?" I ask.

"No."

I hesitate, knowing if I don't ask the right question, I won't get the right answer.

"Snakes, alligators, piranhas?" I probe.

Dionysus rubs his chin thoughtfully as if ransacking his memory, then breaks into laughter. I breathe a sigh of relief.

"Come, Melina. Let us be on our way."

He reaches out and places an arm around my shoulders. His mood is quite chipper. For the first time, I take full notice of how tall he is and feel like a midget by comparison. I gaze ahead at the stream. On the hill stands the figure motionless as a statue.

November 5 A Dream

I dream about a priest I've actually known in real life, who was the assistant pastor of our parish for many years when I was growing up. The priest was young, gentle and nice-looking, and because my family lived right across the street from the church, I visited him often, particularly when I was going through my adolescence. We'd sit in the office of his rectory and have long theological discussions. I was always full of questions about religion, but more than that, I had a mild crush on him.

In the dream, I'm living at my parent's house and I'm my present age. We're preparing to attend a social affair one evening, for which I have no date or escort. I wonder what sort of man I may meet and seem to be dressing according to my expectations. My parents are not only aware of this, they are suspicious of my intentions. Their wariness puts me on alert to be discreet.

We go to the social event. I'm wearing an attractive black evening dress and several men are making advances all at once. I'm trying to select one of these men as my companion or escort for the evening. It seems my parents wish me to quickly make up my mind so it won't appear that I'm "on the make." I'm feeling quite fickle and realize I'm enjoying the idea of being "on the make," even though I'm not. I'm modifying my behavior accordingly. I finally select an escort. For the rest of the evening, I suffer through the gestures and pantomimes of acceptable social behavior in a room full of waltzing strangers. I'm not particularly enchanted with the man I've selected.

The dream shifts and I've already said good-bye to my escort and have returned home with my parents. They turn in for the night. I'm strolling through the dark house on my way to my bedroom when suddenly I see this priest standing in the shadows. I recognize him immediately, as he looks exactly as he did when I was a girl. It seems he saw me at the social event and followed me home. He wants to talk with me and seems disturbed about something. We go to my bedroom.

I sit on the edge of my bed in the darkness. Small children are sleeping in the room, so we must be very quiet. I do not turn on the light. I can see the priest's silhouette against the window and can just barely make out his features. Groping around for words, he begins talking to me and seems deeply troubled. Uncertain as to what I can do to help, I walk over to him and touch his hand to comfort him. He reaches out to me as though he wants to hold me. We embrace. In that moment I understand the reason for his turmoil. He's in love with me and in conflict with his sacred vows. I realize I'm also in love with him. We're both shaking with this realization as we hold each other.

It seems impossible now to resist the power of this realization. He kisses me with his whole heart and soul. We drop to our knees. I yield to him instantly and want to make love with him more than anything in the world. I begin to slip off my black dress. As I'm doing this, I wonder if it will be all right, if I will be violating his vows. Searching his face, I see that he is extremely earnest and filled with desire. I know he is no longer in conflict and has made his decision. This releases the struggle with my own conscience.

The dream shifts and we're now sitting on the bed. A child has awakened and is lying in bed with us. We've not yet made love, although we're both naked. The priest is talking playfully with the child. I'm trying to slip my gown back on to cover my breasts. It seems I can't make up my mind and keep pulling it back off. Now and then the priest catches sight of me doing this and flashes me looks of pleasure.

The dream shifts and I'm lying in the same bed with the child and Ted. On the wall is a large television screen. We're watching a program together in the dark. Out of the corner of my eye I can see the priest standing in the shadows against the wall. He's naked and is waiting for me. I'm unbelievably nervous about his presence in the room and hope Ted won't see him. I'm suddenly aware that to make love with the priest would be a betrayal of my vows to Ted. The conflict inside of me is terrible. My desire for the priest is too strong to shake off.

The dream shifts and I'm standing with the priest in the kitchen of my mother's house. We're fully clothed and talking with each other. We still very much want to make love. The priest reaches out and tenderly embraces me. Suddenly my mother walks into the room and is shocked by what she sees. I pretend my relationship with the priest is platonic. This is extremely difficult and awkward to pull off, given the scenario. I'm doing everything in my power to make my mother buy this, but I'm feeling like a hypocrite. I'm aware that I'm acting a lie, betraying my relationship with Ted and my children, and betraying everything I hold sacred.

My baby son cries out for his morning bottle and I awaken from the dream. I regret it was cut short and I was not able to consummate my relationship with the priest.

November 7 A Dream

I dream that I have no identity. In the dream I'm repeatedly visiting a place or state which represents my interior self. In this state is a large ball or disc of light. Down the middle of the ball or disc is a line. It appears the ball is "in half," yet it is whole. I stare at it in bewilderment. The light of the disc appears at times to emanate in visible lines from the center. The disc then shifts slightly and appears to me as a flat object tilting its face in different directions.

To the right of this ball or disc is another thing, but I now can't remember what it is, nor do I think in the dream it was identifiable. This "other thing" appears to be a necessary counterpart to what I'm seeing, as though its absence would preclude any possibility for me to focus on the image of the disc. It seems it may be some sort of reflector. Even so, this reflector is invisible and seems to be comprised of emptiness or "that which is not." Although invisible, it is as present to me and real as the disc itself. As I watch the interchange between the disc and the emptiness, I'm struck with the realization that I have no physical birth records, that I have not been born.

The dream shifts and I'm standing in the playground of a children's schoolyard. As I watch the children play, my gaze falls on a little girl with a sweet round face, large eyes and long dark hair. Her ears are pierced and she's wearing tiny earrings: one blue and one red. I know these earrings have come from Italy and carry some significance about her personal history. I try to feel further into her personal history and realize she has no parents. She is an orphan.

The dream shifts and I'm sitting in a classroom. The students are approximately my own age, but the feel of the school and curriculum is that of high school. I realize I have a pile of classes to attend, subjects I have no choice about taking. The teacher and students are carrying on a dialogue about the curriculum as if it were our first day at school. I soon discover I must attend an ancient history class on a regular basis, taught by an old curmudgeon who is very strict, hard, and traditional in his methods. The thought of having to endure this on a daily basis is more than I can bear. I speak up and investigate ways I can get out of taking this class. I try to convince the teacher that Old World history is not relevant to my present life or interests. The teacher tells me I have no choice. History is not an elective. I "must" take it in order to graduate.

November 8 A Dream

I dream that I'm walking around in a strange city. The streets are humming with traffic and passers-by are everywhere. Lost or looking for something, I'm trying to familiarize myself with the city's layout in order to get my bearings. As I walk about, I notice the city is quite old and filled with character. Strolling through parks and plazas, I stare up at the quaint buildings, marveling at their architecture.

I'm passing a large complex of buildings when I notice a flight of concrete steps leading down to what I assume is the business district. I approach the steps and begin to descend them. As I do this, I look out over the railing and realize I'm at a very high elevation, as if on a mountaintop. Spread out below me is another city even older than the one in which I've been strolling. As I stare at the art deco architecture and stylish neon lights, I'm amazed at how old-fashioned everything looks. On the corner of the square is a lovely high building with a large clock tower. As I gaze at it, I'm struck with a feeling that the city is operating entirely within a framework from the past. Even the pedestrians exude a slower-paced energy, as though they had all the time in the world. The spirit of the city is so enchanting that I'm utterly spellbound.

I continue walking down the stairway until I reach a bend in the stairs which becomes a landing. In a far corner of the landing, a derelict is sitting in a pile of debris, holding a bottle of spirits wrapped in a brown paper bag. The derelict tells me to "look again," intimating there is something about the city I didn't see. I walk back up the steps and lean over the railing. Spread out below me is a wide, breathtaking boulevard filled with fantasy characters from old storybooks and fables, movies and animation films. Rows of beautiful trees and bushes decorated with thousands of twinkling lights frame the boulevard on each side. It's absolutely spectacular. I'm so excited I can hardly stand it.

I run down the flight of stairs which takes me to the edge of a highway. I suddenly notice I'm holding a package which must reach its destination "overnight." Across the bustling highway is a Federal Express office among a row of business shops. I dart across the highway and inadvertently enter the wrong shop. Approaching a young man and woman standing behind a desk, I try to explain my predicament to the woman. Laughing about it, I tell her that once I crossed the highway, I must have ended up in *The Twilight Zone*. She smiles and tells me the same thing happens to her regularly.

The young man offers to help me look for a Federal Express office. Because he has no phone book, he tells me I must first locate one for him. Concerned this will take me on another wild goose chase, I suddenly remember having seen a phone book in the pile of debris where I ran into the derelict. I dash back to the stairway and ransack the pile of debris. Discovering an old, beat-up phone book, I carry it back to the shop. The man and woman tell me it will take them awhile to look through it. I decide to browse around the area while waiting.

As I meander about, I come upon a store window filled with children's toys. I touch the window and discover I can reach right through the glass. Displayed on three small tables is a tea set, a dollhouse and a blue and white checkerboard cake made of tiny wooden blocks. Captivated, I begin to play with the blocks and tea set. As time passes, I forget completely about the package and the man and woman looking through the phone book. I'm totally absorbed in a world of play, fascinated by the feelings I'm experiencing as I work the blocks to build the cake and arrange the teacups this way and that.

November 10 Interception Of A Conversation With Dionysus

"There's a dreadful voraciousness stalking us within our own bodies," I explain, intensely absorbed in what I'm feeling. "It wrestles us down inside of it and wants to devour us. But what is it really, Dionysus? Who devours? Don't we do the devouring? We turn to the world and ready our jaws, rub our stomachs as if contemplating a monumental meal. It's a hideous appetite, very Plutonian. It's the grotesque stump I encountered months ago in a meditation—the thing that told me it was going to crush my bones between its jaws, swallow me and shit me out the other end. And I was naive enough to ask if this would hurt."

I shake my head in disbelief.

"I've been mystified by this voraciousness all my life. I fear it more than anything, yet when it takes hold of my body and shakes it like a flimsy cage, I feel incredibly alive. I want desperately to sing, dance and write poetry. It seems to awaken a frenzy, a death dance that makes me want to leap into the fire and be consumed by the Dread inside myself—Lord Pluto who will 'take her breath, possess her hair to wrap his loins.' Just look at those metaphors in my poem, 'Saint Bridget's Lamentation.'"

I pull a copy of the poem out of my pocket, unfold it and hand it to Dionysus. As he reads it in silence, I imagine that I'm reciting the poem out loud.

SAINT BRIDGET'S LAMENTATION

perhaps she is Persephone

awaiting envelopment
in earth's musculature
Lord Pluto who will

take her breath
possess her hair
to wrap his loins

she is the garment of glory

she believes light
will heal the grasses

through banishment
her face an invocation
set beside
a long sea

still she cannot
she does not
promise

he will come like a snake
in an orchard of worms

with thick hands
search her throat
squeeze a pulsing light until it
swells in her mouth

in this way he
enjoys destruction
imminent ecstasy
when death is sultry

he will
suck her eyes
steal her eggs
he learns
through devouring

as his muse she
cannot cry out

she believes light
will heal the grasses

Dionysus slowly folds up the poem and hands it back to me.

"The whole thing is a seduction, an orgiastic rite," I continue, sandwiching the poem between my palms.

"And Persephone is the 'garment of glory,' believing light will heal the grasses?" Dionysus asks, raising an inquisitive brow at me.

Feeling self-conscious, I peer into the grass.

"Well, it seems Persephone must give up something in exchange."

"In exchange for what?" Dionysus asks.

"In exchange for her own life, I suppose. But whatever she does, she won't relinquish her vision. That Lord Pluto can't have.

He can rape her, mutilate her, imprison her, but he'll never get her light."

I push my feet out into the grass and slowly wiggle my toes back and forth.

"So," I continue, "he doesn't really conquer her after all. He stays a sorry son of a bitch stuck inside his own ravenous loop, railing inside his own darkness. She knows this, too. That's why she 'cannot, does not promise.' She doesn't have to."

A flush of heat is stealing up my cheeks. I feel I've revealed myself too deeply. I look up at Dionysus. His eyes seem to probe into the very core of my being. A strange, almost fierce light dances inside of them. I avert my gaze to the stream. It is gray. Overhead, a thick blanket of clouds hangs heavily over the woods. Everything seems dreadfully still. I wonder if there will be a storm.

"Soon you must return to Pan," Dionysus says quietly.

His words strike a chord of fear in my chest. My thoughts begin to whirl and everything becomes a blur.

"I don't think I can do that. I don't think I can... "

"Complete what you started?"

"What did I start? All I did was stumble into this place one morning. This whole drama was well into its fifth act."

I stare into my lap and wonder why I said, "fifth." Pan's face looms in my mind.

"I can't do it, Dionysus. I've thought it over for months. I don't get unhinged that way."

"You do get unhinged that way. This is what you fear."

Something is gnawing at the back of my mind. I try to hunt it down, get a fix on it. I reflect on what I said about Lord Pluto, how I called him a "sorry son of a bitch." The phrase just slipped out—even surprised me. Bothered by it, I mentally replay the statement, "He stays a sorry son of a bitch stuck inside his own ravenous loop, railing inside his own darkness. She knows this, too. That's why she 'cannot, does not promise.' She doesn't have to."

I clasp my hands over my mouth. I can't believe what a blind, pompous statement this is and what it says about me. I wonder if Dionysus caught it. I look over at him. How naked I feel in his gaze. I lower my eyes.

"My God, Dionysus, how could you let me get away with that?" I whisper, blinking back a wave of remorse.

I close my eyes against voices of self-reproach, but it does no good. An overwhelming feeling of shame blackens the screen of my mind.

"Pride. That's what it is," I confess sadly. "The ultimate blindness. The cold, superior, impenetrable heart. My God, that's how I see X! Pitiless. No hands extended to the suffering. Even enjoying it."

My remorse is filled with fear. Feeling sick to my stomach, I start rocking back and forth.

"If Lord Pluto is a son of a bitch, then she's the bitch," I continue quietly. "Look how it's set up: she's walled herself up inside the safe fortress of her own virtue, transfixed by her own light. Yes, the delicate flower, the little lamb of God. Her suffering is her soul's orgasm, a stainless rapture heightened by the dark hands that violate her. Her light somehow redeems her own hunger, washes it clean. This is where her pride shines best, the reason she does not promise, does not accept her collusion with Lord Pluto. She doesn't have to, for she's made him the serpent writhing beneath her foot so that she, eyes lifted heavenward, can revel in the sanctified glory of her union with God."

Tears sting my eyes. As I hug my ribcage, my arms feel like tight bandages.

"What's happened to me?" I ask, my voice shaking with alarm. "Why do I think this way? Where does it come from?"

I look up at Dionysus. He's staring across the stream at something in the distance. I rub my eyes and look in the direction he is gazing. The motionless figure has returned and stands on a slope opposite the stream. The figure is that of a man wearing a deep-colored tunic the shade of rust or blood. He looks like a biblical figure: David, Solomon, maybe even Jesus.

"Who is it?" I ask.

Dionysus doesn't move his gaze from the hill.

"You must go and find out, Melina."

My mind begins to reel.

"Now?"

Dionysus gazes at me. His face is very solemn. He doesn't answer. I look again across the stream and study the figure more carefully. My heart is beginning to race.

"Tell me, Dionysus! Who is it?"

My body is very tense. I'm afraid and becoming even more afraid of my fear. Dionysus quietly stands up. His manner is somber. As I look up at his face, cool droplets of rain burst against my eyelashes. I'm confused by what I see in his eyes, a look of pain and sadness. As I gaze more deeply into this sadness, I seem to be falling inside of it. For a moment I feel like a weightless moth fluttering inside the hollow of a dead log. Wherever it leads feels like a haunting journey—a journey of shadows. Yet behind or beyond the darkness I sense a flickering light, a fire. My soul reaches for this fire as though leaning out to touch a star. The star grows brighter, becomes a ball of flames whirling fiercely as it falls rapidly toward earth. I catch my breath and turn away, burying my face in my arms.

I close my eyes, shutting out the look, the shadows, the figure on the hill, everything but the rain. Its gentle cadence in the trees is very soothing. I breathe deeply and listen. The world seems hushed, lulled to a dreamy stillness by the rhythmic murmur. I want to sleep, to curl up inside the rain's sure hands and allow its nimble fingers to tap along my flesh. My body relaxes. Even with my eyes closed, I can see the rain: rain everywhere, bathing the trees, the smooth dark stones, pushing me down into the soft yielding earth. Somewhere a voice whispers, "Do not fall asleep.

Get up. Do not fall asleep," but already my eyes are heavy with the shapes of other things... trees—long dark tunnels of prayer reaching skyward, forming a grotto of stillness...

I'm standing in a grotto of trees, marveling at their height, their stateliness. A feeling of familiarity swells in my body—I've been here before... I've seen all this before. I gaze down at my arms and legs and see that I'm naked. I turn to survey my surroundings. As I do this, a wonderful sensation of floating or moving slowly through water floods my limbs. I raise my arms and wave them to and fro. They seem weightless. Filled with elation, I feel as if I could rise like a leaf in the wind. I extend my arms and reach into the air. I realize I'm trying to walk and seem to need my arms to help me move. My legs rise off the ground with a delicious buoyancy.

I see that I'm moving sideways toward a tree, as though the tree were drawing me toward it. The movement is very slow but deliberate, as if willed by a mind other than my own. My awareness of this seems to press against my brain, shaping and narrowing my focus. My peripheral vision hovers about me like one long-held breath. My body glides slowly through the breath like a moving reflection in a great eye that watches without blinking.

I'm nearing the tree and reach for its trunk to steady myself. I look around. There's something here, a presence. As I gaze into the dark underbrush, my eyes feel very large. I sense small animals stirring, aware of me. Energy expands in my cells and my flesh bristles with invisible feelers. Someone is here, very near. I instinctively turn my face in its direction and breathe the air. A scent fills my stomach and rises in my throat. My heartbeat accelerates. I want to go toward it.

Something hums at the base of my spine, guiding me to the right. I peer across several yards of clearing at an immense tree with large thick roots knotted around the base. Its trunk and lower branches are heavily draped in ivy. Someone is standing motionless beside it. Startled, I slow my movement but can't avert my gaze. I try to make out a face, but it's too concealed in shadow. Feelings of self-preservation flood my chest, compelling me backwards, away. Raising my arms like wings, I try to move in reverse. My arms feel strangely long and willowy. I gaze down at my legs and try to make them rise but they no longer look like my legs; they're very long and bronze-colored. I keep staring at them, trying to comprehend who I am. I attempt to remember, as if I once knew. I peer once more across the clearing at the tree. My head feels elongated, somehow narrower, and I seem to be seeing from the very top of my head.

The figure stirs and the face comes more clearly into view. It glistens. The sound of rainfall swells in my ears, intensifying my focus. Energy shifts in my spine and I begin to glide toward the figure. My eyes widen as I draw closer. It is Dionysus. The suddenness of recognition halts my body as I stare at him. His hair falls in matted tendrils around his face, half of which is bathed in shadow. His eyes appear large and dark and seem to peer out from a cavernous depth. For a moment I think I'm staring into the eyes of an animal. Feeling a wave of fear, I try to remember where I've seen the look before. Something begins to stir in both my breasts. The sensation intensifies and my nipples rise and stiffen. I feel my body weaken as though the life force were being pulled from my breasts. My breathing becomes erratic. It seems at any moment I'm going to collapse inside my own body.

"Give me your hand," Dionysus instructs me, but his lips do not move.

Transfixed, I stare into his eyes.

"Give me your hand," he repeats.

I extend my right hand. He takes it and draws me closer, then places my hand over his left breast. I hold my breath. He strokes my shoulders, reaches up behind my neck and pulls my head back. Energy bursts inside my head as the trees and sky begin to whirl. I close my eyes, feeling his breath on my face. The warmth fills my nostrils, mixes with my own breath. He moves his hand to the underside of my jaw and urges my mouth open. Soft low moans escape my throat. He brings his mouth close to mine and breathes. I clutch his wrist, inhale, nearly gasp, exhale. He draws my breath deeply into his body, holds it, then exhales slowly into my nostrils and the hollow of my throat. My chest rises. Heat is building, expanding in my body. I grope for his shoulder. My hand is moist, slippery.

He lays me back upon the grass and straddles my body between his knees. A mounting force pushes at my temples as if struggling to break free of my skull. I can't think, I can't remember, I can only hear my name on his lips as he brushes his face over my neck and hair.

"What is your desire?" he whispers.

Jagged light streaks up my spine and crackles in my skull. Grasping his shoulders, I feel as if the earth were tilting under my body. I try to call out, but I can't activate my voice. Leaning over me, he takes my hand and places it over his left breast. I close my eyes. The naked torso of a man with outstretched arms appears in my mind: he is showing me a white heart which hangs outside his body. He wants me to touch it. I begin to tremble.

Dionysus brings his upper body close to my face. Reaching behind my neck, he lifts my head to his breast. I falter, then feel his intention urging my eyes open, awakening my mouth. I slowly brush my lips against his nipple, circling it softly. I do not breathe. His hand grips the back of my neck more firmly. My mouth widens. I take his nipple between my lips and begin to suck. A strange taste fills my mouth. I hesitate, pull away. A sweetness lingers on my tongue and clings to the roof of my mouth. I swallow. A strong musk rises through my nasal passages. Energy jerks wildly between my eyes and my mind whirls with images: moist green moss and ruddy soil, coursing woodland streams and massive trees thick with pungent leaves.

The trees move closer into my perceptual field, arresting my vision. One large bough in particular stands out distinctly from the others. It seems so close that I can touch it. I reach out and gingerly stroke one of the leaves, then break it off and smell it. Its spicy fragrance rushes up my nose. My body begins to tingle and instantly I find myself floating high above a meadow of tall lush grass. Lounging in the meadow are several naked women wearing garlands of wildflowers. I stare at them caressing the air and themselves, intoxicated by the perfume of the earth and trees. Without warning, a force beyond my volition impels me toward a fair-skinned woman with strawberry-colored hair. Her arms are draped loosely around the neck of a large animal, whose soft limpid eyes behold her lovingly. I can't stop the movement and realize I'm going to enter her body. My spine stiffens, then relaxes. I ease quietly into her body like water seeping under the crack of a door. She doesn't notice me.

I look through her eyes into the face of an ass. I'm stroking his head playfully and delighting in the sound of my own laughter, the buoyancy of my naked breasts. A deep life stirs within my heart and seems to be pouring out through my eyes, breasts and hands, flooding me with happiness. I'm sharing this with the animal. I feel very tender toward him, as though I know him intimately. I sense that I'm bonded to him through blood ties: we are brother-sister, father-mother, daughter-son. He watches over me and I over him. It is our duty and our joy, and the source of our contentment.

Elation rises in my body and I feel as light as a spring cloud. I'm talking sweetly to the ass, saying things I can't understand. He watches me with his large eyes in which I can see my reflection: how lovely is this woman with the strawberry-colored hair, her childlike smile and wildflowers glowing in his dark eyes. I throw my arms around him and hug him tightly.

CHAPTER 9

TOUCHING THE WOUND

January 12 Session

I close my eyes and see that I'm sitting in the woods near the stream with my arms draped casually around my knees. The air and sky is sparkling clear. Breathing deeply, I drink in the colors and textures of my surroundings. Everything appears fresh and new, as if scrubbed clean by a vigorous rain. A short distance away, Dionysus is sitting quietly on a rock, gazing at the stream. Before him, a large dragonfly flits from one imperceptible thing to the next over the gleaming water. As I rest my gaze on his tranquil form, he slowly turns his head in my direction and smiles at me. At once I'm seized by a sensation of falling backwards into my chest cavity as though it were an elevator shaft. As my perceptual field rapidly contracts, I feel as if I'm shrinking to the size of a child.

At first I feel slightly giddy. My back tingles and I want to shake my legs and wiggle my toes. Instead, I internalize these reflexes and experience a "ballooning" emotional feeling which I can also see as a luminous silver sphere or ball expanding from the center of my body, forming a translucent aura around me. It sparkles like a silver Christmas ornament. I gaze at Dionysus and don't know what to do with myself, as I'm becoming highly energized and want to jump up and run around.

Suddenly a vivid scene from my childhood appears in my mind's eye: an old geezer with disheveled white hair and bristly whiskers is meandering up my family's driveway in a huge truck with a large water tank attached. His name is Mr Trabbish. He spits tobacco and smells strange.

I'm very young, four or five years old. Mr Trabbish climbs out of the truck, spits a wad of brown ooze across the pavement and unwinds a long hose to fill our cistern in front of the house. Bursting with curiosity, I pester him with silly questions about everything he's doing, as well as anything else I can possibly think of. I'm especially interested to know if he has any children. He says he doesn't and would like to take me home to live with him and his wife. I blush, knowing he's just being a nice old man. I play along and tell him someday I'd like to go home with him to be his little girl. Nearby in the front yard, my mother is taking laundry down from the clothesline and spies me pawing all over Mr Trabbish, making a nuisance of myself. She says nothing.

Mr Trabbish finishes filling the cistern and wrestles the python-like hose back onto the truck. He then asks me if this is the day I'd like to go home with him. I tell him yes, I would love to go; of course, I'm playing pretend—something I'm so good at. Delighted, he yells something to my mother about putting me in his truck and taking me home with him. A curious look takes hold of my mother's face as she studies me.

"Go ahead and take her with you," she says. "We won't miss her."

Something in my stomach collapses to the very soles of my feet. I stare at my mother in disbelief, then presume she must be playing along with us—something I've never known her to do before.

Mr Trabbish whisks me off the ground and starts heading for the big black truck. I'm staring at my mother and older brother, Tony, who are both smiling at me and enjoying the scene. I'm anticipating that Mr Trabbish will simply let me sit in his truck for a minute, then the whole pretense will be over and done with. He hoists me up into the cab, slams the door and walks around to the driver's side. I feel as if I'm going to throw up, but I sit quietly and try to smile—I'm becoming frightened of him and don't know what he'll do.

He's now behind the huge steering wheel, saying something to me through a cackling laugh. I tell him I want to get out now.

"Your mother said I could take you home with me!" he exclaims, turning the key in the ignition.

The engine roars so loudly, I fear the truck might explode. I pull on the door handle to get out, but I can't budge it. Seized with a terrible fright, I start to scream. Mr Trabbish is still laughing as he slowly maneuvers the big truck down the driveway. Crying loudly, I bang on the back of the cab, hysterically calling my mother. I push my head out the window and see her and my brother standing in front of the house, smiling and waving as they grow more and more distant.

Something snaps in my brain. Writhing all over the seat, I kick the dashboard and beat on the door with my fists in sheer terror. I think I'll never see my brothers again, my mother and father, my home. I think I'll never know how to find them, that I'll be trapped for the rest of my life inside Mr Trabbish's house. Razor sharp pain stabs at my throat as I scream shrilly, "Let me out! Let me out!"

Suddenly Mr Trabbish stops the truck. He climbs out and walks over to my door. As he opens it, I dive out of the cab, then run as if a thousand bats were chasing me up the steep hill toward the house. Making a beeline for my mother, I throw my arms around her legs and cling to them for dear life, sobbing and shaking.

"That taught you a lesson, didn't it?" she states matter-of-factly.

I'm so relieved to be back home that nothing else in the world matters, nothing at all.

I'm gazing out at the stream as I recall this episode. The big silver ball in which I'm enclosed is now taking on the appearance of a large teardrop. Something sinks inside my chest. I recognize it as sadness.

"I would never do that to a kid," I murmur to myself.

I gaze over at Dionysus. He's watching me quietly. Already I can feel old anger surging from the depths of this sadness, threatening to explode and wreck everything in sight. For a moment I feel horribly destructive. I imagine chopping down trees and hurling huge boulders into the stream, screaming my lungs out in a burst of rage. Instead I sit there, my hands clasped tightly around my knees.

"I just want to say something for the record," I announce, my voice even and controlled.

I pause and stare into the grass, drawing a deep breath.

"Being a kid can really suck."

I look challengingly at Dionysus and find his placid demeanor unbearable. As I continue staring at him, I can feel my blood pressure rising. I jump up and walk to the edge of the stream. The harsh glare on the water is blinding.

"And another thing," I continue, whirling around to face Dionysus. "I don't care what wonderful spiritual wisdom, revelations and transformations come wrapped in the 'childhood tyranny' package—I'm not going through that again, do you hear?"

I'm wagging my finger at him, see myself doing this and hastily drop my hand to my side. I start pacing furiously by the edge of the stream. My face is hot and my eyes feel buggy and popped-out.

"I don't care what kind of miserable karma I've incurred, if there is such a thing as reincarnation, I'll be damned if I tolerate another victimized childhood. I'd rather die a million deaths, be flayed, be burnt at the stake first. Do you hear?"

Tears are beginning to gather behind my eyes, creating pressure. I suck them back, grab a stick from the ground and start banging it against the palm of my hand.

"Okay, so whether I like it or not, the scar is now mine and I have to deal with it—never mind that justice and fairness were completely out to lunch throughout my early life. But first I'd like to know, if it pleases the oh so benevolent court… "

I make a grand gesture to the sky as if some divine tribunal in a celestial realm were listening.

"Why did I have a childhood like that? Did I deserve that? Why did I have an unfeeling mother who was hard, strict, demanding and punishing?"

I pace around some more, then strike a tree with the stick.

"Ha! I'm describing X, aren't I? The thing that lives in me, my mom 30 years ago. Christ, how twisted up. So, did I inherit this darkness or what? Is that all we are, the mutant offspring of our parents' crimes? Where are 'we' in all of this parental mess? Where is the 'I'? Oh please, don't even bother. I know what you're going to tell me."

I wave my hand dramatically at him as if to ward off a horde of flies.

"You're going to tell me there is no 'I,' right? Of course! Just another deluded invention—a crutch, an illusion."

I hurl the stick far out over the stream and watch it fall into the water. I feel poisoned. The hate inside of me is eating me up. I know it well. It always comes in the same ghastly form: cynicism. I stare into the water and suddenly feel exhausted.

"You know," I continue in a faraway voice, "I had a dream last night about a young woman back in the 1950s in her *Leave It To Beaver* kitchen. Newly married, she's wearing one of those ridiculous-looking, frilly white aprons—the kind you have to iron."

I snort in disgust and look over at Dionysus. Gazing at me with his chin propped in his hand, he seems to be listening carefully to my every word. His eyes are very steady and unbelievably green.

"Anyway, she's slaving away in the kitchen, knocking herself out to prepare some million course dinner for her husband who is sitting casually at the table, absentmindedly thumbing through a magazine. By and by she drops something, or klutzes her way through the kitchen and trips over a crack in the linoleum. Her husband takes this opportunity to criticize her. She accepts his crap like a stalwart martyr and bends over backward in her attempts to please him and make amends. At this point in the dream, I'm so angry at her passivity that I go up to her and whisper in her ear, 'Why don't you just tell him to drop dead!' I don't remember the rest."

"Melina."

"What?"

"Why don't you come and sit down."

Sighing, I walk over to Dionysus and look around for a proper place to sit. As I do this, I begin to feel irritable. I realize I don't want to sit down; I don't want to do what he says. I stall.

"Here," Dionysus offers, pointing to a spot on the grass opposite him.

I want to complain, but sit down. I cross my legs and fold my hands in my lap. I realize I'm getting anal and I don't like it.

"Look, Dionysus, before you say anything, I already know X represents a negative masculine dimension of myself, a psychic anomaly my mother was inflicted with also. Maybe X began to crystallize in my psyche partially as a compensation for emotional woundedness—my vulnerability and over-sensitivity in the feeling realm. Maybe he crystallized in a dual role to play cold and hard to my openness and softness, providing a protective layer between me and my feminine side, while also judging and punishing me for the weaknesses of my feminine side, as my mother did not only to herself, but to me."

I take a deep breath, anticipating Dionysus' response.

"Melina, lie down."

I stare at him for a moment, then lie down. The cool grass relaxes me instantly. I gaze up at the sky and treetops. Their visual impact, the calming greens and blues, soothes my overwrought mind.

"Close your eyes, Melina. You are going on a journey."

"Where am I going?" I ask wearily.

"You are going to visit the woman in the chamber of the

Feminine."

"Down in my womb?"

"Yes."

I close my eyes. I don't want to visit the woman, but I know I must.

"How will I get there, Dionysus?"

"The same way as before."

"Do you mean I must get small?"

"Yes."

I take a deep breath and exhale slowly. Focusing on a point between my eyes, I realize it is very easy to get small. Drifting into a white plane of nothingness, I think, "When one gets small, he falls right away. He falls through the universe into his own belly. I must get small and repeat the fall... the fall... the Fall."

January 21 A Dream

I dream that I'm with my former marketing supervisor at the company where I was once employed. She's very excited about showing me what new projects are being launched in the department and is interested to know what I think. A feeling of great activity permeates the dream as we greet other employees and share ideas about the creative enterprises in which they're involved.

At one point in the dream, I'm browsing through a magazine of high-color publicity photos when suddenly the magazine turns into my high school annual. I stare at a photo taken of me and three other girls clowning around in a classroom when I was in the ninth grade. Because the picture is dopey-looking, I examine it closely to make sure it's me I'm seeing. I don't remember ever having seen this photo in my high school annual.

The dream shifts and I find myself in the kitchen of the home of my best friend from junior high school. Surrounded by other old girlfriends, I'm sitting next to Phyllis at the kitchen table, gabbing away and feeling the wonderful sense of closeness and camaraderie we used to share.

The dream shifts and I'm seated at a long table next to my best friend from the first grade, Kathy Dugan. I'm overjoyed to be with her after all these years. On the opposite side of the room is another table at which is seated a young academic-looking man who is asking me questions in a formal, business-like manner. I take my time to answer him as thoroughly and intelligently as I can. After responding to one of his questions, a slightly perturbed look crosses his face.

Addressing himself to Kathy, he remarks, "I keep forgetting you two were once deeply associated."

After hearing this statement, I realize Kathy and I are being screened to see how compatible we are for a joint working venture. Perplexed by his remark, I turn to Kathy and place my left arm snugly around her waist.

"I don't understand what he means!" I whisper in her ear.

Kathy leans close to me and says, "It's your answers, Melina. They're too tight and neatly ordered. You preface too much. There's not enough feeling."

She then gives me an example of this by repeating back to me one of my answers. I'm somewhat embarrassed about the way I'm being perceived. I don't want to be seen as a person who is all head and no heart.

January 22 A Dream

I dream that I'm holding my grandmother in my arms. She has just died and I'm staring into her face in disbelief. Overcome with grief, I lay her down on the ground and, still holding her tightly, weep inconsolably.

Personal Notes

After recording this dream, I sit quietly. I notice my chest feels heavy and constricted, as though I were coming down with a cold. I wonder if the upper respiratory tightness is somehow linked to my emotions. This thought leads me deep into my past. Painful memories rise to the surface of my awareness and I start to cry. I then realize I'm holding all my pain around my heart. I know I must find a way to release the energy safely. I keep crying and some of the pressure lifts.

I'm shocked that I can reexperience old pain in such an immediate way. I resolve that my life's work must center around embracing the wounds of the soul; that only through acceptance, understanding and compassion can I touch the deep love which is pushing with such urgency to be freed. I know it is this extraordinary grace which can restore faith, mend hearts and cradle souls in an enduring peace.

January 28 A Dream

I dream that I'm in a large unfamiliar house with Ted and my two children. Because the house has many rooms and floors, I'm trying to determine in which of the rooms my children will sleep. A disorganized feeling pervades the dream, urging me to provide a sense of order and security for myself and my family. Unable to find rooms for my children on the floor where I'll be sleeping, I must bed them down a great distance away. I finally accomplish this and retire to my bedroom.

Ted is already in bed when I join him and fall asleep. Some time later, something jars me awake. I jump out of bed and sense an extraordinarily evil presence in the room. Realizing this presence is all throughout the house, I grow terrified for my children's safety. I navigate my way to my daughter's room with great difficulty, for the presence is so thick around me that it slows my movements. Finding my daughter, I'm relieved to see she is unharmed.

Clutching her small hand, I leave the room and walk down the dark hallway. The house is so big that I've forgotten where I put my son. It seems I must find him by groping my way through many rooms and hallways on various floors. Suddenly I remember that he's sleeping on the basement level of the house. I open a door that leads down to the basement and slowly descend a staircase with my daughter. At once the vile presence becomes more powerful. Hideous sounds from poltergeist activities issue from somewhere deep in the basement. I know the presence has zeroed in on my son.

I approach his dimly lit room, terrified at what I may find. As awful voices grow loud in the room, I rush in and see my baby in a levitating position above his bed. Invisible forces are tilting him this way and that like a helpless puppet. He doesn't cry, having no idea what is happening to him. Filled with an unbearable fright and repulsion, I know I must physically invade the evil energy field around my son which is holding him captive. I also know if I do this, I may unwittingly excite the evil presence and incur some terrible violence to him and myself.

I firmly take hold of my son, pull him close to my body and run out of the room, dragging my daughter behind me. Utterly terrified, I start running up the staircase. Suddenly I'm halted by a strong feeling that we must loudly recite The Lord's Prayer before leaving the basement. We join together, face the room from which we've just fled and recite The Lord's Prayer as loud as we can.

As I'm saying this prayer, I slowly awaken from the dream. Once fully awake, I feel both sickened and frightened. I try to make myself stay awake so I can shake the feelings and dream images from my mind. It is 4:30 a.m.

February 13 A Dream

I dream that I'm standing in the bedchamber of a large 19th century house. It is nighttime and the room is dimly lit; everything is gray, muted-looking. I'm standing beside an old, heavy Victorian double bed. Lying in the bed on the left side is an older, black-haired woman who looks like a character right out of a Charles Dickens novel. She is lying there looking at me. I notice the covers on the vacant half of the bed are pulled down as if in preparation for someone to join her. I keep staring at the white sheets, feeling she wants me to lie alongside her. I don't want to do this, for she is eerie-looking and I'm filled with a sense of unease.

As I continue gazing at the woman, I feel she is infirmed and may even be on her deathbed. All at once I see another woman lying in the vacant spot on the bed next to her. I keep straining to identify this other woman, but the scene keeps blurring. The scene clears and the right side of the bed is vacant again. I'm now very confused and feel a mounting pressure at my temples.

Suddenly I sense a presence to my left. The presence is invisible, yet I know it is my real-life grandmother who has recently passed away. She's talking to me, but I can't make out what she is saying. It seems she wants me to lie down in the bed next to the strange woman with black hair. A feeling of dread fills my stomach and I awaken from the dream.

Upon Awakening From The Dream: A Meditation

The female force is cool like water. It moves in concentric circles and takes its time. It is gentle but pervasive. When you journey inside of it, your ego gets lost.

Feminine energy goes "through" and "under." It does not rise. It revels in hiddenness, quiescence. It is the bottom of the lake, the dark backdrop of an iridescent surface upon which reflection is cast.

The female force yields, stretches, accommodates. It also swallows; takes everything into itself, births nothingness into life and consumes it in the end through death.

May 5 A Dream

I dream that I'm on a journey with my real-life close friend, Karen. Having just checked in our luggage at an oceanside hotel, we're standing together on the beach, looking out over the ocean.

It is nightfall and we can just barely make things out. Because of the absence of adequate light, the ocean looks nearly black. Watching it quietly, I'm struck by its immensity and power as it spills its dark waves to the shore.

Suddenly the entire ocean begins to swell, rising slowly and soundlessly like a great wall of blackness. My first instinct is to run. I make a beeline for the hotel with Karen following closely behind. More panicked than she is, I can think of nothing else but getting the hell "up" off the ground, knowing it is the only way I'll be safe. Karen's room is on the first floor of the hotel. I leave her to her own fate as I dash up several flights of stairs to the third floor where my room is located. Once inside, I lock the door and feel safe, grateful I got the room on the "upper level."

The phone rings and I pick it up. It's Karen. In a perfectly casual voice, she asks me to come down to her room so we can discuss our evening plans together. Completely disoriented, I can't comprehend how she can be so composed and oblivious to the impending danger outside. I agree to come down. My attitude and manner is very hurried, for I don't want to stay long. Estimating it will be awhile before the ocean hits the hotel, I gamble that I can safely spare a few minutes.

I enter Karen's room a nervous wreck. Dressed to the hilt in sparkling evening wear, she's casually putting on her earrings and is in a very pleasant, chatty mood. I stare out the window of her room and gulp—the great wall of water is only a foot or so away from the window and is slowly advancing. I step away from the window as the water presses against the windowpane. I'm worried the glass won't be able to hold all that pressure, but it does. I look down beneath the window where the wall meets the floor and see that water is seeping in along the baseboard. The carpet is getting soaked. Pointing to it, I babble in a panic to Karen, but she's still not impressed. I run like hell out of the room and up to the third floor.

I jump in bed, throw the covers over my head and try to make myself go to sleep. I desperately want to lose consciousness and figure this is the only way I can achieve oblivion. The phone rings. It is Karen. She's concerned as to why I ran out of her room the way I did, and wasn't I going to come down and join her for dinner in the hotel dining room like we planned? I suddenly feel very badly for having abandoned her. Not wanting to hurt her feelings, I tell her I'll come down to dinner, even though it's the last thing in the world I want to do.

I hang up the phone and walk to the window. Already it's too late for me—even at this height, the wall of water is pushing against the windowpane. As I stare helplessly at it, I realize the building is now completely submerged in the depths of the ocean. I also realize the hotel is no longer a building, but an ocean liner. I can now feel a floating or swaying sensation in the floor of my room, as if the ship were being carried along in the ocean's undercurrents. A small feeling of relief accompanies this observation, although I'm perplexed as to how an ocean liner could survive being under water without sinking.

I go down to the dining room which is very large and filled with scores of passengers. A mood of restlessness and alertness pervades the room, as everyone is aware of our terribly vulnerable situation. Nevertheless, the emotional climate is one of diplomacy and cooperation as passengers attempt to make the best of our predicament, grateful for the safety of enclosure against the danger which completely surrounds us.

May 8 Session

I close my eyes and see that I'm sitting on top of a great hill which overlooks the sea. Everything dazzles and shines as though the earth were a mirror reflecting the sunlight. Gazing down at myself, I see that I'm wearing shorts and a loose, sleeveless blouse. My bare feet are surrounded by tiny blue flowers growing everywhere in the grass. I take a deep breath. The weather feels very Mediterranean. I look out over the hill to the sea below: a wash of turquoise and cobalt, capped by wisps of snow-white sea foam, fills my eyes.

As I listen to the sea, a feeling of quiet exaltation sweeps through my soul. I close my eyes and breathe the feeling deep into my heart. Slowly opening my eyes, I see that Dionysus is approaching to my right and is smiling at me. I watch his bare feet move soundlessly along the grass. He's wearing a long garment belted at the waist by a rope, from which hangs a string of prayer beads. I stare at his tunic and find that I'm very attracted to its homespun, soft-looking texture. I wonder how it feels. Dionysus seats himself relaxedly in the grass and crosses his legs. The afternoon sun blazes in the sky behind his head.

"Hi!" I cheerily greet him.

"Hello, Melina."

His gaze is warm and unabashedly direct. An intense emotion rushes through my chest and rises to my cheeks. Unprepared for it, I blush, then try to conceal it by looking away. Struck by how silly this is, I make myself look at him and try to compose myself.

"It's been a long time, Dionysus. Four months!"

I'm rocking back and forth, wiggling my toes. I'm nervous, but the feeling is not accompanied by a sense of anxiety. Highly energized, I feel like an overcharged battery or a Chinese firecracker ready to spin out.

"Yes, four months," Dionysus echoes.

Smiling, he continues gazing at me as if my insides were completely exposed. I start to fidget.

"Yes, well, quite frankly, after our last session together, I was scared to death to go on," I confess. "I know we're getting into some heavy stuff. I feel as weighty as a planet."

I place my hand over my stomach to demonstrate my meaning. Dionysus' smile remains unbroken as he studies me. Out of nowhere, I'm invaded by a disorienting feeling that I'm lying. It feels extremely uncomfortable.

"I wish you'd stop looking at me like that," I laugh. "Why

don't we just get on with it? I'm open!"

I gesture enthusiastically with my left hand. Again, the feeling that I'm lying gnaws at my insides. Suddenly I feel completely superficial, locked inside a persona that hides my being like a mask. As my sunny mood plummets, I stare into the grass.

"Melina, come here."

Looking up, I notice Dionysus is holding something in his hand. I scoot across the grass and sit crossed-legged opposite him. Gently positioning my right and left knees against his, I instantly feel more comfortable.

"I have brought you something," he discloses, leaning toward me.

Taking my left hand, Dionysus places a beautiful yellow apple squarely in my palm. As I gaze at its smooth skin and pale golden color, I have the most peculiar feeling I've seen the apple before. Its coolness in my hand fills my whole body with a renewed clarity and sense of well-being. I look directly into Dionysus' eyes.

"Do I really have to do this?" I ask softly.

"Yes."

I study the apple, tilting it back and forth in the sunlight.

"Shall I eat this?" I ask.

"You are to hold it in your left hand. It is the apple of Remembrance."

At first I think I hear him say, "It is the apple of Forgetfulness." I then hear "Remembrance." I don't know which it is.

"What?"

"You will know, Melina. Be patient."

As I gaze at the apple in my hand, an odd feeling is intensifying in my uterus. Even though I'm menstruating, the strange sensation in my pelvis feels unrelated to the symptoms of menses. My womb feels like a point of gravity which is pulling my energy into itself. I'm beginning to feel tired and want to lie down. My mouth is getting dry. Suddenly I don't feel very well.

"Lie down, Melina. Sleep. You must sleep now."

"Yes, I'm very tired."

I lie down in the grass on my back. Dionysus is sitting on my right, his body a shield against the sunlight. The shade on my face is soothing. The grass is soothing. Everything, soothing. I think of the apple in my hand. I'm losing the image of it in my mind's eye. Round. Round. Roundness moving up my arm and into my brain. My brain is round. Everything is swirling around. I'm inside a circle, a circle of light.

"Where are you, Melina?"

"Circle."

Spinning rapidly, the circle is beginning to make a sound as its radiance intensifies. The sound is growing much louder, many tones resonating together.

"Are you ready, Melina?"

I focus on the word, "ready." Suddenly, clarity. Everything is pitch black. Space and brilliant pinpoints of light. The sound ceases and I see that I'm poised in the void. My mind feels exceptionally alert as I look around. I realize I'm no longer breathing.

"Where are you going, Melina?"

I gaze into the pitch darkness before me. I'm aware that I'm using my mind to see.

"Into the void."

An electrical force is building at the base of my spine. My whole back-end rises as though it were being maneuvered by a huge invisible machine. My head and upper body begin to tilt at a slight downward angle. Suddenly, velocity; I'm moving rapidly through the void. As my mind penetrates the darkness, I'm aware that I'm looking for something. Yes, the disc... the disc! I pick up speed and see an image ahead. As it becomes more distinct, I realize I've located the disc. Exerting my will to slow down, I experience a strange feeling along my spine and legs of being attached to something long and elastic. A slight tugging sensation registers in my lower body as though something were pulling me back by a resilient line. My speed decreases sharply.

Suspended in utter silence, I watch the beings on the disc from a distance. The disc looks like an immense, ancient sundial suspended horizontally in the void. Its face is illuminated as though by the light of a heavenly body. The underside is completely immersed in shadow. Winged beings are descending upon it from a great height. Others are jumping off of its luminescent surface into the void All at once, a brilliant orange-red beam of light shoots out from the disc and slams into my chest over my left breast. My body reels in circles from the force as my mind crackles with an amazing alertness. A powerful energy is ballooning in my solar plexus. Dionysus' voice pierces the interior of my awareness.

"You are being asked to state your desire, Melina."

I focus quickly: my desire... my desire... what is my desire? My mind is completely blank.

"Do not seek it in your mind," Dionysus instructs me.

Where? Where? I focus on my body and try to feel what it wants. Body signals are coming too fast, too disorganized. I think of love. Yes, that's a good focal point—I desire to love. It doesn't feel right. No, it's something else. I try to remember. What is it? I must already know. I just can't remember. I look in my hand and concentrate fiercely on the apple of Remembrance... remember, remember. Yes! That is what I desire: I desire to remember. Gazing into the void, I focus all of my energy into projecting my intention at the disc.

"I desire to remember."

Instantly I'm propelled toward the disc at great speed. Reaching its rim, I stop about two feet from a winged being. I stare into his dark, saucer-like eyes and wait for something to happen. The being stares back at me and stands motionless. Dionysus' voice breaks the stillness.

"Melina, you must intone the sound of the Ring."

My courage is beginning to wane. Memories of nearly being strangled to death on my last journey to the disc race menacingly through my thoughts. An image of the blue light that emanated from my throat floods the screen of my mind, drawing my entire focus. What is the blue light?

I gaze at the disc and notice grooves or carved notches encircling its outer rim. I then observe what is happening: the disc is rotating very slowly in a counterclockwise direction. Before a being jumps off the disc, he stands at a specific point along the rim at a groove or notch. When he jumps off, a loud vibrational tone issues from the groove. Multiple tones resonate all at once, for there are many beings who descend from overhead, stand at seemingly appointed spots along the rim of the disc, then jump off.

"Dionysus, what are they doing?" I ask, gazing hypnotically at the beings' movements.

"They are maintaining the space-time continuum of the temporal planes."

Observing them closely, I try to conceive of the Keepers as forces operating within my psyche, each Keeper a dynamic of consciousness which, functioning collectively, gives rise to my awareness of space-time dimensionality. The concept is much too large for me. Disoriented, I stare again into the being's enormous eyes. I'm beginning to feel fear.

"I desire to remember," I project fiercely.

The winged being keeps staring at me. I open my mouth and try to intone the sound of the Ring in the void. As strange noises rise from my throat, I feel a powerful urge to find the tone that is blue. I can see this color clearly in my mind. It is mantle blue—the color of Our Lady's cloak, the Lady Mary from heaven. A sound swells from somewhere deep within my skull. I try to intone it, but I can hardly hear my voice. Energy begins to swell in my stomach. I don't know how I know this because I can't feel my stomach. It seems my stomach is in my mind.

"Melina, use the force within your solar plexus."

I drop my awareness into my stomach. This is difficult because I must rely on memory to "feel" or locate my body as though it were an idea suspended outside the realm of form. I can't sense my own gravity. I have no frame of reference but my memory.

The phone in my office rings loudly. Startled, I pull out of the session.

July 7 A Dream

I dream that I'm standing in a field at the edge of a wood. Nearby is a small stream. As I look around, it's clear I'm in another time in history, a medieval period. Every detail of my surroundings is extraordinarily distinct, particularly the warm brilliance and slant of the sunlight as it clarifies grass and foliage, releasing the earth's pungent fragrances. By this, the whirring of insects in the trees and the dryness of the field, I know it's summertime.

I see that I'm standing with Francis Bernardone of Assisi. Wearing a plain brown robe which looks very worn, he is a small, slightly built man with a slender bearded face and nut-brown hair. His overall bearing is one of poetic sensitivity, underscored by an ascetic, if not devotional, sensibility. We've been talking together, but I now can't remember what we've said. Men on horses are advancing through the woods, heading in our direction. I know they are warlike and mean to do us harm. I close my eyes and receive a clear mental impression of them boldly killing Franciscan friars by piercing them with long heavy lances. I look at Francis' hands and see that he has not yet received the stigmata. For some reason I think this makes him even more vulnerable to cruelty and senseless mutilation. I'm filled with a sense of danger and know we must run.

I look around and see what appears to be a high ruin on the side of a nearby hill. An arched tunnel made of old stones leads through the hill. I start running toward it, urging Francis to do the same. He follows but doesn't keep up with my pace, and I must keep stopping to wait for him. I can now see the men approaching on horses. They've spotted us and are galloping toward us. All at once I find myself inside of Francis' body. His physical form is difficult to operate in a hurried manner, for his disposition doesn't lend itself to the raw urges of self-preservation as does mine.

Still inside Francis' body, I finally enter the tunnel. It is dark and cool. I'm trying to use my mind to maneuver him along the side of the tunnel, his back to the wall, and out of the way of horsemen who will thunder into the tunnel at any moment. We move slowly along the tunnel wall, feeling our way with our hands. The wall curves at a sharp left, revealing a smaller tunnel which detours off the main one. I feel that Francis is drawn by wherever it leads, less to escape danger than to fulfill some purpose. We enter the smaller tunnel. At the back of the tunnel is a grotto fashioned naturally of large rocks. In the center of the grotto is a beautiful waterfall. I feel that Francis wishes to stand in the waterfall and pray.

Suddenly I see that I've departed from his body. Myself once more, I watch Francis climb over the large stones. As he stands under the waterfall with his eyes raised to heaven, I know he has found union and peace with God. I also realize this union is our only true protection and that joining his soul to God is all that has ever mattered to him. As I watch him, I'm filled with a sense of awe and reverence. Francis looks in my direction, his eyes entreating me to join him in the waterfall.

I climb the stones and enter the waterfall. We hold each other. Overwhelmed with tenderness, I feel as if bandages around my heart were loosening and dissolving. Every fiber of my being begins to burn with love for Francis. It grows all consuming. Unable to bear the intrusion of our clothes as we hold each other, I long to be naked with him. Francis looks at me with an expression of sadness, as if to say he can't join with me in flesh, but only in "soul." Filled with grief, I struggle with feelings of shame for my own need.

I suddenly find myself standing alongside the grotto, beholding an ethereal radiance emanating from Francis' body. In that moment, I know he has been cleansed by the waters and transformed by the Holy Spirit. He steps down from the waterfall and approaches me. Feeling there is yet a phase of the holy ritual I must complete with him, I gaze into the waterfall at a beautiful white sanctuary candle floating just beneath the water's surface. Lifting it in both of my hands, I offer it to Francis. I know he must step upon the candle and mold it with the warmth of his feet, thereby "sealing" a sacred mystery.

Personal Notes

I slowly awaken from this dream, saturated with the numinous tones of its life: the feelings of intimacy with Francis, the sacred ritual we performed, the palpable richness of the field, tunnel and waterfall. The sense of immediacy, realism and presence I experienced throughout the dream is beyond my ability to recapture with words alone. Such poverty of language leaves me feeling mystified and strangely sad. Gently hugging my sense of disorientation as I record the dream, I realize all I have of this experience is what I can salvage from memory, the dream gone forever.

I go about the affairs of my working day, shelving the dream for more practical concerns. Returning to it by late afternoon, I find the dream's sacred tone has been reabsorbed by the formless—an inevitability I was hoping I'd be spared. As I reflect on the dream in a mood of detachment, I begin to feel uneasy about the larger-than-life image of Saint Francis, fearing it may be indicative of my excessive preoccupation with spiritual life. Alarmed by this possibility, I look up the word, "infatuation" in the dictionary: *to inspire with a foolish or extravagant love or admiration*. My insecurity mounting, I retire to my office and read over the recorded dream, wondering what might be gleaned by observing the images through a more rational, circumspect lens.

Why Saint Francis? Archetype, yes... but it could have been any archetypal dream-person with numinous overtones: Buddha, Saint Matthew, Angel Gabriel, Yogananda... yet it wasn't. The specificity of Francis' image—ascetic, brown robe, stigmata—simply won't be replaced by facsimiles, however evocative of the sacred. I'm beginning to smell the holy odor of Catholicism all over the spiritual beauty of the images, enticing my soul with intimacy, union and ecstasy via baptismal waters and transformation by the Holy Spirit. A paralyzing thought: what if the Roman Catholic Church were itself an archetype, sending its parade of saints into my dream-scapes with their tattered robes and halos, their tonsures and bare feet—the soul's images of a remembered spiritual life...

Closing my notebook, I lean back in my chair and gaze out the window at the cerulean blue sky. Viewing the dream from a rational perspective has given me a lift, cushioning my anxiety against the soundness of reason. Still, some part of me realizes this approach is a defense against feelings of loss: loss of the ensouling depth and tenderness evoked by the dream's sacred overtones.

Closing my eyes, I dare myself to reenter the dream, the waterfall, the embrace. What courage it takes to allow the heart its vulnerability, the soul its breathtaking lovers.

July 21 A Dream

I dream that I'm watching my mother with my two older brothers, Tony and Paul. Here they are toddlers, and it's clear I'm somewhere back in time, early 1950s. My mother is sitting in a low overstuffed chair typical of the period. Tony and Paul are playing at her feet, sometimes climbing up on her lap or straddling one of the fat arms of the chair.

I look closely at my mother's face, marveling at how young

and different her features appear in contrast to the way she looks today. I stare at her and take everything in: her short, sable-colored permed hair, the smooth roundness of her face, the youthful, almost girl-like expression in her eyes, her cherry red lipstick. Noticing she's having difficulty with something, I realize she's trying to pose for my father who is fidgeting with a camera perhaps six feet in front of her. I then realize I'm seeing what the camera sees, as if my eyes were the lens itself. Unable to view what is behind or around me, I can't even see my father. The angle and depth of my focus changes according to my father's manipulation of the camera. I realize I have no form; my awareness is inside the camera and therefore "hidden."

I continue to watch my mother and see quite plainly that she is unhappy. Attempting not to show this side to the camera, she maintains her composure despite the gymnastics of Tony and Paul, who seem oblivious to what is going on around them. I'm certain her unhappiness is lost on my father.

As I watch my mother, I begin to know what she is feeling. Her youthful emotions and drives are in sharp conflict with the maternal and wifely responsibilities that now enfold her life. Observing her closely, I sense her frustrated ambitions, feelings of confinement and loss of personal empowerment and freedom to indulge and express the inner life of her emotions. I see how this overall disconnectedness interferes with her capacity to relate to the moment—her inability to truly relax and enjoy her babies playing at her feet and in her lap. Instead, I sense she feels burdened and is putting up with it, masking her feelings and clinging to a "role" of motherliness in order to support my father's perceptions and expectations of her. I can see this split quite clearly and feel her deep confusion, her sense of "alienation."

Growing self-conscious that I'm seeing too much and too deeply, I begin to feel vulnerable and sad. As my father continues to focus his camera on her from different heights and angles, I can do nothing but watch this scene of her over and over.

I finally awaken from the dream. The images of my mother, her fragile youth, hopes and dreams tangled about her like vines choking a rose, press heavily on my heart.

Personal Notes

Throughout the morning, I can't seem to shake this dream's hold on me. I consider phoning my mother, then decide I must allow the dream's weight its own passage. Staying inside the emotional climate of the dream reawakens an old feeling from my childhood which seems connected to the seasons, a "fall into winter" feeling. There's a chill about it I can still feel, carrying me back in time to the way my inner mental world used to be as a child. When I allow myself to inhabit that world, I can sense the presence of something large and heavy encircling my brain as though it were an actual band of substance. The band now appears in my mind's eye as a large silvery ring: I sense my brain as Saturn, around which hovers an incredibly weighty hoop of steely coldness.

The pressure this band exerts on my brain I can also feel in my chest as a "sinking" feeling, a gravitational pull which affects both my spine and stomach, drawing energy "downward." This energy loads up in my solar plexus and rotates around my navel as a dark moving ring. Often, energy can't extend or move beyond the ring. Because of this, a strong force field gathers and pulls me into it. Comprised of fear and anxiety, it is dark and womblike. Whenever I'm in this force field, my head is always tilted downward as though I'm waiting to be born.

October 17 The Earthquake

5:00 p.m., Tuesday. I preheat the oven to 450 degrees, massage a bloody roast with fresh parsley and crushed garlic clove. I've planned this day meticulously: the lamb roast, the hour I will place it on the oven rack, the savory dinner my family will devour as we watch the World Series. I glance up at the large wall clock: 5:02 p.m. I recheck the oven temperature, calculate minutes per pound out loud. My preteen daughter answers from the adjoining room where she struggles through her math homework, calls out that I'm "prehistoric" because I talk to myself. Suddenly, an overwhelming smell of burning paper. I reel around and face the oven, see gray smoke rising from its tight silver mouth. I leap to the sink to wash blood off my hands, change my mind, grab a towel and yank open the oven door. Through the billowing smoke, a blackened pizza box threatens to burst into flames. "Oh shit!" I cry at the top of my lungs and my daughter flies into the room.

"Oh shit." The sound of my voice carries through the open window to the hot, still air where nothing green has stirred all day. I stare blankly at the kitchen faucet running full blast over the charred cardboard. I replay the reel in my mind, see myself carrying the smoking box to the sink, wonder if I did it fast enough, wonder what would have happened if... My heart is still pounding. I turn and gaze at my daughter frozen in the doorway. I memorize her brown hair and eyes, yet do not realize I'm doing this. Muted sounds rise from the den: droning voices of ABC sports announcers, the din of happy fans pouring into the stadium. My daughter opens the refrigerator and reaches for an apple. I place the roast in the oven and forget to look at the time.

BOOM! The house reels as though hit by a massive wrecking ball. Tons of earth heave beneath the kitchen floor. I clutch the counter, hear myself cry, "Run!" My daughter streaks passed me, her body a blurred mass vaulting out the backdoor. Wine bottles and cookbooks fly off the baker's rack. My brain goes haywire: "Earthquake! Earthquake!" I race for the door as a deafening rumble convulses glass and plaster, hurls plants and dishes to the floor. I reach the backdoor, hear raw force groaning through the support beams and ceiling. A realization stuns me: "My baby is on the second floor!" Dread shoots through my veins, splits me in half. My instinct for self-preservation continues running out the door while my body leaps wildly up the split-level staircase which leads to my son's room. "Must get to my baby, save my baby, faster, faster, I'm not going fast enough." Each stair is a jerking plank beneath my feet. I'm thrown into the wall, cut my shoulder and do not feel it. The violent shaking rages to an inconceivable pitch. I look up, feel the blood drain from my face. Walls are buckling, are planes of whiteness moving in all directions. "Oh God... this is the big one."

I reach the top of the landing, turn the corner, run down the narrow hall, the snaking gray tunnel. I think I'm taking too long and won't make it. The French doors of my son's room swing wildly on their hinges. Through them I glimpse a frenzied whirl of shapes: the dinosaur mobile, toys and books toppling from their shelves. I pull the doors open, see my wide-eyed boy frozen to the mattress as his crib bolts back and forth across the floor. I reach for him with a fierce strength, my hands like talons of a gigantic wild bird. I clutch his small form to my body. "Walk slowly... don't drop him... get him safely out of the house." Objects fly off the bureau and crash to the floor. Tangled tree limbs lunge at the windowpane. "Don't look at this... shut it out... leave now."

I move toward the swinging door, falter, feel the lurching weight of the house pressing around me on all sides. "You will die here." Something snaps between my eyes. I no longer feel my body; it doesn't exist. I pass through the doorway, move weightlessly down the narrow gray hall, descend the winding steps. "Place your foot carefully upon each step... look only at your feet... nothing else matters." I hear the backdoor slam behind me, feel the swelling redwood deck lift me onto the grass where my daughter lies facedown, her arms strapped over her head. I stand numbly, watch the stucco walls of our house shudder as enormous waves of energy snake beneath my feet. "How long... how much longer?" I try to pray, try to conceive of what to do, how to shut off the gas line, the water line, how to survive...

The earth stills. The house remains standing. My inner reality, the cherished home where I live and dream, is shattered.

CHAPTER 10

DESIRE AND THE FORBIDDEN

February 24 Session

I close my eyes and see that I'm walking toward the stream in a very familiar area of the woods. This spot seems to have become my meeting place with Dionysus. Gazing ahead, I see Dionysus stooping over what appears to be a campfire. Smoke is rising from it and the smell of burning wood fills the air. He looks over at me, smiles and stands as I approach. It seems as if centuries have passed since I've been here. I'm extremely happy to see him.

"Hello!" I call.

"Hello, Melina!"

We embrace. He's so tall. I hold him tightly. My heart is doing somersaults.

"What are you doing?" I ask, pointing to the campfire.

I see that he's caught some fish and intends to cook them. Nearby is a round of bread, cheese, and a flask which I imagine is filled with some beverage.

"Are you hungry?" Dionysus asks, nodding invitingly at the food.

Filled with anticipation about sharing his meal, he looks very happy.

"I've just eaten. I'm not very hungry," I answer.

I think about what I'm saying. I'm hungry, but not for food. Feeling a moment's discomfort, I look into his eyes and hope he understands. Dionysus studies me quietly for a moment. I begin to feel a bit nervous.

"I want to talk to you. May I?" I ask, motioning to a spot away from the campfire smoke.

Dionysus grabs the bread, cheese and flask, and walks with

me to a spot beneath a magnificent tree. It's so incredibly lovely in this place. I now realize how much I've missed being here. It's been nine months, long enough to have conceived and birthed a baby.

Dionysus seats himself and tears off a small portion of the bread. Sitting cross-legged, he looks perfectly at ease. He takes a bite of bread, then gives me his full attention. I fold my hands in my lap and stare into the grass.

"I've been thinking a lot about coming here," I begin, trying to collect my thoughts. "What I mean is, before I entered this place just now, I thought about it for weeks."

Dionysus uncorks his flask and takes a long sip. I can feel my pulse beginning to accelerate. I don't want to get so nervous that I screw up what it is I want to tell him.

"Well, recently it's occurred to me, that is, I've finally realized... "

I stop. I'm sure I haven't realized anything. I position myself closer to Dionysus so that my right knee is touching his left. Immediately I feel more comfortable. I look directly into his eyes and find my voice.

"I think I'm in love with you, Dionysus."

I hold my breath and gaze down at my hands. Now what? I look into his eyes and wait. He pulls off another small portion of bread and munches it. Waiting for him to speak is becoming unbearable. I break the silence.

"The problem is... well, it feels very uncomfortable falling in love with a god, you know, someone who's not real, an abstraction."

Dionysus stares at me, chewing quietly.

"Are you getting this?" I ask.

"Yes."

"Do you understand?"

"Of course."

I hold my breath again. This is not going the way I had hoped.

"I don't think you're really getting what it is I'm trying to say, Dionysus."

"Maybe you are not really saying what it is you want me to get."

I blush. My thoughts begin to race. What is it I want him to get? What response am I looking for?

"This is a god-awful lonely feeling, for one thing," I explain quietly. "It seems the last thing I needed in my life two years ago was to stumble into an incredibly intoxicating god in my own psyche. I mean, it's not as if I can ask you to leave, right? And sure, I could choose not to come here, but that would be impossible, now wouldn't it? That would be like trying not to live in my own body."

I stop and stare at him. His mouth is full of bread. Nonetheless, he looks completely absorbed in what I'm saying.

"Is it possible for you to stop eating while I'm explaining this?" I ask politely. "It's hard to concentrate while watching you chew your food."

"I am hungry," he answers simply. "You are, too."

He tears off another piece of bread and munches it, gazing thoughtfully at me. I begin to feel restless.

"Why are you always hungry?" I ask. "Why are you always stuffing your face with food? Doesn't anything quell your appetite?"

Dionysus swallows slowly. A somber look steals across his eyes, making them look deeper, smokier. It's clear his disposition is changing, and rapidly. He places the bread in the grass and moves toward me. His eyes look very focused. Startled by what is happening, I begin to feel breathless. He places his hands on my shoulders and tilts me backward in the grass. On all fours above me, his presence seems to fill the whole sky.

"Dionysus, I... "

"Be quiet."

Leaning forward, he brushes my face and shoulders with his

breath, then pauses and inhales. I realize he's smelling me. He brings his face close to my neck and hair. I hear him breathing deeply.

"Melina, you smell like a rabbit," he whispers.

All at once I feel like lion's prey waiting to be devoured. A frantic energy slams the space between my eyes like a burning arrow. Overwhelmed, I start to whimper. I can't seem to stop it. Dionysus places a finger to my lips.

"Shh... "

Something heavy and soft lands on my chest. Looking down, I encounter the wide-eyed gaze of a brown rabbit nestled between my breasts. I gasp, then freeze like a statue. Dionysus pushes the rabbit up to my chin.

"Smell the rabbit, Melina. Tell me what it smells like."

I hesitate. The rabbit looks wild and I'm afraid it will bite my face.

"It won't hurt you," Dionysus assures me. "Look."

He caresses the rabbit's fur with slow deliberate strokes, relishing the softness between his fingers. I tilt my head forward and gingerly sniff the rabbit. Its long whiskers twitch.

"What does it smell like?" Dionysus asks again.

I close my eyes and try to place the scent. It is a combination of smells and I must separate them.

"Wind... softness... grass."

"And wild things," Dionysus murmurs, gazing at me through heavy-lidded eyes.

He resumes stroking the rabbit, gently combing his fingers through its glistening fur. I can feel the rabbit's warmth sinking into my body as it rests contentedly between my breasts. Growing more and more relaxed, I look up into Dionysus' eyes. The space around us seems to be thickening into a pale, honey-colored haze.

"What wild things?" I ask dreamily.

"Wild mushrooms."

"What do they smell like?"

Dionysus lifts the rabbit from my chest and places it in the grass. Leaning forward, he brings his lips to my ear.

"They smell moist," he whispers.

I catch my breath and close my eyes. The word explodes in the back of my skull and thunders through my body like a waterfall. Everything is whirling fast. His lips brush my cheek.

"Moist, Melina. What does it make you think of?"

My awareness falls to my vagina, the moisture gathering there. I hear my breathing growing deeper. He brushes his fingers across my cheekbones and temples, gathering my hair in his hands, moving his mouth to my other ear.

"Trees. What do they make you think of?"

I envision his phallus, remembering how it felt inside of me during my first encounter with him and the lion.

"Hear me whisper to you, Melina. What does it make you see?"

I struggle to find my voice.

"Say it," he prompts, tracing the curve of my ear with his lips.

"Mouth."

"Petal... " he whispers.

"Tongue."

"Take... "

"Receive."

"Receive... "

I pause, drawing a deep breath.

"Open."

My legs feel like the ocean. They want to yield, open beneath him. The power of it is all-consuming. Dionysus cups my head in his hands and lowers his face to mine. A fierce light dances in his eyes as his fingers press against my temples.

"Feel what is happening inside your body, Melina. Revel in the joy of your soul as it bends to meet me. Tell me now that I am an abstraction. Tell me that I am not real."

At once I feel that I'm falling into something so powerful and deep in my body that to resist it would break me into a thousand pieces. His hands move up and down my stomach and thighs, loosening my clothes. Removing them easily, he coaxes my legs apart and strokes my inner thighs. Inhaling sharply, I clutch the grass, pressing my fingers deep into the soil. The urge to yield pounds wildly in my chest, sending waves of heat through my spine and limbs. I close my eyes as he leans into my body, his mouth engulfing my breasts, his tongue caressing my nipples.

All at once a tremendous internal force collapses inside my stomach. Falling wildly through a large silky cord at my navel, I feel as if I'm being yanked out of my flesh and pulled into Dionysus' body. Losing the rhythm of my breathing, I push against his stomach with my fists as I start to hyperventilate. Dionysus grabs the back of my neck and presses two points at the base of my skull.

"Breathe slowly, Melina. Relax, breathe slowly."

My breathing shifts, easing the constriction in my chest, but I'm still pushing at him with my fists as though my reflexes had gone haywire. Dionysus takes both my arms, places them close to my body and holds them there. Gradually my body relaxes. I stare up at his face in a daze, the sky a vivid blue corona around his head. My mind is still whirling. I want to curl up into a tight little ball for protection—protect my stomach. I try to do this but Dionysus counters my effort, tightening his hold on my arms.

"The child is afraid, but the woman is not," he explains quietly. "Allow the child her fear, for it will run its course; afterward, the child will not even remember the reason for it. If you allow her this, she will allow you your passion, for it is the child who holds the key to your pleasure and you who hold her courage."

Dionysus releases my arms and leans over me. His breathing is deep next to my ear.

"I will wait, Melina. I will help you."

His words awaken a deep ache in my heart. It feels very old... as old as the world. Tears sting my eyes. I place my hand lightly on his cheek.

"Why will you wait?" I whisper. "Why do you want to help me?"

Something fills his eyes like sunlight on water and begins to whirl. The whirling expands, begins to move toward me. His mouth opens. Tiny aureoles of light spill out and twirl like heavenly bodies in the space between us. Spellbound, I watch the light as it spins into delicate rings of color and falls into my eyes. Spiraling deep into my body, the multi-hued rings penetrate my heart, awakening the memory of a poem I wrote years ago ...

IN TWILIGHT WE MOVE IN TECHNICOLOR

from your mouth, the shapes of

syllables, falling
light-petals

you say

we have traveled the length
of our limbs, climbed

the far slope

I breathe
the silk of your

tongue, sail
your red kite

February 25 Session

I close my eyes and see that I'm walking toward an area in the woods where Dionysus is resting under a large shady tree. His feet are crossed at the ankles and his eyes are closed. There's a luster about him, yet I see no outward appearance of light. Slowing my steps, I approach him quietly so as not to wake him. As I drink in the serene beauty of his face, the memory of our last encounter pulses through my body like tiny ripples of electricity. My legs begin to feel loose. I quietly seat myself in the grass at his left side. Looking down at myself, I see that I'm wearing red shorts and a loose sleeveless blouse. My feet are bare. The way I'm dressed reminds me of summer. I inhale deeply, liking the way I feel. I listen to the quiet rhythm of Dionysus' breathing as he rests. Glancing over at him, I'm startled to see that he's watching me. A warm rush of energy steals up my cheeks.

"I hope I didn't wake you," I say softly.

"Not at all."

We stare at each other.

"You have not had much sleep," Dionysus observes.

"It was you who kept me up until 4:00 o'clock in the morning," I confess, smiling. "After yesterday's session, I couldn't sleep for anything. Too wired."

Dionysus smiles and slowly sits up.

"And for whom are you saving yourself?" he asks.

"Ted, of course."

I grab my toes and pull them back and forth. Dionysus now seems roused to full wakefulness. His eyes are very sparkly, revealing his delight in what I've been saying. Feeling somewhat shy, I want to shift off the subject. I reach into my pocket and pull out an old poem I had written years ago which I recently discovered tucked away in a file. I'd completely forgotten that I'd written it at all.

"I'd like to share a poem with you, if I may."

No sooner do these words leave my mouth when I'm

overtaken by a feeling of revulsion. I realize I don't want to read the poem and wonder what compelled me to think otherwise. I place the piece of paper on the grass between us.

"There's something about this poem that disturbs me," I acknowledge quietly.

A gray, cloud-like mass steals across my peripheral vision. I turn my head quickly to either side, but I can't detect anything responsible for it.

"Read the poem to me, Melina," Dionysus suggests, repositioning himself comfortably in the grass.

I gingerly retrieve the paper and read the poem to myself. A knot begins to gather in my stomach.

"Look, something strange is going on here. This poem is about Francis of Assisi, or seems to be, yet I honestly don't have a clue as to why I made him a central figure in this work. I also had a very powerful dream about him several months ago. In addition to that, I recall quite clearly seeing a white statue of Saint Francis in the church lawn of that place I journeyed to—the one where the old priest lives who, oddly, recited to me a poem about the town of Assisi. Furthermore, what is the reason you wear monk clothes and prayer beads when we meet? There's a strange motif gathering gravity here and I think it's odd that I should be the last to know what it could possibly mean."

Dionysus props his chin in his hand.

"Read the poem, Melina."

I stare at the poem and stall, wrestling with feelings of uneasiness. Pushing through my resistance, I shake my head and breathe deeply.

WHAT WE COULD HAVE SAID

I worship the Saint Francis stump;
this red candle, its tangled rivulets
a paraplegic. On its left side,

a carefully poised lung; on
its right, a nubile breast.
I want to press my lips
to its oily stigmata, stroke each
bone and fractured rib. But moment
by moment my cells collect
odor. They count me. Your photo
watches from the wall, watches
my thinness. I will lie down
like a rug, like Astroturf
swallowing distance, defining
the hollow of this landscape.

I fold up the paper and tuck it under my foot. I then remember a sequence in the Francis dream where he must step on a white candle with his bare feet to "seal" a sacred mystery between us. I vividly recall how I held the candle out to him in my two hands, placing it on a rock. I then realize the poem evolved out of the image of a candle, and that distinct references to stigmata occur both in the poem and in the dream. I look up at Dionysus. He's watching me steadily.

"I've never had any particular devotion to Saint Francis when I was growing up," I explain, mystified by the eruption of a saint in my psyche. "He, like any other saint in the Catholic archives of overachievers, received the homage due him on his appointed holy day. Other than my fondness for The Prayer Of Saint Francis, he means very little to me. I'm sure he must be a symbol for something in my unconscious."

"He is not a symbol, Melina."

"What is he, then?"

"A man."

I pause, unsure of his meaning.

"What?"

"A man under the same spell as you."

I wince at his use of the word, "spell."

"Please don't use 'spell,' Dionysus. It doesn't fit and it's not accurate. We're not talking about sorcery or magic. We're talking about religion, devotion, a disciplined way of life. With regard to Saint Francis, who was the exemplar of spiritual virtue, the use of the word, 'spell' is almost sacrilegious."

I look down at my foot and feel positively anal. I could just imagine my father saying those very words. Dionysus leans back against the tree.

"We should not have this discussion right now," he remarks.

"Why not?"

"You are not receptive. Your mind is too tight. Your body is wailing with need."

"What?"

"Go take your shower. As you stand in the water, recall your dream with Francis under the waterfall. Observe how you felt with him. Then... "

He stands and helps me to my feet.

"Make love."

Personal Notes

I leave my office and head for the bedroom. It's Sunday afternoon and my son is taking his nap. As I enter my bedroom thinking about the previous day's session with Dionysus, I break into a wide grin. Ted sees me glide into the room with this smile on my face and throws me a friendly but suspicious look. Sprawled across the bed reading a book, he's aware that I've been holed-up in my office doing session work. As I undress for my shower, I can't stop smiling and notice that Ted is eyeing me from the bed. I wonder what in the world I'm smiling about. I suddenly realize I feel very happy.

While taking my shower, I find my thoughts drifting aimlessly. I try to recall my dream with Saint Francis as Dionysus suggested, but I can't focus—the dream simply doesn't hold my interest. I dry off and dress skimpily, catching a reflection of my body in the mirror. I notice I've lost some weight and realize loss of appetite and adrenaline overdrive are responsible. Wondering if it's apparent, I lay across the bed next to Ted and ask him if I look thin. I throw my legs up in the air and scoot around the bed, demonstrating different angles, then burst into laughter. I feel so energized. I throw my arms around him. He gazes sleepily at me and smiles.

Ted asks me what I've been writing about. Composing myself, I relax across the bed and tell him I think I've made some progress. As the smile comes back to my face, he knows I'm speaking in a sexual context. I then ask him if he'd like me to share the material. To my surprise he says no, then buries his head in my shoulder, moaning that he can't possibly compete with a god, saying it feels too "scary." I'm not sure how seriously to take what he's saying. Placing my arms around him, I gently stroke his hair and tell him the work in which I'm involved is a psychic process; names and faces in the archetypal world have no real meaning. What matters is what and who I am in this moment with him. While offering him reassurance, I mentally tell myself I'd better really believe what I'm saying or I'm in big trouble.

Later we make love. Ted has an extraordinary ability to lose himself inside the power of the moment, fully surrendering to his instincts and emotions. When this takes place, it seems the full potency of the archetype I've been working with awakens in both our bodies, drawing us deeply inside of it. I try to meet this energy completely through my heart, soul, mind and body. How perfectly this activity completes the circuitry of my session work, providing an immediate framework for grounding and wholeness. I wonder if this is the reason Dionysus is always so interested in how often I make love.

Much later that night, while sleeping deeply, I hear a voice whispering in my ear. The language is very sexual and shakes my mind awake. As I listen to it, hands move up and down my stomach and thighs. I squint at the bedstand in the darkness where clock numbers are glowing red: 2:35 a.m. I become disoriented. The voice whispers in my other ear. As I listen, my breathing accelerates. The lingering thickness of sleep pulls me in and out of a dreamlike state, flooding me with a sense of re-enactment: everything about this moment feels exactly like my encounter with Dionysus in the grass. Palpable and hypnotic, it completely arrests my sense of space and time.

I call out to make certain it is Ted. He answers in a low wild voice. I feel my night clothes slip away from my body, his mouth on my breasts. I sink completely. As I fold my hands around his phallus, I see myself in my Saint Francis dream, lifting the white candle with both my hands out of the grotto waters, holding it out to Francis. In this moment, holding Ted and holding the candle are one and the same. Startled by this realization, I wonder what it could mean.

February 27 A Dream

I dream that I'm examining or closely watching Pan as though to familiarize myself with who or what he is. I'm studying all the details of his physical features. Pan is cooperating by holding his head and body at different angles so that I may examine him, all the while staring fixedly at me. I have the sense that what I'm doing is being guided or orchestrated by his mind or will. This is a strange feeling. I particularly remember the jet-black color of his hair and how the laugh lines around his eyes curve like slender talons.

At times I have a sense of floating above and around Pan as I study him. Whenever I'm in this floating state, I'm drawn or pulled into his body, as though the force of his physical gravity were stronger than my ability to maintain my awareness outside of it. This is a very weird sensation, as I seem to move in and out of him like a weightless balloon. At different intervals throughout this movement, he bangs a set of drums. A great deal more is going on in this dream, but I now can't remember it.

Personal Notes

The weekend has caught up with me and I'm tired. As I think about my dream with Pan, I feel a slight unease. I don't know what's making me feel uncomfortable.

Today I clean my office. A large portrait I sketched of Dionysus is propped on a rocking chair. I place it out of view in a large drawer, then gather all my tablets, poems and session work and put them all away. I don't want any of this material to be in my line of focus for awhile. While tidying my desk, I contemplate Dionysus, Pan and X, reflecting on the darker side of sexuality. My gaze wanders to the "fat" book I had Ted purchase for me nearly two years ago, which is still sitting on a nearby shelf: *The Marquis de Sade: 120 Days of Sodom*. I haven't looked at it since the day I brought it home from the bookstore, telling myself back then I'd never open it again. Given this resolve, I wonder why I've kept it. I now question whether I was too severe in my judgments—or too frightened of my impulses.

I pull the book down from the shelf and open it. The language and imagery is as boldly lurid and assaulting as I remember. I flip through the pages and skip around, looking for "reason" and "emotion" in the cesspool of images. I find only the dark madness of Sade's characters embracing "ecstasy" in forms that debauch, murder and rape the mind, soul and body. Sickened, I close the book.

February 28 A Dream

I dream that I'm walking on a beach with a small group of people I don't know. Within this group is a man who strikes up a casual conversation with me. In all respects, he seems to be a "man of the world." Unsure of where I am and where I'm going, I find comfort in carrying on a dialogue with him. During our conversation, he predicts we'll see a man wearing a robe and holding a stone in his hand. I look to the left and see, walking near the water's edge, a man wearing a robe and holding a stone in his hand. I turn to the man of the world and tell him he was right.

The dream shifts and I find myself gazing out the dining room window of the house in which I live in real life. The lower floor of the apartment building next-door is being renovated. The landlady is busily replacing the heavy window coverings with green cafe curtains and seems very excited about the changes she's making. Stepping outdoors to get a look at the front of the building, I'm surprised at how its entire character has changed, appearing lighter and more contemporary. The landlady tells me the lower floor of the building will now be used by a lovely French cafe next-door to expand their facilities and seating capacity. Thinking this is a marvelous idea, I'm excited about the upgrade and expansion.

The dream shifts and I'm waiting to be seated in the French cafe along with the small group of people with whom I walked on the beach. It's lunchtime and the place is hopping with activity. As I listen to the group chatting gaily in French, I wonder how I'm able to understand their conversations, as I'm completely unfamiliar with the language. I pick up a French menu and scan it, unable to comprehend a word of it. I then notice I'm holding a sheet of paper in my left hand. Peering closely at it, I'm relieved to see that I've somehow translated the French menu into English. All at once a light wind blows the paper out of my hand and sails it into the dining room. I watch it dip and bob over tabletops as it disappears in the bustling lunch crowd.

The dream shifts and we're now seated at a table in the French cafe, joined by the "man of the world." Out of nowhere, an attractive dark-haired woman approaches our table and seats herself. Instantly sensing an awkwardness in the air, I realize she has something to do with the man of the world's past. It's clear she means to make him uncomfortable by her presence and I strongly suspect trouble is brewing. He handles the situation with aplomb and doesn't resist her presence. It appears by his manner that he's setting an example for the rest of us. I'm not thrilled we'll have to put up with this situation throughout our entire meal.

March 1 A Dream

I dream that I'm on the top floor of a skyscraper, sitting on the floor of an apartment with someone I don't know. We're relaxedly watching television when the program is interrupted by live footage of a terrible earthquake. A large area of land swells and bursts open. Destruction is everywhere. As we watch this, I realize the earthquake is taking place in a nearby vicinity. Staring in horror at the disaster taking place on the TV screen, I know this is the "big one."

All at once the skyscraper in which we're sitting begins to tremble and sway. We can't save ourselves, for there is nowhere to run or hide. I spread my hands out on the floor and advise my companion to do the same, saying, "There's nothing we can do but ride it out!" I close my eyes, realizing we're really in for it. I'm extremely aware that we may not come out of this alive.

The dream shifts and I'm journeying with my real-life friend Karen and her four sisters to unfamiliar lands and destinations. At times we all split up into pairs and go our different ways. At the end of our journey, Karen and I reunite with her sisters and happily relate our travel experiences. Aglow from sun exposure, all four women are wearing brightly colored, tropical print blouses. I sense there will be a wedding.

The dream shifts and I'm kneeling in the grass under a large tree in a natural setting, performing a ritual. At times it seems I'm standing outside myself, watching what I'm doing. A small glass vile filled with golden-yellow liquid is positioned next to me in the grass. Peering into the glass, I can see the golden liquid changing alternately from the shape of a crescent moon to a perfectly round sphere like the sun. I'm kneeling over it with my hands folded. As I watch this from outside myself, I realize I'm taking a vow. I'm deeply struck with the knowledge that this vow is being made to or with "myself."

A nearby invisible presence tells me to look at the grass, "how new and green it is." I gaze at the grass, marveling at its brilliant color. The presence then positions me a distance away from what I'm seeing and tells me to look again from this vantage. Staring at myself in the grass, I now see that the area of land on which I'm kneeling is a huge chunk or mass of earth suspended in the air like a small floating island. Filled with wonder at this revealing perspective, I notice how slight the surface layer of grass is in contrast to the rich dark earth beneath it.

March 7 A Dream

I dream that X and I are engaged in an intensive, problem solving endeavor, putting various formulas to the test and performing trial-runs, as well as taking an idea from its concept phase and working it through to physical actuality. While engrossed in this endeavor, I become intuitively aware of an Eastern Indian girl and a young man who are making plans to be wed, and whose betrothal is inexplicably linked to my activities with X.

X gives me some advice. I take it. I now can't remember what it is.

March 12 A Dream

I dream that I'm walking with an older man who is part beast. We're betrothed to each other and there is something he wants to tell me or show me about himself. He's sad because he fears that once I know what it is, I won't want to marry him. I feel great compassion for him and know I'll marry him anyway, no matter what it is he reveals.

The dream shifts and I receive a phone call from my real-life brother Tony in Switzerland. Extremely upset, he tells me there's a contract out on him and that he will die on December 19th. He wants to come home and see the family for the last time and instructs me to tell no one of his upcoming death.

The dream shifts and I'm with my brother Tony in a family setting. He looks very grim. I know in my heart he's saying farewell to all his loved ones who know nothing of his predicament. It's a terrible weight to know what is in store for him and that I can do nothing to prevent it.

March 16 A Dream

I dream that I'm seated at a long table around which are gathered my friend Karen, her father and other members of her family. The talk is casual. At one point, Karen's father tries to make a comment, but the conversation around the table distracts the others from hearing him. Noticing this, I turn and give him my full attention. He seems quite grateful and extends both his arms across the table toward me. I look down at his hands and see they are the hands of Pan. I keep staring at them. They're somewhat discolored—brownish and overlarge. His nails are thick and curved like talons.

I feel compelled to offer him my comfort, sensing this is the reason he extended his hands to me. I slowly place one of my hands in his. I'm very aware that what I'm doing could be easily misread by those seated around the table. I'm struck with a strong sense of the "forbidden."

March 16 Session

I close my eyes and see that I'm strolling through the woods, looking for Dionysus. It's early morning and the atmosphere is exceedingly peaceful. Dew still clings to the leaves. How rich the trees and grass look, how full and deep. My heart expands.

I walk through a cluster of trees and find Dionysus sitting quietly against one of them. His face is upturned to the eastern sky, his eyes closed against the unfolding sunlight. I watch him. How I've grown to love him. This feeling smarts a bit, carrying with it a strange wave of sorrow. As I continue watching him, I feel a strong internal force pouring out to him from the center of my body. It's as though my physical form were melting down into myriad shadow-forms, flowing and moving against each other like a whirling cluster of soul fragments. The feeling of "melting down" intensifies. A strong sense of disorientation and wistfulness pushes from somewhere deep within my being. It is becoming so powerful that I feel I'm being involuntarily pushed forward out of my body toward Dionysus. I close my eyes. A dream is coming that I don't want to remember. It feels very old, as though I must have dreamt it before I was born. What is telling me this? Where is it coming from? Everything within me trembles.

I try to touch the dream from a distance. When I do this, my heart swells. It's as if I'm pushing my hand into a painting that gives, that yields and receives me into its life. I try to pull myself back from the dream so that I can observe it, but now it's becoming so vivid and dimensional that I feel myself being enveloped inside of it. My feelings about myself are changing. My body is changing, my clothes and hair. The air is becoming sweeter, lighter. I feel that I'm wearing a blue dress. I hold my breath, afraid to open my eyes. I open them.

I see a man standing before me across a clearing in the woods. Every detail about him is exceptionally clear. He's wearing a brown, coarsely woven robe. His hair and beard is dark. His arms are outstretched to me. Something in my body begins to sing and at once I feel myself rising slightly off the ground. This feeling of buoyancy fills me with an indescribable sense of delight, of extraordinary freshness and simplicity. Suddenly I want to sing the word "clear" over and over, praise the petal and leaf, the dewdrop. The sound of distant bells fills the woods. I remember time, the tolling of the hour, the clock on my office desk. I look at the man whose arms are outstretched to me. I know I must leave. I also know I'll be back.

Personal Notes

I pull out of the session and gaze about my office. How still and solid everything looks. I feel myself, my body, sitting on the loveseat, physically locked to this spot. How long have I been sitting here? It all seems strangely incongruous to me in a way I couldn't hope to explain to myself. Across the room, propped on the rocker, is the portrait I sketched of Dionysus. I stare at it, then tell myself I must put it away and pack for a business trip to New York. The hour is later than I want it to be and I have a million things to do.

Before taking my shower, I weigh myself. I blink at the scale, perplexed that I'm losing more weight. The scale must be wrong. What is happening? I realize my weight loss is directly related to my session work, the inner fire of Eros. Will I eventually be burnt down to a mere skeleton? Can I hold this heat without causing physical harm to myself? I undress and look at my reflection in the mirror. What is happening?

I go to make the bed and lie down in it instead. Outside the window, the spring air tousles the white plum blossoms. As I watch them float through the air like eyelets of lace, a fragrant breeze fills the room and spills over my body. A feeling of arousal which has persisted for the last few weeks gently rises and falls within me. Although subtle, it has remained as constant as a clock ticking or the heart beating, with or without my conscious involvement. I find this peculiar, as I'm menstruating and temporarily shut down to sexual desire.

I attempt to locate the source of the pulse spilling through my body. Closing my eyes, I surrender to my body's rhythms, removing all barriers. Sinking rapidly inside a powerful energy field emanating from my solar plexus, I sense my body is in the throes of making love. The energy is very deep and seems to be rooted just above my navel. With my barriers removed, I can feel my complete emotional involvement in this lovemaking. It is overwhelming and nearly frightens me. With whom or what am

I making love? I try to see a face, but I can't—only white outlines, energy dancing in undulating waves. I think if I lie here like this for two solid weeks without moving, I should be perfectly content and want for nothing.

I quickly rise from the bed and start my shower. Standing under the soothing stream, I remember Dionysus' words, "Go take your shower. As you stand in the water, recall your dream with Francis under the waterfall. Observe how you felt with him." Instantly a detail of the dream crystallizes in my memory: "I look at Francis' hands and see that he has not yet received the stigmata. For some reason I think this makes him even more vulnerable to cruelty and senseless mutilation."

Concentrating on this image, I reach for the razor to shave my legs, see the blade is new and caution myself not to draw blood... *blood, stigmata.* I wonder why my dream-self would perceive the absence of stigmata as making Francis more vulnerable to cruelty and senseless mutilation. Is it because he has not yet received the supernatural marks that so often confer sainthood? Does being "favored by God" exempt one from the often senseless cruelty of living an ordinary human existence? If it does, then one might postulate that truly living in the life of God is the soul's ultimate protection against the ravages of mortal being. Is this what I really believe?

I nick my ankle, same spot as always and can't stop the bleeding... *bleeding wounds of Christ, the sacrificial lamb.* My God, do I have a saint complex? A collage of childhood fantasies erupts into my mind's eye: soaring as a heavenly angel over oceans and skyscrapers; donating chests of gold coins, all dug up from my backyard, to the world's poor and homeless; making the blind see and the lame walk; gladly choosing crucifixion over yielding to the temptation of scarfing a Hershey's chocolate bar during Lent. I smile as a thick wad of suds flops to the shower floor.

I wonder if it is the emotional life evoked by such images for which the soul longs, or is it simply longing itself the soul loves, with or without an object? Oh, but how compelling is the object. I close my eyes and revisit the lovely clearing in the woods where the monk, arms outstretched, beckons me into a delicious life so hauntingly familiar, yet unknown to me. What is it that feels like a dream I don't want to remember?

I wrap a towel around my hair and head for the vanity, telling myself to sober up. Certainly the monk's presence in my inner life calls forth my feelings of love for Jesus. That's plain, given my Catholic history. And what better figure to stimulate the profound memories of this love than Saint Francis, whose hands and feet are marked with the wounds of the crucified Christ? A strong memory surfaces: seven or eight years old, I'm lying on the couch, thoroughly absorbed in a children's book about the life of Christ. My mother calls me for dinner. Dazed, I place down the book and gaze about me at the suddenly absurd-looking objects in the room: the clunky black telephone, the maple chairs covered in puke-green vinyl, the electric skillet heaped high with chop suey, my brother picking his nose in the far corner of the room. In that moment, I feel sucker-punched by my own life—*no, it simply can't be that I was born two thousand years too late. I must be dreaming this: the color TV bulging from the corner, that strange-smelling glop in the electric skillet, these dark-haired people milling around me.*

Trying to conceal my sense of shock, I seat myself at a table filled with flying arms and plates. All the while my heart is sinking by degrees: *to think I can never walk with the apostles or hear firsthand the blessed words of Our Lord*. My father makes the sign of the cross and nine heads bow. Finding my plight too terrible to endure, I implore God to send me back in time to the days when Christ walked the earth, believing I could, through prayerful begging of His sympathy, blast through the time barrier walling me off from the savior of the world. "Suffer the little children to come to Me."

My mother loads up my plate with chop suey, tops it off with

Chun King crispy noodles and places it before me. I blink at it, waiting for it to disappear. Minutes drag by—it sits there as heavily as my 65 pound frame in a time zone filled with pine knot paneling and butterscotch-colored linoleum tile. Tears well up in my eyes as I lower my head over the blur on my plate—*why have you abandoned me, God?*

Retreating to the woods after dinner, I perch myself on a fallen tree trunk and cry the very light out of my soul: luminous mercurial balls seep out of my insides and float off, some following the narrow creek winding east toward the neighbor's property, while others, too heavy to float, sink into the ground, saturating the poison ivy and salamanders. Feeling invisible and forgotten, I watch my soul leak out in silvery bubbles the size of volleyballs as if that's what souls always do when they are sorrowful: cry themselves back to God as they waft like balloons over buildings and treetops until, reaching a point of final departure, they ascend to that pure, secret place of Heaven.

Refocusing on the present, I gaze at my face in the mirror and remember the hour. All that packing to do and so little time. Surveying the features of the grown woman staring back at me, I wonder to what degree that astonished, disappointed child still lives inside me. How much is she influencing my interior life? I search for her in my eyes, but I see only a woman in love. Whether it is with Christ, Dionysus or life itself, I hardly care, for my eyes reflect a mysterious inner universe: a soul immersed in the inexplicable rhythms of quiet exaltation.

Later in the afternoon in the midst of packing for my trip, I'm overcome by an urge to stop what I'm doing and enter a state of inner silence. Retiring to my office, I have an unexpected and enormously powerful experience with "the clear." I can't possibly find the words to adequately describe this experience with so little time. I must wait until I return from New York. Perhaps by then... perhaps... I will have found my voice.

Ted and I make love in what seems an ocean of liquid fire.

Falling asleep in his arms at 2:30 a.m., I bless the clear note still singing in my body, the wealth of feeling rising in my heart.

March 17 A Dream

I dream that I'm standing in the kitchen with my brother David at a family gathering at my parent's home. We're talking together when suddenly my grandmother, who in real life is deceased, breezes into the room in her usual chipper style. Talking animatedly, she is in a bright lively mood. I'm observing her for a long time before it dawns on me that she's dead and her presence in the room is a physical impossibility. Spooked by this realization, I make hand signals at my brother to get his attention. He looks over at my grandmother then back at me and whispers, "Melina, she is both alive and dead simultaneously."

March 18 A Dream

I dream that I'm riding with Dionysus in a carriage through an English countryside. Bathed in diaphanous light, the carriage and landscape appear delicately surreal and seem to belong to an age in the past. As we journey, Dionysus silently bids me to observe his being or essence. I do this by examining his image or physical presence. He then shows me an interior aspect of himself, transfiguring his form into the image of light on water. The juxtaposition of his physical form and the image of light on water is repeated over and over and seems quite intensive. I have the definite sense he is trying to bring my awareness of these two aspects of himself into alignment: to integrate them into a whole.

March 20 Session

I close my eyes and see that I'm sitting against a large smooth rock, facing Dionysus. Above us, the boughs of an incredibly large tree provide deep, relaxing shade. Dionysus is quietly observing me, as if waiting for me to speak. I have a lot on my mind and hardly know where to begin.

"I suppose you know I've made contact with a man on the East Coast to review the material I've compiled regarding my journeys and sessions with you."

I stop and study Dionysus' face to see how he's taken what I've said. He's still observing me intently. I begin to feel slightly uncomfortable.

"This man is a psychotherapist, a Jungian," I continue. "I'm corresponding with him."

"What is his name?" Dionysus asks.

I think about the man's name and find that my tongue stubbornly refuses to move.

"I don't want to say his name in here," I mumble.

"Why?"

"I really don't know him yet."

Dionysus leans back leisurely and crosses his arms behind his head.

"Why are you sharing the material with him?" he asks.

The question stirs up many feelings, causing me to focus deeply. I choose my words with care.

"One day I'd like to have this material published. Both spiritually and creatively, it would fulfill my deep longing to assist the labor of souls as they travel their own life journeys. Because there's a lot of meat in this work and a great hunger in the world, I thought it wise to enlist the aid of a person with a knowledgeable background in psychology to provide a backdrop, a foundation for a work of this type."

The expression in Dionysus' eyes hasn't changed. Like a Svengali, his probing gaze seems to penetrate to the hindmost corners of my soul. I continue staring at him and don't know what else to say.

"Go on," he urges.

I stare into my hands.

"So far it's been difficult to make a connection with this man in a way I would like."

"In what way would you like to experience this connection?" Dionysus asks.

"I don't know... "

My thoughts trail off. I realize I'm trying to lose the thread of this.

"Melina."

"Okay!"

I pull myself together and try to pinpoint my dilemma.

"What I'm dealing with is fear. It seems important that I have some common basis with this man, a point of reference. So far our 'common basis' is nonexistent. It's become clear to me that I'm not corresponding with a person, but with a mental construct—an impenetrable posture that has been rigorously conditioned and preprogrammed. I've never encountered anything quite like this before where the quality of humanness between two people is absent, a dumb note in the exchange. There's no soul in our communication, not because I don't desire it, but because it's not a 'permissible' dimension he's extending in our communication. Without it, we're nothing but oil and water in a tight glass box. Shake it and there's the illusion of elements merging. But that's all it is—an illusion, an appearance— nothing one can build soul on, nor can one hope to creatively weave the threads of love, faith, compassion and wonder into a picture that inspires and broadens the dimensions of the human spirit. Pictures are 'symptoms,' it seems."

This last statement reverberates inside of me, causing me to feel troubled and sad. I don't want to abort my correspondence with the man, yet I realize I may have no choice.

"I don't know, Dionysus. I keep thinking it's me. Maybe I'm not being adaptable enough to his methodology. Whichever way I cut it, I can't help but strongly feel his language postures are well-maneuvered techniques designed to narrow my psychic field, rendering it a claustrophobic cell stripped of the voices of the human heart."

My feelings of disappointment deepen. I caress the grass with my fingertips as if to assuage a deep ache.

"Where does fear fit into the picture, Melina?"

I think this over for a few moments.

"Because I want our work together to bear fruit, I fear that I'll invent the point of reference, the common basis in our exchange. Let me rephrase that. I feel my subconscious mind will invent it and impose it on my experience with him. The idea of this happening, the possibility, is becoming a barrier to my sense of ease about our correspondence."

Dionysus' eyes are becoming very sparkly and energized. He leans forward in the grass and smiles impishly.

"Perhaps you should dance with him," he suggests.

I sit upright and stare at him.

"What did you say?"

"Perhaps you should dance with him. You want to touch him, don't you? You want to feel him as a reality in your work."

My head is spinning with the strangeness of this idea—dancing with a psychotherapist. I lean back on my hands and study Dionysus for a long time.

"I don't know what he looks like. I can't dance with air."

Dionysus smiles. Rising to his feet, he takes a courteous bow.

"Allow me," he offers.

"Allow you to what?"

"Allow me to take on his form."

"No!"

I leap from the grass and throw my arms around his shoulders.

"I don't want you to do that!" I cry, restraining him with a bear hug.

Dionysus offers no resistance. Relinquishing my grip, I step back and try to compose myself.

"Don't you see, Dionysus? If I dance with this man, I'll simply be adding fuel to my need to invent some common basis between us."

"You are inventing nothing."

Dionysus seats himself comfortably in the grass and looks at me with a placid smile. I find it irritating and turn away.

"You're just making matters worse," I grumble. "Obviously you don't understand my position here, the dilemma I'm experiencing."

I plop myself down in the grass and sigh deeply.

"Your only dilemma is that you will not allow him to become tangible in your world, Melina. You are resisting your desire to do so."

I push my finger into the grass as a scowl creeps across my face.

"What do you mean by 'tangible'?" I ask.

"You know exactly what I mean."

"Oh, really? Tell me, who could possibly know what 'tangible' means in a place like this?"

A long interval of silence ensues. I pull up blades of grass and pile one on top of the other as though building a tower. All the while, I'm trying to make sense of the bizarre turn in our conversation.

"I honestly can't make heads or tails of what you mean, Dionysus."

"All you need do is simply desire to remember."

"Remember what?" I ask.

"Remember this man."

"But how can I possibly remember a man I've never met?"

"Through dreaming," he answers quietly.

I stare at him in amazement, then close my mouth.

"No."

"No, what?"

"Are you suggesting I dream him up?" I ask incredulously.

Dionysus slowly extends his left arm out to his side, then gently lowers it to the grass.

"I am suggesting you open to your desire to remember him."

"One can't remember a person she's never met."

"You have met him."

"I have never met him."

"You are choosing forgetfulness."

"You are choosing impossibility."

I jump up from the grass and pace a distance away. This has become much more complicated than I had intended. As I try to understand the riddle of his words, I find myself sinking further inside a maze of convoluted logic without exits. With frustration mounting, I pace back over to Dionysus.

"What you're suggesting is only adding to my dilemma, contributing layers, not eliminating them," I point out. "If it's a past life you're alluding to, it can hardly be relevant to my present situation. Those kinds of labyrinths can get a soul entangled and distracted, lost."

I stop and catch my breath. Dionysus' chin is propped on his hand. He's watching me with mild amusement. I sit down on a rock and cross my legs, wondering why I don't leave. I've made a solid stand. What else can come of my being here? As I think it over, I start to feel rotten.

"Why don't you dance with him?" Dionysus persists. "He will not bite you."

Too tired to argue, I lie back in the grass and exhale loudly. Dionysus is grinning at me in such an openly friendly way that I catch myself breaking into a smile.

"All right, I'll dance with him. But no presto-chango acts from you. Keep your distance."

I emphatically wave him off. Dionysus rolls his eyes and blinks.

"Well?" I ask, motioning to the space between us as if it were a stage.

"Well, what?"

"How do I get him here?"

"He is already here."

I sit up and scan my surroundings.

"Where?"

Dionysus points to a large tree across a clearing. Lying beneath it is what appears to be a man sleeping.

"Is that the psychotherapist?" I ask.

"Yes."

I hesitate. I don't like any of this. It's beginning to feel ridiculous.

"You don't think I'm going to walk over there and wake him out of a dead sleep, do you?" I balk.

"No, Melina. You must enter his dream."

"But I don't know how."

"You do know how. You must simply desire to remember."

March 21 Session

I close my eyes and see that I'm sitting against a smooth rock under a large tree, exactly as I was in my last journey. Dionysus is seated in the grass to my right. I'm gazing across a long stretch of grass at the man who's lying under a tree. I'm trying to make out what sort of clothes he's wearing, but I can't see anything in particular.

"Are you ready?" Dionysus asks quietly.

I keep thinking about "remembering" this man through "dreaming." I'm positively stumped about it and don't want to enter an experience with the man in this manner.

"I told you I would dance with him and that's all," I whisper, scrutinizing the form beneath the tree. "I don't know anything about 'remembering' him, nor do I care. Let's dispense with the remembering and dreaming part, all right?"

I look over at Dionysus. His face is disturbingly sober.

"You will not be able to dance with him unless you desire to remember him," he warns. "To do this, you must enter his dream."

I bite back frustration, feeling this is a ploy designed to manipulate me into the experience "for my own good." I throw up my hands.

"I haven't the faintest idea how to do what you're talking about."

"It is simple, Melina. Allow your desire to remember him bring you to his side. Then lie down next to him under the tree and rest."

This is beginning to sound so off the wall that I can hardly endure it a moment longer. I raise my voice, not caring if I wake the dead.

"Why don't you just speak plainly and tell me what I'm really doing is attempting to remember myself? It's my own dream you want me to remember. Why am I being maneuvered to play it off on him?"

Pointing to where the man is lying under the tree, I'm beginning to feel wretched. I stand up and walk over to Dionysus, seat myself next to him and place my right knee against his left. I look into his eyes.

"I don't need another mirror, Dionysus. You are my mirror."

"He is not a mirror, Melina."

"What is he, then?"

"He is a man."

I stare into the grass.

"He is a psychotherapist," I correct him.

"He is a man."

"What's that supposed to mean?

"You must go and find out."

I look over at the man under the tree and sigh, resolving to get this over with. I stand up and amble across the grass toward him. All the while, I'm thinking about how to resurrect a desire to remember him. This confuses me, so I focus on my desire to know who he is. With each step, I ask in my mind, "Who are you? Who are you?"

I'm now standing at the man's back. His clothing is the color of mud and has the texture and appearance of old sackcloth. I think he must be poor. Some sort of hood is pulled over his face. I roll my eyes. *I don't want to see his face so I invent a hood. Great.* I stand there. Then I remember that Dionysus told me to lie down next to him. I decide to lie down facing him. I walk around him and sit down in the grass at his side, then look at his face. The hood creates deep shadows over his features. I sigh, wondering how much more elaborate my process could possibly get.

As I lie down next to him, the word "hermit" comes to mind. I think, "I'm lying down with a hermit. I wonder what he is dreaming." I close my eyes and relax instantly inside a calming stillness. I want to forget everything now and just sink into the peace and solitude of the surrounding landscape. I sense the trees around me, the soft grass beneath my back. I imagine the sky over my head, the clouds drifting slowly and the words, "infinity"... "rest"...

I detect a faint sound that's familiar to me, the soft scratch of a pen moving across paper. Opening my eyes, I see the hermit seated at a very old desk which appears to have been roughly hewn from a tree. He seems to be deeply absorbed in the labor of writing. I stand and quietly approach him from behind, then peek over his shoulder. There on the desk is a large piece of parchment. The man is holding a quill and writing something in black ink. A small inkpot is positioned on the desktop to his left. At rhythmic intervals, he stops and lowers the tip of his quill into the inkpot. As I gaze at the calligraphy, I'm struck by its overwhelming beauty. Archaic and ornamental, the style is strongly reminiscent of sacred manuscripts hand-rendered by monks in the Middle Ages.

All at once the man stops writing. He picks up the parchment and hands it to me without looking up from his desk. I take the parchment and stare at it, unable to make out a word of it. I hand it back to him. He holds it for a moment, then places it on the desk. Not knowing what to make of this gesture, I decide to lie down and try to sleep my way through this. No sooner do I recline in the grass when the hermit seats himself next to me. He takes my right hand and places something inside of it, then gently closes my fingers. Slowly opening my hand, I see that he's given me a single blade of grass. As I gaze at it, I feel touched and inspired. I sit up and gather some soil at the base of the tree. Taking the hermit's left hand, I open it and place the soil in his palm. It feels very right to do this, natural.

We sit quietly. The tranquility of the woods is extremely soothing and seems to fall in folds of featherlight silk around my body. Sinking into the stillness, I try to pick up impressions about the man, but the effort is making me sleepy. Gazing dreamily at his form, I feel that I'm being drawn into the shadows his hood creates over his face, the darkness in the folds of his cloak. Growing sleepier, I lean into the grass and lie on my side. Something tells me not to fall asleep... "Do not dream, do not dream." I'm beginning to drift. The trees, everything, whirling... sounds of music and a feeling of lightness...

I'm dancing with the hermit. Amused by something we are discussing, I'm laughing as we glide over the grass. I try to listen more closely to what he's saying, but I'm arrested by the melody of ancient instruments quietly rising and falling in the space around us. I gaze up at the trees swaying in the sunlight and feel their life speak to my soul. The language feels very old... the hermit in whose arms I'm dancing feels very old. I ask the sunlight to take me out of this dream and into the root, the source of all Light. Closing my eyes, I breathe the sun's warmth into my being as if to seal a prayer.

The man is speaking to me again and draws me closer. As I attempt to hear what he's saying, I feel my heart open. Words begin to form on my lips. I turn my face to his ear.

"Is this your dream or mine?" I whisper.

"We're having the same dream," he answers.

"I don't remember you," I confess.

The man laughs delightfully.

"I don't remember you, either."

"Then why are we dancing with each other?" I ask.

"It is what we desire."

"Will our desire help us to remember?"

The man stops and looks at me for a long moment before answering.

"Remembering will help our desire."

CHAPTER 11

CONSUMMATION

March 22 A Dream

I dream that I run into the very first man with whom I fell in love years ago. He is visiting from out of state and, by some coincidence, our paths cross. As we engage in conversation, he stalls and seems troubled. It soon becomes clear that our running into each other was no coincidence: he's been tracking me down and is struggling with something he wants to tell me. Uneasy about his reemergence in my life, I try to keep our discourse breezy and inconsequential. His troubled mood does not lift. Through much effort, he finally tells me he and I have a child—a child I don't know about.

The implications of this revelation are staggering and fill me with a sense of complete disorientation and anxiety. It's clear he wants me to take some responsibility for this, to help him. I'm at a loss as to how to make space for this "intrusion of the past" into my life. I don't want to get entangled with this man again, nor do I feel he wants much personal involvement with me. His focus seems to be centered around "our child" and needing my help.

March 23 A Dream

I dream that I'm in a large city with a little girl over whose care I have charge. She and I are traveling with family and friends, staying at different places throughout the city. Divided into small groups, we must find accommodations where we can.

The dream shifts and I'm sleeping in a single bed with the little girl. I keep waking up, anxious the little girl might wander out of bed and stray off while I'm asleep.

The dream shifts and I'm standing with the little girl on the corner of a busy thoroughfare in the heart of a big city. Holding an assortment of little treasures she's collected, she keeps running ahead of me. I'm worried she'll dart out into traffic. Suddenly she tosses her treasures high into the air. A loud bursting sound fills the air as thousands of tiny silver-gray balls rain down onto the sidewalks and streets. A continuous pattering noise accompanies this shower like the sound of a pearl necklace when it breaks and falls to the floor.

I run around the corner after the little girl and cry, "See? I told you if you weren't careful, you would break it!"

I scan the streets, searching for her treasures. The tiny balls are raining down so thick, I must squint to protect my eyes.

The dream shifts and I'm in a large room with members of my family who are seated around an oblong table. I'm naked. My mother is holding me in a compromising position while some of my brothers take turns whipping me with a belt. Others around the table are watching this and touching themselves. One of my brothers puts his phallus in my mouth.

The dream shifts and I'm sitting on the floor with my oldest brother with whom I'm very close in real life. We're quite happy to be together, for he's come to the States from Switzerland and we've not seen each other in awhile. He's talking to me in a sensitive and dear way. All the while, I'm smoking a cigarette with my eyes closed. I'm so sleepy, I can't seem to keep them open. This feels very weird and I'm trying my best to respond to him as if I were fully awake. He comments that I look better than the last time he saw me.

"But you just saw me at Christmas," I answer.

He says he knows the time has been short, but it's true nonetheless. I light another cigarette and still can't keep my eyes open. Gazing at the cigarette I just lit, I ask him if I just smoked one. He says yes. I laugh at myself and put it out.

Personal Notes

I awaken from this dream very slowly, as if I'd been drugged. My head feels thick with sleep. The dream images cling heavily, moving in and out like swirling batter. I lie quietly and watch the images, taking note of what I'm feeling. I'm peculiarly sensitive and feel disoriented. I notice a strange sensation in my abdomen, as if two small hands were pushing from the inside-out, on either side of my navel. As I lie there half-awake, I hear an inner voice distinctly say to me, "Cry the shame out."

I close my eyes and contemplate the dream with my mother and brothers. It reeks of incest. I'm at a loss as I reflect on it, having no incestuous secrets and knowing of none in my family. As I continue thinking about the dream, my feeling of sadness deepens. The sensation of hands pushing from the inside of my abdomen increases. I begin to feel pain. I also become aware that I'm somewhat sexually aroused. I lie there and allow myself to feel it all.

A painful memory moves into my thoughts: I see myself as a small child, lined up with my brothers in the kitchen, waiting to be spanked. Our pants are pulled down to our knees. My mother has taken a kitchen chair and placed it in the center of the floor. When it comes our turn, each of us will have to bend over it and endure the belt, as we've all been guilty of breaking one of her rules. The shame of this ordeal is worse than the spanking. As I recount this experience, my heart sinks with pain, not only for myself, but for my brothers. I feel like crying, but the tears do not come.

March 23 Session

I close my eyes and see that I'm standing in the woods watching Dionysus labor over a small campfire. He's busily preparing a meal of fish and bread. Pausing from his toils, he looks up at me and smiles. I smile back weakly. I'm not exactly sure this is where I want to be.

Motioning for me to sit, Dionysus continues with his preparations. Spotting a low smooth rock, I quietly seat myself and watch him roast two fish on a stick over the fire. The wood crackles and hisses as furls of gray smoke rise into the air. Dionysus is squatting. I take note of his bare feet and robe. I sigh. I'm tired.

"Melina, why are you here?" Dionysus asks, his voice melting into the surrounding stillness.

As I gaze at him, my ears fill with the sound of hot wood crackling. It's very peaceful.

"I'm here to finish business," I answer softly.

I stare into the fire. Suddenly I feel sadness.

"Do you know what this business is?" Dionysus asks.

The question doesn't interest me and my mind begins to wander.

"I'm not sure what I know anymore."

I look up from the fire and search Dionysus' face. His eyes fill with softness.

"Come, Melina. Let us eat our meal."

I seat myself in the grass, moving closer to the fire. I'm not hungry and say nothing. Dionysus pushes one fish off the stick onto a flat rock. He hands me the stick with the remaining fish, then breaks a round of bread and offers me a portion.

"Relax, Melina. Eat."

He sits leisurely in the grass and proceeds to eat heartily. I stare down at my food and toy with it.

"I'm thirsty," I murmur.

Dionysus pauses over his fish and observes me quietly.

"For what are you thirsty?" he asks.

As I listen to his words, my mind starts getting fuzzy. I feel as if I'm going to fall asleep. I gaze at the smoke rising from the campfire.

"I don't know," I answer dreamily, my voice trailing off.

I realize I'm trying to make myself disappear, vanish into smoke. Dazed, I look inquiringly at Dionysus.

"Eat, Melina. You will need this nourishment to carry you."

I pick up my fish and take a small bite. It's surprisingly delicious. Feeling a wave of hunger, I sample the bread. It has a light nut-like flavor.

"I'm thirsty," I repeat.

"For what are you thirsty?" Dionysus asks again.

This time a pang of anxiety shoots through my chest. A flurry of responses reels in my head, heightening my confusion.

"Water?" I whisper.

Dionysus studies me. His look is very penetrating and my heart begins to pound. Placing his fish aside, he slowly stands and approaches me, then kneels in the grass before me, his face only inches from mine. Overwhelmed by his nearness, I try to swallow and start to cough. Dionysus continues looking directly at me. I gaze into his green eyes. They're filled with a deep stillness.

"For what are you thirsty, Melina?" he asks quietly.

Something rises in my throat, but I can't speak. I keep staring into his green eyes. They're very moist. The moisture collects and begins to fill his eyes. I hold my breath, feel pain in my chest. A tear gathers at the corner of his right eye. I watch it move slowly down his cheek. Dionysus raises his hand to his face and gently lifts the teardrop with the tip of his finger. My hands begin to tremble. My dry lips part as the pain in my chest tightens around my heart. He moves his hand to my mouth and places the teardrop on my tongue. It bursts, filling my mouth with its saltiness. In that instant, everything within me shakes loose, crumbles like a tower to the ground. I collapse in his arms and weep deeply.

Personal Notes

After the session, I feel quiet and spent. I want to lie on my bed, curl up into a ball and hold my arms around my stomach for warmth. I can't. Recharged from an afternoon nap, my little son is waiting for me to rescue him from his crib.

When Ted arrives home from work, he finds me lying quietly on my bed with our son. I make no attempt to greet him as he strides toward me, his upbeat energy filling the room like a town parade. Lounging beside me on the bed, he casually remarks that I look as if I were under a spell. I ask him what he means.

"You seem to be only half present and look as if you wish you were totally gone," he answers, gazing curiously at me.

I say nothing. We study each other, trying to feel out the situation and where the rest of our evening might wind up. Lying on the bed between us, our son is listening to music on a portable CD player with earphones, robotically blinking his eyes to the beat. As we quietly gaze at his ridiculous face, the tension between us thickens.

I mention to Ted we should have fish for dinner, barbecued outside on the grill. He replies that he was just about to suggest the same to me. I note the coincidence and let it pass. Evening shadows lengthen across the room, deepening the silence between us. All the while Ted is staring at me as if he were seeing an apparition. Finally he launches into a lengthy inquisition about why I'm behaving strangely. I'm tired and don't feel like talking. My voice is tight when I answer him. Clearly getting the message, he loudly objects and we start to bicker. Thank God my son takes out his earphones and interrupts us, for it's been eons since Ted and I have had a full-blown quarrel and I'm not in the mood to handle one tonight.

Later, when Ted comes home from the store, he shows me the fresh trout he's bought, then unveils a surprise: two decadent-looking pieces of chocolate cake to "fatten me up." I gaze dolefully at the dark wedges displayed on frilly paper doilies, knowing full well I won't eat any. Holding Ted close, I thank him anyway and ask him to forgive my earlier behavior.

"I'll forgive you," he warns, scooping me up in his arms, "if you'll remain mindful not to take your dark moods out on me."

I make a mental note of this and try for the rest of the evening to be more outgoing and civil.

The children are tucked in bed for the night when I climb the stairs to take my shower. Despite the day's toll on my mind and emotions, my body is singing with desire. How strange I feel, so electrified and alive, yet so fragile and exposed. Tonight I'm ovulating and the arousal I've been feeling over the last few weeks is peaking. Aware of this fact, Ted is downstairs watching *Mr Roberts* on cable, gearing up his strength. I smile thinking about the friendly ultimatum I gave him earlier in the evening, "If I don't make love with you tonight, I'll go crazy." Any man who lives with an ovulating woman knows this to be true. He also knows it's during this time a woman will throw her sexual weight around without batting an eyelash. I reflect on the curious balance of power between the sexes as I undress for my shower. An ovulating woman will become like Kali; she will get what she wants. It is futile for a man to resist her, for his pleasure is guaranteed if he engages her desire—his agony inevitable if he does not.

Gazing into the mirror at a face that looks pale and thin, my heart sinks. I want to wash it all away, revive myself. I step into the shower and open my body to the heat, placing my arms behind my head and my back to the pounding stream. It spills over my shoulders and breasts, my stomach and thighs. I spread my feet apart. The heat penetrates my vagina. My nipples rise and a delicious heat spreads throughout my cells. Energy rises in my spine, shimmers and awakens me to its inner life. I embrace it with my whole self. When I do this, the cells in my body seem to merge as one voice. I can feel their resonance fill me with powerful desire. I tilt my head back and open my mouth. Steaming water spills over my face and tongue. I caress my breasts and stomach, drinking in the love pouring from my hands, the celebration flowing from my heart.

When Ted comes upstairs to take his shower, he finds me

brushing my wet hair in front of the mirror. He stares at my nakedness from a distance. I can tell by the look on his face that he's wondering what he's in store for. This leads me to wonder what I'm in store for as well. We glance at each other and say little.

Later, lying in bed, I watch Ted walk across the dimly lit room to adjust the blinds at the windows. I look at his body as if seeing it for the first time. It is beautiful to me, a form I'm still discovering even after seven years of loving him. He slides into bed next to me and holds me in his arms. Speaking to each other with our hands, we move them slowly, our bodies sinking into an ocean of stillness. Ted's breathing deepens. He places his lips to my forehead and kisses it with quiet tenderness. My mind is instantly bathed in a delightful calm. He kisses my nose. My entire body smiles and feels comforted. He lifts my chin and lightly places his lips on my mine. I feel his finger enter my mouth and touch the tip of my tongue. As its saltiness fills my mouth, my mind reels in amazement. I pull back and stare at him, half-expecting to see Dionysus. I keep blinking.

He moves toward me, reaches behind my neck and pulls me to his breast. I taste the sweetness of his body with a new hunger. Heat is rushing out of my mouth and nostrils. I breathe this heat down his stomach and groin, then take him deeply into my mouth. Dream images of my mother and brothers invade. I let them come. They do not bring pain, for my desire is too full. My heat purifies them. My love takes them in. The expansion in my heart grows so intense that I can endure it no longer. I fall backward on the bed and catch my breath. Ted leans over me, whispers that when I climax, I shouldn't bring the energy up into my head. He tells me to push it down, push it out like I would push a baby out. I feel his warm breath between my thighs. I close my eyes. He says, "Melina, push it into my mouth."

Personal Notes

In the morning I rise early. I haven't had much sleep, for I've been up half the night with stomach cramps and the runs. Despite the mild discomfort, I feel energetic and happy. I go about my usual morning chores before beginning my day's work, intuitively feeling my body is undergoing a necessary process of release. Unconcerned, I let nature have its way.

It's Saturday and spring is spilling through the windows. I'm tidying the kitchen and singing when my daughter wanders through, eating a waffle. I stop and kiss her full on the lips. The front doorbell rings and I answer it. A high school boy is standing there holding up a can of God knows what. He launches into a sales pitch, calling his product, "Amaze." I nearly laugh out loud. As he pauses to catch his breath, I tell him my life is amazing enough, actually too amazing, and I couldn't possibly stand any more excitement. He stands there stunned, then wishes me a good day. I wish him the same and bolt the door. As I head for my office, I instruct my daughter that unless God Himself is standing on the doorstep, I don't want to be disturbed.

My phone rings all morning. Family and friends want to know about the outcome of my meetings in New York. My brother Tony calls from Switzerland and asks me to send him a copy of my children's book as soon as it's published. Phoning from Ohio, my brother Dominic has me in stitches for the next hour, laughing about everything under the sun. Not until mid-afternoon am I finally able to settle down to my work. My stomach is still jumpy and I must run to the bathroom often. Energy in my body seems to be going haywire. Now and then it leaps into my head with a white brilliance. I can hardly concentrate. The arousal within me has not abated. My cells are singing and dancing like a happy fountain under the sun. I'm mystified as to how I can feel this way and also have the runs.

I try to focus on my work, but a sensation of gravity is building in my body. Extremely sexual, it pulls my awareness to the chair across the room at my desk. Glancing over at it, I remember my experience with the Voice—that which named itself the Holy Spirit and which I called "the clear." I quickly look away and tell myself to concentrate on what I'm doing. My command doesn't take hold.

I walk across the room and sit in the chair. My body is tingling. I place myself in the same position as the one I remember from my experience with "the clear." Once I've accomplished this, I tilt my head over the back of the chair and relax, then ask myself what on earth am I doing. I have no idea. I wait to see if I can feel the Presence, the Voice. I don't. I dismiss it and tell myself one can't expect to have this type of experience twice in the same week. I decide to enter the exercise anyway, with or without the Voice, to see what might happen.

I close my eyes and feel the warmth of my hands resting between my thighs. As I relax inside the sensations of my body, a mild wave of guilt pushes at my conscience. Allowing it to be there, I quietly observe it. I decide to tolerate this feeling and proceed with the experience. This posture creates a strange feeling of duality, bringing my observer-self to the fore. Immediately, all spontaneity collapses and is replaced by a "gap." The gap starts filling up with a crippling sense of self-consciousness. I remove my hands and take a deep breath. The observer-self scatters and my mind becomes a blank. I know I must start all over again. I reach deeply for my courage.

I find my position again. I'm trying to keep the toes of my left foot in contact with the toes of my right as I was guided by the Voice, realizing this will help ground the circuitry of energy. I'm finding that my legs are too short or the chair is too high to do this comfortably and I'm compensating by straining thigh muscles. I abandon the one-on-one contact. Instead, I curl the toes of each foot inward toward each other and allow them to rest on the floor a slight distance apart. I close my eyes and tilt my head back, surrendering to a state of deep relaxation. A feeling of peace settles over me. My mind begins to float and everything becomes milky-looking. The whiteness sharpens as if it were absorbing light. I'm watching it for some time when a Voice speaks to me from somewhere above my head.

"Open your eyes."

I open my eyes to a view of spring clouds passing overhead through the ceiling skylight. Feeling a strong Presence, I try to sense its proximity to me. My awareness is instantly drawn to an expanse of space just inches above my eyes. As I focus on its crystalline energy field, it's as if I'm gazing upon or into "the clear" or *that which is clear*—a transparent, numinous body of scintillating clarity. I have no other way of describing this. The expanse of clearness is very distinct and seems to be set apart spatially from all that is around it. As I gaze into it, I'm filled with a sense of delight, of freshness and "newness" at what I'm experiencing. The Voice comes again.

"Do you want to die?"

The words move through me like an ocean surf on a calm day. I let its power roll slowly through my being. I have no emotional response to it whatsoever.

Again the Voice asks, "Do you want to die?"

As my concentration deepens inside an inner stillness, I feel my heart open.

"If I die unto You, yes," I answer.

Instantly the Voice responds, "Receive Me."

Energy rises and sweeps through my body, heightening my sense of arousal. I feel myself becoming loose, open. I bring my awareness to the warmth of my hands between my thighs. I begin to breathe deeply.

"Open your mouth," the Voice directs.

I relax my jaw, allowing my mouth to fall open.

"Open your mouth wider," the Voice instructs.

Pangs of self-consciousness begin to invade. Wrestling with anxiety, I try not to lose the rhythm of my breathing. I open my mouth wider. Instantly my connection with the Presence intensifies and the energy in my body soars. Unprepared for this dramatic shift, I completely lose my rhythm and focus. I bolt upright in my chair and stare down at my desk. My heart is beating rapidly. I hear myself say aloud, "I can't do this. I just can't do this." I gaze out the window at the white plum blossoms and ask for help. I then lean back in my chair and collect myself, knowing I must find my way back to a state of repose.

As I sit there, I call to mind the Hindu and Tibetan doctrines of Tantric Yoga that regard the sexual force as a mysterious power belonging to the realm of Kundalini, the vital force in the human body which, when aroused, wills the expansion of the human being into the divine. Could the involuntary awakening of this universal force be the trigger for what is now happening in my body and consciousness? Closing my eyes, I can feel the energy in my body converging in the area of my womb. As I observe its movement, my thoughts gravitate to my birth experience with my son. I recall that if a woman can keep her mouth loose and open while she is giving birth, it will expedite her cervical dilation. The physiological link between a birthing woman's mouth and the uterine mouth is very powerful; they work together. As I allow this awareness to burrow deep into my cells, I feel it clarify the Voice's instruction, "Open your mouth wider," as well as my posture toward what I'm doing. I realize I'm a servant in this experience, one who mediates in the creative process through cooperation. My cooperation is my willingness to receive, to open, to allow. There's nothing I need do but focus on my desire: to want what is happening the way I would anticipate the birth of my own child. In this way, my involvement becomes manifold—I'm at once the birthing mother, the midwife and the emerging infant.

I reposition myself in the chair and breathe deeply, then tilt my head over the back of the chair and focus on "the clear" before my eyes. Desire rises in my body and I collapse inside of it. The Voice comes again.

"Extend your tongue."

Approaching this gesture slowly, I'm reminded of Communion, the sacrament of the Holy Eucharist. I extend my tongue as if receiving the Host, He Who is the Bread of Life. Energy rushes like fire to the tip of my tongue.

"Extend your tongue further," the Voice directs. "Widen your mouth."

The screen of my mind fills with the primal image of a serpent emerging from a dark cave, its eyes raised to the sun's burning heat. The tip of my tongue begins to stiffen and tingle. Cool air rushes in and out of my mouth as the warmth of my hands penetrates between my thighs. My arousal is escalating and it's becoming difficult to keep my eyes open.

Suddenly an enormous release, first in my stomach, then throughout my chest. Waves of energy rush into my throat and burst inside my open eyes. At once I see a tiny pyramid in each of my eyes, outlined in dazzling white light. The interior of each pyramid is gloriously clear. The Voice speaks from inside my eyes.

"Can you see Me?"

Awed, I stare into the pyramids. The Voice comes again.

"Can you see Me?"

Wonder fills my heart. I feel like a child looking at the world for the first time.

"Yes. Yes, I can see You!" I answer.

I close my eyes, unable to gaze a moment longer at the radiance, the sheer diamond-like purity of "the clear." After some moments, I rise from my chair and walk slowly across the room to the loveseat. With every step, I take note of how I feel. A powerful calm radiates from the center of my body to the tips of my fingers and toes. My mind is filled with a tranquil, steady awareness, one which seems to be absorbing its own state of peace. I seat myself on the loveseat and gaze at the bookcase on the opposite wall. Everything looks extraordinarily distinct. The solidness of objects and their richness of color fill my eyes in a new way. I realize what I'm seeing is the "groundedness" of form, the magnetic power of gravity sustaining and clarifying the physical universe. I feel this gravity resonating in my being like a massive vertical pillar around which my consciousness and physicality spin in their appointed orbits like moons around a planet. It is an awesome feeling.

I lean back and breathe deeply. I notice my stomach cramps have completely vanished. All pressure in my lower abdomen has been replaced by a warm and pleasant calm. The soothing absence of discomfort fills me with great peace. I close my eyes and say a prayer of thanks. I resume my work.

April 7 Session

I close my eyes and see that I'm resting naked in Dionysus' lap. My head is nestled in the crook of his left arm. Completely undisturbed about my unclothed condition, I feel deeply relaxed and at peace. I gaze up at Dionysus resting comfortably against the trunk of a large tree. Now and then he looks down at me. His eyes are filled with a deep calm. My awareness is drawn to my arm draped loosely over his legs and my hand nestled in the cool grass. The earth next to my bare skin feels wonderful. I draw air deeply into my lungs and exhale slowly. My face relaxes into a smile.

"Dionysus, may I tell you something?"

Dionysus holds my gaze in a peaceful way. For a moment I feel as if I'm going to fall into the "deep" resting behind his eyes.

"Something wonderful is happening to me and my relationship with Ted. It's as if a very old dream, one I can't even remember, is slowly coming to life."

I pause, uncertain I'm articulating this right.

"Is this making any sense to you?" I ask.

Dionysus closes his eyes and smiles.

"You are remembering through dreaming," he answers, "yet what you are remembering is not a dream."

"What is it?" I ask.

Dionysus looks down at me. His eyes focus as if upon a deep thought.

"Do you truly desire to know, Melina?"

A slight wave of nervousness steals through my stomach. I comb my fingers back and forth through the grass.

"I don't know... yes... I think."

Dionysus' smile widens. He places his finger lightly on my forehead and runs it down my nose, mouth and chin, pausing at my throat. He then traces a vertical line from my throat to the area between my breasts.

"You think, or desire?" he asks, resting his finger upon my heart.

My heartbeat jumps. I close my eyes. Fear comes.

"I'm afraid."

His finger moves slowly down my stomach, then pauses just below my navel. My awareness falls to my womb. He traces his finger over my pubic bone. Suddenly I feel it resting in the lips of my vagina. I breathe deeply.

"Look, Melina."

He lifts his hand. On his finger is a cherry-red smear of blood. I inadvertently gasp.

I pull out of the session. Realizing I'm due to start my period, I check myself. The sight of fresh blood unexpectedly weakens me. Feeling vulnerable and disoriented, I'm uncertain as to whether I want to reenter the session. I close my eyes and see that Dionysus is still holding up his finger smeared with blood. He brings it close to my face.

"What do you see?" he asks.

A torrent of strange images rushes into my mind's eye. As I try to distinguish one image from another, I feel my ears flushing with heat. I clasp my hands over my ears and shut my eyes.

"It is time, Melina. You are ready to remember."

I can feel the images exerting an overwhelming force over my sense of will, making it nearly impossible to resist their pull. Inundated with their moving shapes and textures, I feel as if my eyes were being pulled backwards to the base of my skull. Panting, I cover my eyes.

"I don't know, Dionysus... I don't know... I don't think I can... "

Everything becomes a blur. I pull out of the session.

April 10 Personal Notes

It's late afternoon when I feel the urge to sketch. Bringing out a tablet and pencil, I know I'll sketch a man. At first I'm very casual about it, not caring what shows up on paper. As the head of a man comes into view, he looks strangely familiar. I soon realize I'm sketching X. I don't like the fact that I'm sketching him, but I feel compelled to complete the drawing just the same. When Ted walks into the room, I ask him to comment on the portrait. He stares at it thoughtfully, then says it looks like a young boy. Amazed, I examine the portrait, wondering how he could see a young boy in so diabolical a figure.

Much later in the evening, after the children are in bed, I retreat to my office. Ted becomes wary when I do this, never knowing in what state of mind I'll emerge. He follows me into my office and hangs around. I patiently wait for him to leave.

It is very quiet. Feeling a strong desire to meditate, I light a candle and put on some music, then seat myself comfortably on the loveseat. The muted glow of an ebbing full moon pours through the overhead skylights, filling the room's dark contours with a silvery luster. I close my eyes, releasing the day's concerns. Instantly a feeling of peace falls over me. I enter it fully and begin to drift into a deepening feeling in my heart, an expansion. I lean back, sinking further inside a sense of engulfment. A soft light fills my mind and bathes me in its quiet and warmth. I listen to my breathing becoming deeper, fuller.

Suspended in a world of stillness, I begin to notice the inner light filling with soft shapes. I watch these shapes as one would watch the drifting movement of distant clouds in a half-sleep, unaware of the passage of time. As the shapes become more distinct, I realize I'm looking at sunlight filtering through the boughs of a great tree. The light streams down upon the verdant surroundings in a diffused misty way, deepening the shadows that snake across the grass. Mesmerized, I watch the play of light as it stirs above a patch of grass and slowly condenses into a pillar of radiance. Gazing dreamily at this movement, I notice the body of a man crystallizing in the light. His flesh gleams like snow under moonlight. He moves toward me out of the softly whirling mist. I see it is Dionysus.

I gaze about the wooded landscape, its towering trees heavy with age and shadows. Recognizing where I am, I can feel all of my senses becoming enlivened. I look down at my naked body glowing with a pale light. Astonished, I move my arms through the air and notice the accustomed feeling of gravity is absent. Turning toward the light stirring in luminous waves upon the grass, I see that Dionysus is approaching me. He slows his steps and extends his hands to me. As I gaze at his nakedness, my eyes fall to his phallus. It is erect and distinctly flesh-toned, standing out markedly from the moonlit pallor of his body. I notice the head of his phallus is unusually wide. I feel a moment's fear.

Advancing toward me, Dionysus takes my left hand and leads me to the whirling light falling through the leaves of the great tree. With every step, a vaporous light exudes from my body, expanding and contracting as my feet glide weightlessly over the grass. Arriving under the tree, we stop and he embraces me. As his phallus presses against my body, my arousal climbs so fast that I become winded and reel backward. Dionysus holds me firmly against the tree. Heat begins to pour from my mouth and hands, my nose and ears. Everything in my body seems to be collapsing and rushing into him. An electrifying force instantly flows back to me, sending charged currents of energy rippling through my cells.

Dionysus takes me in his arms and kisses me deeply. The energy in my body intensifies, swells like fire in my chest. Struggling for breath, I throw my head back as a fierce sound rises from my throat. Frightened by what is happening inside my body, I cling to Dionysus with all my strength as jagged arcs of light leap across his shoulders. They penetrate my arms and hands like liquid fire and sweep through my body. Tears burst from my eyes as he probes my inner thighs with his phallus. The heat of his breath rushes across my face as he explores my mouth. I respond with equal hunger, the energy in my body soaring to a wild pitch. I've gone over the edge and can't stop. I don't want to stop.

I kiss him with a desire so deep in my soul that I can barely breathe. Its power is taking me over, consuming me. I yield to it with my whole self. I taste and breathe him. I touch, drink and embrace him. I can no longer tell the difference between my mouth or his, his hands or mine. His fire is my own; our desire is one.

His phallus pushes between my thighs. I clutch his shoulders and close my eyes. An inner voice cries, "Open your eyes and see Me!" I open them and behold my image reflected in Dionysus' eyes. A wild look of pleasure flashes through them as he thrusts himself inside of me. Gasping, I grab him around the neck, burying my face in his shoulder. He pushes me back so that I'm gazing into his face. His eyes flash ecstatically as he lifts his voice.

"Feel me!"

He penetrates deeper and I cry out, unable to keep my eyes focused. He places his hand behind my head, steadying me.

"Look at me, Melina. Feel me!'

He thrusts again. Breathing rapidly, I feel as if my very being were about to die. I try to tell him this but he's respirating hard, his stomach swelling and collapsing against mine like a great bellows. Deep moans escape his throat as he grips my hair, pulling my head back against the tree. I grasp his forearms, my gaze riveted to his face as his eyes roll upward. All at once he rears his head, releasing a cry like roaring wind. It thunders in my ears and strikes the core of my soul.

I cover my breasts with my hands and slowly drop to my knees. Physically weakened, I can't stop the violent trembling in my body. Dionysus kneels before me and gathers me in his arms. Gently we rock back and forth in the grass, our breathing rising and falling sharply in the stillness. Sinking into the lulling rhythm, I close my eyes as flickering currents of energy in my body ebb to a soothing radiance. The radiance spills into my mind like soft mist. I breathe deeply, then feel a hand touch my thigh. I open my eyes. Kneeling on the floor before me is Ted in the glow of the candlelight. He is looking at me wonderingly. I extend my hand to him. He lays his head in my lap and I stroke his hair. We do not speak.

April 13 Good Friday Session

I close my eyes and see that I'm walking toward a grove of large shady trees in the woods. Beyond the trees is the stream. Even from this distance, the water looks unusually calm. I glance up at the sky and notice the sun is not very bright. I wonder if a good rain is coming, even a thunderstorm. Gazing ahead, I spot Dionysus sitting in the grass under one of the large trees. Wearing a long, coarsely woven robe, he is seated in the manner of one meditating in an Eastern tradition. Seeing him this way has a strange effect on me. A feeling of quiet falls over me.

I'm now standing before him. His eyes are closed as if he is absorbed in prayer. Sensing my presence might disturb him, I suddenly regret having come here. I stand quietly, wondering what I should do next. Dionysus slowly opens his eyes as if awakening from a deep sleep. He gazes at me wordlessly, his eyes filled with a profound stillness unlike anything known to me. Staring into them, I feel my breathing slow. Everything in my vision begins to fade except his eyes. I can't draw my gaze away. I begin to feel energy being pulled from my chest. It creates a strange sinking sensation in the trunk of my body, drawing me toward him. I seat myself in the grass to his left and fold my hands in my lap. Dionysus is now watching me. My anxiety is beginning to mount.

"Do you believe I am the Resurrection?" he asks, his voice deathly still.

His words stun me. My head begins to reel as answers collide in my mind like an explosion of glass. I stare at him in utter confusion. A reply begins to form. I feel its heaviness in my mouth as though it were a stone upon my tongue.

"Yes," I whisper.

He extends his hand as if he were holding something in his palm. Looking into it, I see nothing—only emptiness. I gaze at him in confusion.

"Look into my hand, Melina."

I stare into the palm of his hand. I see only his flesh, and that it is beautiful and good. Suddenly the ground heaves violently beneath me, pitching me into a large expanse of milky vapor. I fall rapidly, the vapor rushing passed my body like icy fingers. Bands of cloud-like forms enshroud me in a tunnel of whiteness as I plunge deeper. I rake the air and struggle to breathe.

All at once my feet touch down onto something solid. I crouch low to the ground and shut my eyes, throwing my hands around my body. I don't want to see what is here. I don't want to hear anything. I press my hands to my ears as my heartbeat drums at my temples. I try to think of a way to get back to Dionysus, to get out of wherever I am. I try to imagine where I could be. I move my hands away from my ears and listen. I hear no sound. I open my eyes and stare down at my feet. I'm crouched on a floor of old gray stone. Glancing to my left, I notice the stones form a wall which gradually arches at a ceiling. I realize I'm in the passageway of the chamber of the Feminine.

Standing quickly, I press my back to the wall on my right and look around. It's strangely lit in here, as though by a torch or lantern. I stare into the passageway, knowing that further down it angles to the left and opens into a small chamber. I hesitate, then walk softly in the direction of the chamber, tracing the cool stones of the wall with my fingertips. A moist, musty odor pervades the air and reminds me of the smell of an old crypt: stone, ivy, earth and dust. It produces a strange mixture of feelings within me.

I'm now at the bend in the passageway. From here I can see the small open doorway of the chamber of the Feminine. Cool air flows out of the chamber into the passageway. Reaching forward, I caress the air as I walk slowly into the room. To my right, beneath a massive crucifix hanging on the wall, is the prayer kneeler. I don't see the woman. I look around the dim room. It is small and sad like a deep and forgotten secret. A tremendous sigh wells up within me. The sadness hangs in every corner of the room, breathes in every molecule. As I gaze at the prayer kneeler, my eyes fall on the rich velvet cushion. Deeply attracted to it, I approach the kneeler and extend my hand. The feeling of the velvet is unbelievably exquisite. As I drink in its deep, rose red texture, I realize the color is one that is closest to my heart.

Running my fingers over the smooth wood of the prayer kneeler, I wonder what it would be like to kneel here and place my folded hands upon the cushion. I gaze up at the body of Christ nailed to the cross. At once I feel a strong desire to pray. I position myself on the kneeler and fold my hands upon the cushion. Warm and soothing, the velvet yields beneath my hands. I close my eyes and think of the woman, what she must have felt when she knelt here. I envision her fragile face and light hair, her long, pale blue dress fastened at the waist by a thin sash, the prayer beads tangled in her clasped hands. I wonder who she is and why she cries so inconsolably. Wanting to pray for her, I bow my head. Instantly my heart is seized with the pain of her inner torment. It rakes my insides, jarring the memory of an inscription on a holy card I memorized as a child: "O all ye that pass by the way, attend and see if there be any sorrow like unto My sorrow."

I hold my hand to my chest and breathe deeply, trying to shake it all away. Opening my eyes, I gaze up at the crucifix. Immense and ornate, it strikes me as strangely medieval and has a heavy effect on me. I close my eyes again and hear a faint sound behind me. I turn around and search the room. A figure stands near the far wall in the shadows. I strain to see more clearly. The figure steps forward into the light. It is X. Overwhelmed with fright, I stand up quickly. The prayer kneeler crashes to the floor. I run for the doorway. X throws himself in front of me, barring my passage. Not daring to look at his face, I step backward to the wall where the crucifix hangs.

"Going so soon? I wouldn't hear of it!"

The room explodes with his wild laughter. Recognizing his words from *The Wizard of Oz,* I recoil at his mutilation of a childhood treasure. Glancing at a window on the right wall, I'm relieved to see it's open and large enough for me to crawl through. I inch my way toward it, staring down at my feet. X does not stop me. I reach the window and realize I'll have to turn my back on him to crawl through it. Petrified, I stall.

"I'm going through this window," I inform him loudly, trying to control my voice.

X says nothing. I quickly turn around and hoist myself up onto the sill. I pass through the window and crawl out onto the grass. Seized with fear, I crawl faster, then jump to my feet. I turn around. X is standing but an arm's length away. His arms are crossed at his chest and he's smiling at me.

"What do you want?" I cry.

"You."

"Why?"

"You know why."

"No, I don't know why, I really don't."

I slowly back away from him and look around. Trees loom in every direction, but I don't recognize where I am.

"I'm going now," I announce quietly.

I turn around and start walking. Everything in my field of vision becomes a sharp tangle of shapes and colors, offering no relief of exit or escape. A feeling of being trapped overwhelms me. Suddenly my feet start racing as though I had no control over them, hurling me into the mad tangle before me. The sound of footsteps pounds in my ears. Realizing they're not my own, I run faster.

"Stop! Stop!" I scream.

Hands grip me by the shoulders and push me to the ground. X's velvet cloak spills in heavy folds around me.

"Stop what? I haven't done anything... yet."

He grabs my wrists and pulls them over my head, pressing them deep into the grass. He lowers his face to mine and kisses me. His mouth is very hard and I gasp.

"Please stop! I don't want this! Please!"

"You always want this—this and more!"

He kisses me again. Dark shapes tear and claw inside my brain. I pull my mouth away and gasp for air. He laughs loudly, then releases my wrists. I quickly cross my arms over my breasts and turn my face sharply to one side. Suddenly I feel his weight lift from my body. I stare up at his tall form standing in the grass to my right.

"You are free to go," he pronounces, smoothing the folds of his cloak.

Staring at him in disbelief, I sit up in a daze, then rise to my feet. I back away slowly, turn around and walk as quickly as I can without breaking into a run. My eyes drink in the trees and sky as if I'd just awakened from a long dark dream. My pace quickens. An inner voice cries, "Don't look back! Don't look back!" Shutting my eyes against the temptation to look, I envision Lot's wife, her body freezing into a pillar of salt as she steals one last glimpse of Sodom. I quickly banish this image from my mind and fix my gaze on the green of the trees, the blue of the sky.

Suddenly a sound like rushing wind howls in my ears. A terrible heaviness presses at my back and I whirl around. X grabs me by the shoulders and pulls me tightly to his chest. I struggle frantically, staring into his eyes. They're filled with wild excitement.

"Did you really think it would be that easy? Did you?" he shouts.

His hot breath sears my face. I start to choke. He throws me to the ground and straddles me.

"You're not free! You've never been free!"

He holds my face in his two hands and begins to exert pressure. I push desperately at his arms.

"Such a beautiful face you have, Melina."

He pushes his fingers into my flesh. Blood rushes to my face and I cry out.

"How your loveliness enslaves you... and this!"

He presses his fingers to my mouth, pulling my lips over my teeth.

"One could simply peel this off, couldn't he? Then what would you be? Yes, what would you be without this lovely face you wear?"

He throws his head back and laughs insanely. The sound of it fills me with dread.

"Please stop! Please!"

My voice is wild and shrill. I feel I can't breathe. He releases my face and draws his hands slowly down my neck and chest, cupping them over my breasts. Terror freezes in my limbs and pushes sharply in my throat. I turn my face to my shoulder and shut my eyes.

I pull out of the session, unable to maintain my focus. I feel sick to my stomach and my heart is throbbing in my ears. Gazing out the window, I exhale deeply, running my fingers several times through my hair to relieve tension. All the while X's face is frozen in my mind's eye. I feel completely in the grip of his energy.

I walk downstairs and sit outside in the sunlight. Ted is weeding the garden. From time to time he looks over at me, trying to read the darkness in my face. I say nothing. Finally he joins me on the deck and asks me what's wrong. I briefly recount my experience with X, my voice strangled with feelings of despair. I tell him I don't think I can continue with the experience, that I don't have the courage and can't go through with it. We quietly hold each other.

"Trust your inner strength, Melina. Trust yourself," he consoles me. "You can do it."

I listen to his words as if in a half-sleep. I'm very tired.

I return to my office. Sitting at my desk, I stare down at the paper scrawled with words. A sinking sensation pulls in my stomach and chest. I pick up the pen and breathe deeply. I close my eyes.

"Look at me! Look at me!"

X is kneeling over me, shaking me by the shoulders. I stare down at my nakedness and cover myself with my hands.

"Don't hurt me!" I cry.

"But you want me to hurt you, don't you?"

"No!"

"You like it, don't you?"

I struggle to push him off.

"No! No!"

I feel his hand groping between my thighs. He digs his fingers deep into my flesh. I bite my lip as tears flood my eyes. He leans close to my face and grins.

"So, you think Dionysus is the Resurrection."

He gestures lewdly between his thighs, then grabs the back of my neck and pulls me up to watch what he's doing.

"He makes himself rise, doesn't he?"

I push my hand into his groin as hard as I can and kick him with my knees. He pulls back. I roll over and crawl frantically through the grass. He grabs my ankle and yanks me toward him. I kick wildly with my other foot and scream at the top of my voice. He lunges at me, crushing me beneath his weight.

"Struggle, bitch! You know how much I like it when you resist me!"

I swing at him with both my arms. He grabs them in midair and pins them to either side of my body. He pushes his face into my hair. I hear his breathing in my ear.

"I'll just have to tie you up, won't I?"

Something freezes in my brain and I go limp. Inner voices fill my ears: "It's all a dream. Don't believe it. It's not real. None of this is really happening." A strange glaze fills my eyes and everything begins to look diffused and fuzzy. I feel him pull me up off the grass by my wrists and drag me to a tree. We stop beneath it and I gaze at it in a daze. He presses my back against it. I watch him stoop and pick up something off the grass.

"Remember this?" he asks, waving it in my face.

I stare into the soft fabric of a pale blue dress. It looks very old and delicate. A thin sash is tied loosely around it.

"I asked you a question!" he shouts.

"No."

He throws it to the ground. Again he picks up something off the grass. He raises it to my eyes.

"What about this?"

He is holding what looks like a monk's robe. It's very worn, nearly tattered, and is tied with a yellowed knotted rope. It seems somehow familiar to me and raises a mixture of strange and sad emotions.

"Well?"

Confused, I struggle with my feelings.

"I don't know... "

His face flushes with anger as he pulls the knotted rope from the robe. Casting the garment to the ground, he twists the rope around his hand.

"I will burn you with this. I will burn you... "

My eyes are becoming heavy. I close them. Something rises within me which feels familiar and very old... a dream... one I have no memory of ever having dreamt. All at once a searing pain tears across my flesh. I cry out and fall to the ground. X grabs me by the shoulders and shakes me violently.

"Get up, whore! Get up and feel what I'm going to do to you! Then you'll remember!"

He releases me and rises to his feet. I drop to the grass. Energy is draining out of my body. I stare up at him as if in a dream and gaze at the sunlight shining through the leaves above his head. I watch the soft rays pour down over his face and body. Something strange and delicate begins to stir within my chest. I feel it collect in my heart like a soft mist. It rises and fills my eyes. At once I'm flooded with the sense of a presence within me which is distinctly feminine and filled with grace. A feeling of floating seems to lift me slightly off the ground.

Suddenly a form rises from my body and stands beside me. It is the woman from the chamber of the Feminine. She is holding a small round jar the color of bronze, marked with the symbol of the cross. Lifting a lid, she places her two fingers in the jar, then raises them to X's brow. She gently anoints his forehead. As the ointment glistens on his skin, I recognize it as chrism—sacramental oil used in the rites of baptism, as well as in the rites of the dying.

I watch her kneel in the grass before him. She dips her fingers into the jar and touches the ointment to the palms of his hands, then bends and anoints his feet. Rising slowly, she takes his hands in hers and looks quietly into his eyes. I'm breathless as I watch her: her nakedness in the sunlight, the soft waves of her hair, her eyes embracing him as if she knew his innermost soul. She bows her head as though preparing to speak. When she raises her eyes to his, they are filled with tears.

"Long have I placed the burden of my sins on your shoulders, made you carry my cross to Golgotha, nailed you to it and rejoiced in my redemption by the shedding of your blood. Long have I held you in contempt, castrated you for the blade that severed me at birth, forced my loneliness upon you, blamed you for my disappointments. Long have I abandoned you to the shadows of my days and the secrets of my nights where the sun neither brightens nor warms, where love and pity roam homeless. Long have I kept you the prisoner of my judgment, gave you crumbs when you pleaded for bread, lashed you with my denial, bruised you with my scorn. Long have I enslaved you in the tyranny of my righteousness! Oh, my soul, forgive me! Forgive me!"

She bows her head for several moments, then slowly turns and gazes at me. Her face is filled with openness and peace. She extends her open hand to me. Glowing in her palm is a sphere like that of the moon. Sensing its warmth, I move closer and peer into its lovely pale light. All at once I'm pitched forward into a soft milky radiance as though I were being propelled into the sphere's innermost core.

The sphere gently rises and begins to float. Instantly I experience an indescribable feeling of joy and lightness. I close my eyes and focus on the soothing motion. Long moments pass before I sense a stillness, a cessation of movement. Slowly opening my eyes, I see that I'm gazing into a hand. I look up. Before me sits Dionysus, his open palm extended to me, his eyes filled with ineffable silence.

Personal Notes

No sooner do I finish the session when Ted walks into my office. Worried about my emotional state, he wants to know how I am.

When he is seated and calmed, I read the session aloud, pausing frequently in order to handle its intensity. When I near the end of the statements made to X by the woman from the chamber of the Feminine, a surge of emotion floods my heart. Unable to continue, I cover my face and weep. Ted holds me. After some moments, I resume reading the session.

When I've finished, I lay the material aside and lean back quietly on the loveseat. I gaze over at Ted sitting in the rocker. Struggling to digest the material, he looks pale and perplexed. He fires off dozens of questions: what did X mean when he said, "I'm going to burn you with this"? Did he actually strike me? What is the significance of the blue dress? What was it I started to remember? Where did the woman come from? Am I sure she was addressing her statements to X? What does all this mean?

I have no immediate answers to his questions and feel a sense of removal from his turmoil. My emotions are completely preoccupied with the woman from the chamber of the Feminine. Her spirit rests like a hand on my soul, silencing its aches and vanquishing its struggles. Awakened to feelings of renewal and hope, I have no other thought but to unite my mind and soul with her lingering presence in my heart. Like a restorative flame, her abiding grace fills me with a deep sense of promise and seems to absolve the crimes and cruelties of X.

As Ted proceeds to air his questions and concerns, delicate scenes of medieval life and figures of a monastic order flash in and out of my awareness like fragments of a dim dream. Hauntingly familiar, they seem inexplicably joined to the woman from the chamber of the Feminine. As I experience their inner movement inhabiting my soul, my feelings of intimacy with the woman deepen. Extraordinary feelings of tenderness and devotion sweep through my being as the scenes and figures coalesce into an immense body of collective experience from a long-ago age: joys, labors, prayers, agonies and hymns of yearning and praise. Fully cognizant of my identity as my spirit melds with human souls from centuries passed, I also feel an expansive sense of being other than myself—other than the face and eyes through which I gaze out at my office, the small sanctuary of my existence.

I leave my office and find myself gazing into the mirror over my vanity. There's no doubt I look as though I've been through a terrible ordeal. The face in the mirror is pale and bedraggled. It's little wonder that Ted, who must gaze into this mess, often becomes distraught over my welfare. In the meantime, Ted is ransacking bookshelves all over the house for mythological material. Later I spot him in the den reading *Dionysus: Myth and Cult* by Walter F Otto. Like so many books I've stockpiled for later perusal, it's one I've not yet read. For the next few days, Ted's nose and soul is buried in it.

On Easter Sunday, I attend church services as a way of celebrating a sense of victory I can't quite name. I close my eyes and think of this victory as life itself: life into death and death into life. I drink in the lighted white candles and Easter lilies, the little children in frilly bonnets and scrubbed white shoes, the dome of the church thundering with organ music and jubilant voices. A baby with dark almond eyes drools all over her mother's new dress, grinning at me. A feeling of peace overwhelms me, flooding my soul with gratitude.

As the service nears its close, the church resounding with a glorious organ postlude by Bach, I find myself gazing at a large stained glass window of Christ which extends from the altar to the ceiling. He stands in a simple pasture, his arms outstretched and beckoning. The royal blue of his mantle fills my eyes. Lost in its serene brilliance, I barely notice my eyes are filling with tears. My heart is speaking, but its language is unfamiliar, unconstrained by thought or time. How delicate and precious is its life, as deep within me as my earliest memories of being in this world. As I quietly breathe its mystery through my body, I bless each travail that has led me to this moment, this view of a window suffused with light, for I realize this is the pause between contractions—a respite from the rhythms of human suffering that hasten soul's movement through the emotional confluences of daily life.

I take stock of my surroundings and discover the church has nearly emptied. Reaching for my daughter's hand, I step out into the sunlight.

BOOKS

O is a symbol of the world, of oneness and unity. In different cultures it also means the "eye," symbolizing knowledge and insight. We aim to publish books that are accessible, constructive and that challenge accepted opinion, both that of academia and the "moral majority."

Our books are available in all good English language bookstores worldwide. If you don't see the book on the shelves ask the bookstore to order it for you, quoting the ISBN number and title. Alternatively you can order online (all major online retail sites carry our titles) or contact the distributor in the relevant country, listed on the copyright page.

See our website **www.o-books.net** for a full list of over 500 titles, growing by 100 a year.

And tune in to myspiritradio.com for our book review radio show, hosted by June-Elleni Laine, where you can listen to the authors discussing their books.

MySpiritRadio